FOURTH EDITION

INDIANS OF TODAY

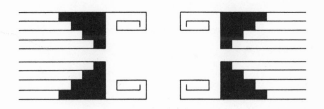

Editor and Compiler
MARION E. GRIDLEY

I.C.F.P; INC.

12/12/72

DEDICATION

Dedicated to *Indians of Today* . . . wherever they may be.

Sincere appreciation and thanks are extended to the William H. Donner Foundation for the generous grant which absorbed the costs of publication and production thus making this volume possible.

ACKNOWLEDGEMENTS

Cover and Book Design	Carla Bach
General Editor	John A. Hurst
Director: Art and Production	Carla Bach
Associate Director: Art and Production	Arvid Casler

FOREWORD

This fourth edition of *INDIANS OF TODAY* salutes the many outstanding American Indian leaders who have made, and continue to make, significant contributions to the lives of their people and to the Nation. There has long been a need for positive recognition of Native leadership in areas other than the Arts, Sciences, and the Professions.

We begin this decade of the 70's in the midst of unprecedented public interest in the Indian people. *INDIANS OF TODAY* will enhance and enrich this public support by bringing alive the personal qualities and special attributes of Indian leaders.

The Nation needs to acknowledge the Indian heritage as all of us seek to make peace with nature and to bring to a halt the senseless destruction of what is left of our natural resources. The Indian way is providing essential leadership to this effort. I recognize and support the determination of Indian people to take the lead in restoring to our land the pride and dignity that is an essential part of our Indian heritage.

We owe our Indian leaders much. Their outstanding accomplishments will provide inspiration for today's young Indian men and women who, emerging as leaders of the future, will continue unbroken the ancient tradition of our people's dignity and pride.

Through *INDIANS OF TODAY,* we pay tribute to their individual achievements and to their continuing contributions to the betterment of the lives of all people.

Louis R. Bruce
Commissioner of Indian Affairs

TO YOU ... THE READER ...

The first edition of *INDIANS OF TODAY*, published in 1936, was a natural outgrowth of the special exhibit demonstrating Indian Progress on display at the Century of Progress Exposition in Chicago.

Although the first edition of this book contained just 128 pages, each of the next two volumes grew not only in the kind and the content of the biographies, but in the number of pages required on which to report them! It has been particularly gratifying and a continuing personal delight to Marion Gridley to see and to record the ever-increasing number of stories of Indian successes and achievements. In earlier editions, one of her problems was finding people to include in the book - and then, somehow getting their story! Now, the question is - how to include - within space limitations, the many Indians who serve in positions of responsibility and importance.

Throughout its existence, the editorial thrust of *Indians of Today,* has been to present Indian people in terms of personal accomplishment rather than in the perspective of national prominence. This kind of editorial approach can only help break down the stereotyped image of the American Indian so prevalent in the minds of the general public. This composite picture of success and achievement, presented in the dignified biographical form used in each edition of *Indians of Today*, produces possible and attainable "aspirational images" for today's young Indian. This feeling has often been expressed by readers in this way, "I walk a little taller . . . and hold my head a little higher, because of *INDIANS OF TODAY.*"

A new and exciting dimension has been added to this, the fourth edition of the book . . . that is, the inclusion of young people . . . who, though just starting out in life, have already demonstrated ability and shown promise of potential greatness. In addition, Eskimos as a native people, are included in this volume.

With so many in similar professions, such as education, art, science, as well as the ministry, the selection of biographies by the editorial board was made solely on the basis of ancestry (i.e., at least one-fourth Indian blood); and careful recognition of particularly unusual life stories or contributions of an individual. Some, who justifiably belong in the book, do not appear because no response to our request for biographical information was forthcoming.

Marion E. Gridley, the compiler and editor of all editions of *INDIANS OF TODAY*, has been closely associated with Indian people since the 1920's. Her intense and compassionate interest in the American Indian can be traced not only to her childhood but perhaps to the early history of the Gridley family itself.

The Gridley family first came to America in 1620 and were among the founders of the present town of Farmington, Connecticut in 1640. History tells us that the Gridley's were good friends of the Tunxis Indians who inhabited this area. These people so trusted the Gridley's that they asked them to negotiate land sales for the Tunxis tribe. Later, other members of the Gridley family lived among the Oneida Indians in New York State. In this area the Gridley's started a school for Oneida children. The name Gridley appears again among those Cherokees at Spring Place Mission, (the Georgia Colony), the name Gridley taken by a Cherokee from the list of donor's to the Mission.

Throughout her entire life Marion Gridley has studied the many facets of Indian life and its culture. Before and during the time she was married to Chief Whirling Thunder, she lived among Indians. Two honors, of which she is exceedingly proud, are the ceremonials of adoption by the Omaha and the Winnebago. She was given the Omaha name of "Little Moon Beam." Her Winnebago name is "Glory of the Morning."

She has preserved . . . and can relate at will . . . many of the legends, customs, habits, family situations, and tribal traditions with which she is so thoroughly familiar. With her unusual insight and understanding, coupled with the application of a tremendous in-depth knowledge and background, Marion as a nationally-known, and prize-winning writer, has been able to partially fulfill her personal ambition . . . to help Indians find their way toward an equal place in society.

A short, forty years ago the direction of the footsteps of the Indian was wavering, unsure, and hesitant. Today the stride is firm and assured and the journey toward success has begun. Many of the Indian people whose biographies appear in this volume will proudly attest to the fact that Marion's actions, personal interest, and gentle leadership even during times of great stress, gave strength and impetus to effecting some of the changes we see today.

When people work closely on such a project as the publication of a book of the magnitude of this one, they often learn personal things about one another. Many times during these past few months I have asked Marion, "Why? Why give so much? Why exert so much energy?" In answer I received the kind of "Gridleyism" with which I have become so familiar.

Drawing on her childhood experience as a Camp Fire Girl, she said quite simply, "one of the laws of the Camp Fire Girls impressed me deeply. It was this. 'Love is the joy of service so deep that self is forgotten.' "

And then she continued, "I have tried to make this my way of life. Giving freely of my time, my experience, and of my professional skills - while serving as a volunteer - has been my way of saying - 'Thank You!' for the privilege of living."

One evening, after we had checked the very last of the page proofs and packaged them to send to the printer, we all admitted to being more than a little tired. As we stood waiting for the elevator, Marion turned and said wistfully, "Time and the years have a way of catching up with each of us. This is the last *INDIANS OF TODAY* that will come from my pen. I ask that it be my memorial."

In answer to her, I can only paraphrase an old Indian saying, "To share what you have shared is to live forever!"

John A. Hurst, Vice-President
Production and Manufacturing

Publisher's note:

Part of the proceeds of the previous volumes were used to further Indian causes. Some of the revenue from this edition of Indians of Today will be given to selected Indian graduate students in need of financial assistance. It is sincerely hoped that those students who receive financial assistance, will express - through their own lives in the future - the extension of the hope and confidence that will be placed in them.

BEN REIFEL (DAKOTA-BRULE) UNITED STATES CONGRESSMAN

Mr. Reifel is the only Indian in Congress and the first Dakota Indian to be elected to the House of Representatives. He is completing his fourth consecutive term and has announced that he is not running for re-election.

Born in a log cabin to a full blood Indian mother and a German-American father, Mr. Reifel worked on his parents' small farm until he was ready for college. His mother spoke little English, but "in spite of her limitations, she was instrumental in shaping her children's lives . . . and to help us know what was essential to bridge the gap from old to new," her son says.

Schooling was not gained easily, but the unusual ability that Ben demonstrated soon brought him special notice. He was assisted to enter college to major in chemistry and dairy science, for he was keenly interested in agricultural improvement. After graduation, he was appointed farm agent in the Indian Service, working on his home reservation. Twenty-one years later, he returned to this reservation as the first Indian superintendent in its history.

Still in the Indian Service, as an organization field agent, Ben helped Indian groups form business councils under the Indian Reorganization Act, of 1932. Later, he was a tribal relations officer and then Area Director for the Aberdeen office of the Bureau of Indian Affairs.

Dr. Reifel was elected to Congress in 1960, easily defeating two formidable opponents in the primary and winning a sizeable plurality in the election. In each successive election he won by larger margins.

On May 19, 1970, during the discussion of a bill having to do with Department of the Interior appropriations, Congress-woman Hansen made these remarks:

"... may I also point out that to the sorrow of every Member of this Congress, this is the last year my very distinguished colleague from South Dakota, Congressman Ben Reifel, will serve in the House of Representatives and the last year he will participate in one of our bills.

"The gentleman from South Dakota has been one of the Nation's outstanding members, contributing not only to the knowledge of our committee, but to the support of programs financed by this committee across the nation. I am proud to have had the privilege and opportunity to serve with him and I deeply regret his leaving us. It is not only this gentleman's competence and ability, but his deep and abiding love for humanity which have been daily reflected in the activities of this Congress. He has always been in the forefront of those who care about people and programs meaningful to the United States. It is his kind of America which will keep this country from burning. May I say on behalf of our committee: 'We are sorry you are leaving. May you send someone in your place as conscientious as yourself, who loves humanity as deeply as you do.' "

During his career, Dr. Reifel has collected bulletins, maps, reports and other material pertaining to the Plains area and its people. This gives him valuable insight into the problems of the locale and Indian-white relationships.

"Indians must recognize what their problems are," he says. "The plans that evolve must be Indian plans for which they are willing to struggle to complete. Indians cannot, without disastrous consequences, disregard any elements of modern life if they wish to have a meaningful part in the America of Today."

BIRTHPLACE: Rosebud, South Dakota, September, 1906.
MARRIED: Alice Johnson. CHILDREN: Loyce Reifel Anderson.
EDUCATION: South Dakota State College (B.S., M.S.); Harvard University (M.A., Ph.D.).
SCHOLARSHIP: Faculty Scholarship; John Hay Whitney Fellowship.

3

HONORS: Outstanding Indian Award, All American Indian Days (1956); Indian Council Fire Achievement Award and honorary life membership (1956); Boy Scouts of America Silver Antelope Award (1960); Certificate of Merit, Dakota State College (1970). MILITARY SERVICE: U.S. Army, World War II - France, Germany. (Lieutenant Colonel, Army Reserve).
ORGANIZATIONS: Arrow (president); Rotary; Masons; Elks; National Easter Seal Society (board); Upper Midwest Regional Educational Laboratory.
CONGRESSIONAL COMMITTEES: Appropriations Committee, ranking minority member, Interior and Related Agencies Subcommittee; Legislative Subcommittee.

FRELA OWL BECK (CHEROKEE) REGISTERED NURSE

Mrs. Beck comes from the distinguished Owl family which has so many members who are outstanding in their personal accomplishments. Her career has been as a nurse - staff nurse, nursing instructor and relief supervisor.

BIRTHPLACE: Hayward, Wisconsin, December 9, 1939.
MARRIED: George S. Beck. CHILDREN: Emil, Amy.
EDUCATION: Northfield School for Girls, Michigan State University, School of Nursing (B.S., with high honors).
SCHOLARSHIPS: Board of Home Missions, Congregational and Christian Churches; Association on American Indian Affairs.
HONORS: Alpha Lambda Delta; Tower Guard; honorary member, Honors College.
ORGANIZATIONS: Michigan Nurses Association; Child Study Club; Shiawassee District Nurses Association (past treasurer); Mary Guild (secretary); Tots Thru Teens Child Study Club (president).

CLARENCE ACOYA (PUEBLO-LAGUNA) SPECIAL ASSISTANT TO COMMISSIONER OF INDIAN AFFAIRS

As a boy, Clarence Acoya spent his summers herding sheep and working in the fields. In high school, he was a counselor in private camps. Somewhere along the way he became interested in business administration and prepared for a career in that field.

This training, he says, has given him an appreciation of association with people at various levels. He has held a number of positions where his talents in his chosen profession have been put to the test. He has been executive director for the New Mexico Commission on Indian Affairs, treasurer for the Pueblo of Laguna, Project Director for the National Congress of American Indians on Ford Foundation projects, and administrative assistant to the Mayor of Tucson.

BIRTHPLACE: Albuquerque, New Mexico, October 20, 1930.
MARRIED: Peggy Freeman. CHILDREN: Wendell.
EDUCATION: Albuquerque Indian School; Bacone College (Scholarship); University of New Mexico; Yale University (fellowship).
MILITARY SERVICE: U.S. Marine Corps, 1951 - 1954.
ORGANIZATIONS: Bernalillo County Medical Center (past board member); American Indian Athletic Hall of Fame (President); National Indian Training and Research Center (board); National Congress of American Indians.

ANDREW ACOYA (PUEBLO-LAGUNA) ARCHITECT-PLANNER

Andrew Acoya is believed to be the first Indian from the Southwest to attend Massachusetts Institute of Technology. He is specializing in low-income housing and planning for under-developed areas.

In 1969, he was project director for a squatter housing project in Bogota, Columbia and was a member of a project to study self-help housing in the United States.

He believes that a great fault of the American people lies in the fact that they believe that minority or "inferior" groups of people exist. It is his hope, he says, that one day the "minority peoples" will come to believe in the simple statement that "no one can make you feel inferior without your consent."

BIRTHPLACE: Fort Wingate, New Mexico, June 24, 1943.

EDUCATION: University of New Mexico (B.Arch.); Massachusetts Institute of Technology (M.Arch.).

SCHOLARSHIPS: Laguna Pueblo; Bureau of Indian Affairs; Massachusetts Institute of Technology; John Hay Whitney Foundation Fellowship.

PROFESSIONAL PAPERS: Seven on architectural and housing subjects.

ORGANIZATIONS: NAHRO; M.I.T. Rocket Club; M.I.T. Architectural Group II.

LEONARD S. MARCHAND (KAMLOOPS-CARIBOO) MEMBER, CANADIAN PARLIAMENT

Mr. Marchand is the first Canadian Indian elected to the House of Commons. He is the Member of Parliament for the Riding of Kamloops-Cariboo in British Columbia.

In 1960, he was employed as a research officer with a Department of Agriculture Research Station. He took educational leave from this position to enter university training. He again took leave from his research work in 1965 to become Special Assistant to the Minister of Citizenship and Immigration, Indian Affairs Branch.

Mr. Marchand has long been active in promoting closer relations between the Indian and non-Indian communities.

BIRTHPLACE: Vernon, British Columbia, 1933.
MARRIED: Donna Parr. CHILDREN: Lori Anne, Leonard, Jr.
EDUCATION: Reservation schools; University of British Columbia (B.S., Agri.); University of Idaho (MS., For.).
PROFESSIONAL PAPERS PUBLISHED: several relating to range management.
ORGANIZATIONS: Mika-Nika Club (a founder). North American Indian Brotherhood; National Indian Council; Agricultural Institute of Canada.

HELEN HARDIN (PUEBLO-SANTA CLARA) ARTIST

When she was six, Helen won first prize for a drawing. Encouraged by her mother, the famous painter Pablita Velarde, she soon entered art competitions for children. She sold her first painting at the age of nine.

In high school, she competed in many student art competitions and designed and supervised school projects requiring artistic ability.

Her first one-man show was held when she was nineteen. She has co-exhibited with her mother in many public events. During a visit to Bogota, Columbia, a one-man show was held for her at the United States Embassy and was attended by many dignitaries.

Helen paints under her Indian name, "Tsa-sah-wee-eh," which means Little Standing Spruce. Unlike her mother who uses ground earth paints, Helen paints with casein and acrylics in a style that is contemporary and rarely traditional, though clearly representative of Indian culture. A serious student of the designs and art of her heritage, she is a young modern thinker who uses old ideas to form contemporary art.

BIRTHPLACE: Albuquerque, New Mexico, 1946.
MARRIED: Terrazos. CHILDREN: Margarete.
EDUCATION: University of New Mexico; Special School for Indian Arts, University of Arizona.

EXHIBITIONS: Six and numerous gallery showings.

AWARDS: Two first awards, among others.

PUBLISHED WORKS: *American Artist* (April 1965); *New Mexico Magazine* (March/April, 1970).

ILLUSTRATOR: *Runaway Boy* (Raton Jemez).

ORGANIZATIONS: National League of American Pen Women; New Mexico Council of American Indians; New Mexico State Fair Committee.

SPECIAL ACTIVITIES: Speaking to school classes on Southwest Indian Culture.

JAMES SEWID (KWAKIUTL) CHIEF AND TRIBAL LEADER

James Sewid, a well-known Indian fisherman who operates two purse seiners, has been prominently engaged in the salmon fishing industry in British Columbia for more than 40 years.

Sewid was born into a rapidly distintegrating Indian culture. As a child he received unusually intensive training and special treatment from his elders because he was heir to "many names." Early in life, he learned that these names carried great responsibility, and in spite of poverty, illiteracy, family breakdown and social conflict, he lived up to his responsibility. He became the leader of the progressive group in his tribe and was their first elected chief when the traditional system of hereditary chiefs was eliminated.

Sewid entered the fishing industry at the age of ten and at thirteen married a high-born girl of his tribe. He went through great inner conflict with respect to traditional practices but is now active in reviving tribal traditions.

Recognized across Canada as a leader by Indians and non-Indians alike, Sewid was selected by the National Film Board of Canada to portray many of his accomplishments in a film, *No Longer Vanishing.*

Chief Sewid has been an innovator throughout his life. As a child, playing on the beach, he constructed from discarded items the first little automobile in Alert Bay. He introduced an electric light plant into Village Island, making it the first remote village to have such a convenience. He created the light company as a new type of social organization, and was made chairman of it. He paid the village school teacher from his own pocket to secure the extension of the school year. It was he who changed the traditional band structure from hereditary to elected chief. He instigated new ways to solicit and use band funds; developed the intertribal council, a new kind of political structure; and he originated a bi-racial committee to deal with juvenile delinquency. He built a community house and developed an arts and crafts organization.

In 1969, his autobiography, *Guests Never Leave Hungry* was published by Yale University Press. It tells of his work and of his activities as chief and describes new economic developments and institutions that he has initiated to benefit his people.

Sewid moves back and forth between two cultural worlds. Seldom does he draw upon European culture but presents new ideas which have to be adapted to a bi-cultural environment. He identifies with both cultures and draws on the best from each. He has remained socially anchored within Kwakiutl society, living in traditional communities, but he is a leader in the Anglican Church. He has participated in political activities on provincial and national levels. His marriage was both Anglican and Kwakiutl.

BIRTHPLACE: Alert Bay, British Columbia, Canada, winter, 1913.
MARRIED: Flora Alfred. CHILDREN: Dora, Eugene, Oswald, Daisy, Alvin, Louisa, Harold, Lucy, Emma, Wilhelmina.

ORGANIZATIONS: Native Brotherhood of British Columbia (past vice president); Indian Fisherman's Development Board (chairman); Masons; Board of Trade, Alert Bay.

HARRISON BEGAY (NAVAJO) ARTIST ✱

The paintings of this artist, it is said, have exerted greater influence on Navajo artists than any others. He is internationally known and is distinguished by his softened colors and delicate lines. He is also recognized by a characteristic "stopping of action" so as to give a seeming appearance of static to motion. Another characteristic is the attention to detail, a quality which the artist has developed to a high point. He has painted many scenes associated with the industries of his people.

In some of his works, the lines are so fine that it seems impossible that they could be made with a brush. The colorings are often almost ethereal. Although Begay's unique style has influenced others, he has never been equalled in perfection.

BIRTHPLACE: White Cone, Arizona, November 15, 1917.
EDUCATION: Reservation schools; Santa Fe Indian School.
HONORS: *Palmes de'Academiques* of French government (1945); *American Indian Painters; Southwest Indian Painting.*
MILITARY SERVICE: U.S. Army, World War II, three years European Theatre, Iceland.
EXHIBITIONS: More than 25 major exhibitions, more than 35 public and private collections.
AWARDS: Thirteen, including two Grand Awards.

✱ *See art section*

11

MILLICENT MAXINE NATCHEES (UTE) TRIBAL SECRETARY

Maxine Natchees is the first member of her tribe to hold the position of secretary to the Tribal Business Committee. She is also secretary to the administrative manager of the tribe.

In World War II, her father was the first American soldier to enter Berlin.

In 1969, Maxine was selected "Young Career Woman" for the State of Utah by the Utah Federation of Business and Professional Women. She has travelled extensively to promote the interests of young women in business and professional careers.

Maxine leads a busy life and has many interests. She is frequently a delegate to national conferences; attends special classes, acts as adult advisor to a member of the tribe's Junior Business Committee; and is active in all of the reservation events.

BIRTHPLACE: Fort Duchesne, Utah, April 2, 1943.
EDUCATION: Utah State University.
HONORS: Outstanding Young Women of America; "Maxine Natchees Day" on Ute reservation; First Runnerup to Miss Indian America XVI (1969).
ORGANIZATIONS: All-Indian Girls Basketball Tournament (past secretary); Volunteer Entertainment Committee (past secretary, chairman); American Legion Auxiliary Post 126 (past historian).

JOE SANDERS (CHERO-KEE) EDUCATOR)

Joe Sanders' grandfather was the High Sheriff of the Cherokee Nation; his father was the first sheriff of Cherokee County after Statehood; his brother has been sheriff of the same county and all three sheriffs used the same jail.

Before pursuing an educational career, Joe, himself, was a highway patrolman. Both of his parents were educated in the schools operated by the tribe; both were teachers and their six children also teachers.

Mr. Sanders has been a teacher in Arizona public schools and on the faculty of Arizona State University and Eastern Montana College. He has represented Indians off reservations before the Federal Civil Rights Commission. Most recently, he was Director of Indian Education for the State of Arizona. He now teaches language arts in a junior high school and is trainer - educator for the Headstart program in 9 schools in Maricopa County.

BIRTHPLACE: Tahlequah, Oklahoma, December 12, 1912.
MARRIED: Lake M. Hill. CHILDREN: (2).
EDUCATION: Northeastern State College (BS); Arizona State University (MA).
SPECIAL ACTIVITIES: Scholarship Chairman, Southwest All Indian Basketball Tournament Committee, founded 16 years ago to assist young Indians obtain a college education. Funds have been granted to more then 200 Indian students to further their education.

13

LaDONNA HARRIS (COMANCHE) CIVIC LEADER

Mrs. Harris was reared in the home of her grandparents where Comanche was the primary language. Her grandfather was a member of the nationally-known Troop "L" at Fort Sill. A proud Comanche, he wore braids all of his life. He always dressed in his best suit to watch television because he figured that if the people could be seen, they must be able to see those watching.

Long active in the field of minority rights and poverty, Mrs. Harris has been especially interested in mental health. She has devoted many hours working for improvement of the care of the mentally ill. Her interest in education goes back to the days when she worked to supplement her husband's income so that he might graduate from the university he was attending. She also helped further his political career which led to his election to Congress as Senator from Oklahoma.

Mrs. Harris has also been extremely active in work for Indians, not only in Oklahoma but across the country. She is the founder and first president of Oklahomans for Indian Opportunity, a nationally-known Indian self-help organization. More recently, she created Americans for Indian Opportunity which will promote the cause of Indians, Eskimos and Aleuts. She was also instrumental in organizing an information-workshop pilot program for Indian Community Action Programs.

Appointed by President Johnson as a member of the National

Indian Opportunity Council, she chaired its Committee on Urban and Off-Reservation Indians.

BIRTHPLACE: Cotton County, Oklahoma.
MARRIED: Fred Harris. CHILDREN: Kathryn, Byron, Laura.
HONORS: Outstanding Indian of the Year, American Indian Exposition; National Education Association Human Rights Award (1969); Southwest Region Anti-Defamation League Human Rights Award (1968); New York Chapter, American Jewish Committee Human Rights Award (1969); Delta Sigma Theta (honorary member, 1969).
ORGANIZATIONS: Women's National Advisory Council on Poverty (past chairman); National Rural Housing Conference; Southwest Center for Human Relations Studies (executive board); National Steering Committee, Urban Coalition (chairman, Health Task Force); National Association of Mental Health (board); Joint Commission on the Mental Health of Children; National Health Council (board).
SPECIAL ACTIVITIES: 1970 National Health Forum (chairman); University of Oklahoma (Board of Visitors); Antioch College (Board of Trustees); National Board of Directors, Girl Scouts.

ROBERT WILLARD (TLINGIT) EXECUTIVE

Robert Willard's father was the founder of the Salvation Army in Angoon, Alaska. Robert's own career of public service began as a clerk with the Alaska Division of Tourism. The work entailed public relations in promotion of the Alaska Ferry System.

In 1961, he became a State Trooper, the first Alaskan Native to be a member of this group. It was his responsibility to provide law enforcement for 47 villages in an area that covered 58,000 square miles. Patrol of the area was primarily by aircraft, riverboat or by dog sled in the winter months.

He mext became a member of the Juneau police force and in three months was elevated to Sergeant of Police and Shift Commander. Later, he became Department Training Officer. He retired from police work to become an investigator with Alaska Legal Services Corporation. He was assigned to introduce the OEO legal services program to Southeast Alaska. His work as area field representative and government liaison officer launched his involvement in the Native movement and in community affairs as they relate to Indians.

After an unsuccessful fight against Urban Renewal, Mr. Willard began to advocate "coalition" of minority groups. This concept became a reality when it was realized that Indians had been counted by the city of Juneau in order to qualify for the HUD program. Mr. Willard was chosen the spokesman for several coalition organizations and demanded and secured from the City Council an apology to the Natives - the first one in history. He was unanimously elected to chair the Model Cities program and Native people were put in control of the Model Cities policy board. Two natives were elected to the Juneau City Council and one was elected to the Area School Board.

Another major accomplishment of Mr. Willard was the securing of $752,000 for the assistance of 700 Indian students who had been denied grants-in-aid for college training. He obtained an additional $60,000 to finance an additional 25 Native students who had been unsuccessful in getting educational help.

Early in 1970, the Governor of Alaska appointed Mr. Willard Executive Director of the Alaska Human Right Commission.

BIRTHPLACE: Tenakee Cannery, Alaska, June 26, 1936.
MARRIED: Ruth Jamestown. CHILDREN: Dennis.
EDUCATION: Public schools.
MILITARY SERVICE: U.S. Marine Corps, one year.
ORGANIZATIONS: Tlingit-Haida Central Council (Anchorage delegate); Alaska Native Brotherhood (president, Anchorage camp).

SPECIAL ACTIVITIES: Governor's Council on Administration of Justice (advisory board); Governor's Labor Task Force. Numerous other committee and civic assignments.

HOWELL ORR (CHEROKEE-CHICKASAW) ARTIST AND ART TEACHER

Howell Orr, a descendant of the last chief, or "king" of the Chickasaw Nation, is especially interested in the work of Mexican muralists and in the technique of batik painting.

He has been art instructor in several public schools, and now teaches at the Valley High School in Las Vegas, Nevada.

He is accomplished in egg-tempera, watercolor, casein, oil, acrylic, fresco, pyroxylin, collage, lithography, woodcuts, batik, sculpture, mural painting, ceramics, textile, photography, and weaving. He has his own line of original lithographed Indian-design Christmas cards.

BIRTHPLACE: Washington, Oklahoma, May 20, 1929.
MARRIED: Deborah Montgomery.
EDUCATION: Chilocco Indian School; Bacone College; Northeastern State College (B.F.A.); University of Tulsa; University of Gto San Miguel Allenda, Mexico (M.F.A.); University of the Americas, Mexico City; University of Nevada Southern.
MILITARY SERVICE: U.S. Ski Patrol, Europe and Korea, four years.
EXHIBITIONS: More than 20; several public and private collections; several awards.
ORGANIZATIONS: American Federation of Teachers; Nevada State Democratic Central Committee League of Young Democrats.
SPECIAL INTERESTS: Indian dancing and lore, Mexican culture and history.

VINCENT LITTLE (MO-HAVE) AREA FIELD REPRESENTATIVE, BUR-EAU OF INDIAN AF-FAIRS, HOOPA AREA FIELD OFFICE

Mr. Little came to his present position with the Bureau of Indian Affairs from that of a secondary teacher at Phoenix Indian School; an enrollment officer at Western Washington University; a Tribal Operations Officer at that same agency; and an assistant super-intendent at Lapwai, Idaho.

He has recently been nominated to participate in the Executive Interchange Program for 1970 under the direction of the President's Commission on Personnel Interchange.

Active in community programs Mr. Little has organized the Hoopa Valley High School Booster's Club for the purpose of encouraging parent participation in school affairs. He also encourages community participation in sports activities.

BIRTHPLACE: Los Angeles, California, February 22, 1931.
MARRIED: Betsy Calnimptewa. CHILDREN: Stewart, Gregory.
EDUCATION: Phoenix Indian School; Phoenix College (A.A.); Arizona State University (B.A., M.A.); George Washington University.
ORGANIZATIONS: Hoopa Valley Chamber of Commerce; Kiwanis; Veterans of Foreign Wars; High School Booster's Club (president); P.T.A., American Indian Foundation, Humboldt State College.

BENJAMIN PEASE, JR. (CROW) TEACHER, ADMINISTRATOR, JOB CORPS CENTER DIRECTOR

Mr. Pease's maternal grandfather was Whiteman-Runs-Him, a Crow Indian Scout with Custer who survived the Battle of the Little Big Horn.

Widely-known and respected, Mr. Pease takes great pride in his Indian heritage while achieving enviable goals in our modern world.

He has served more than 20 years as a teacher and school administrator in public schools of the State of Washington. As Center Director for the Job Corps, he has responsibility for 210 young men and a staff of 56 employees.

As president of the Indian Festival of Arts, held annually in LaGrande,Oregon, he helps to preserve ancient culture and to encourage the contemporary talents of young Indians.

BIRTHPLACE: Crow Agency, Montana, June 15, 1923.
MARRIED: Margery Jordan. CHILDREN: Janine, Benjie, Joel, Linda.
EDUCATION: Linfield College; University of Oregon; Rocky Mountain College (BS); University of Washington; Washington State University (M.Ed.).
HONORS: All-around Athlete awards.
ORGANIZATIONS: Kiwanis (board).
SPECIAL ACTIVITIES: Pilgrim Congregational Church (chairman of board); Representative at large, United Church of Christ of Idaho-Washington Conference (1969-70).

FRED KABOTIE (HOPI) ARTIST, CRAFTSMAN, ART TEACHER

The first of his tribe to receive national and international recognition as an artist, Fred Kabotie's influence has been far-reaching. He is outstanding among artists of any race.

When Fred was about six, his family who were strict traditionalists, sought to escape a government attempt to force them to abandon their customs. They joined with others from the village of Oraibi and established a new village, which they named Hotevilla. Eventually they were made to return to their original homes where the children were placed in schools for the first time. The men of the families were sent away to Carlisle Indian school, in Pennsylvania.

However, when a day school was opened, Fred would be spirited away each morning so that he could not attend. Finally, he was sent away to Santa Fe Indian School as a disciplinary measure. In the fifth grade he was assigned to color maps. The wife of the school superintendent was excited by his use of color. She encouraged him and later had him illustrate a book she had written for children. The little book attracted much attention and Fred illustrated another as well as a magazine story which was later published in book form.

When he graduated from high school, Fred was employed by the School of American Research and the Archeological Society of New Mexico to paint Indian dances. Later, he painted Hopi life and ceremonies for the Museum of the American Indian. He was also commissioned by the Fred Harvey Company to paint a large mural of the Hopi Snake legend in the Indian Tower on the south rim of the Grand Canyon.

With his initiation into a Hopi men's secret society, Kabotie's future was determined, for he has remained among his people since that time. His work and name usually appear whenever Indian art is mentioned, but his work as an educator has prevented him from painting extensively since 1959.

Kabotie reproduced the pre-Columbian Hopi paintings in the Awatobi ruin in Arizona when it was excavated by the Peabody Museum. This reproduction toured the United States. In 1941, he sponsored the organization of the Hopi Silvercraft Cooperative Guild, a non-profit group of silverworkers who utilize and adapt ancient Hopi designs in their products. The original members were fourteen war veterans. He did not receive any salary for his services but was motivated by his love for the fine products of his people and a desire to keep the traditional designs alive and productive.

Many honors have come to this gentle Hopi artist. His works have been exhibited from coast to coast, and in foreign countries. It is said that he has painted almost every ceremony of his people. He is a master of detail and fine balance.

BIRTHPLACE: Shungopavy Village, Arizona, February 20, 1900.
MARRIED: Alice Talayaonema. CHILDREN: Hattie Lou, Michael (a rising artist).
EDUCATION: Santa Fe Indian School.
HONORS: Guggenheim Foundation Fellowship (1945-46); Indian Council Fire Achievement Award and honorary life membership (1949); *Palmes d'Academiques*, French Government (1954); Certificate of Appreciation, Indian Arts and Crafts Board (1958); Achievement Award, University of Arizona (1961); *Who's Who in American Art; American Indian Painters; Who's Who in America; Who's Who in the West.*

AWARDS: four grand awards, among others.

ILLUSTRATED: *Tatay's Tales; Swift Eagle of the Rio Grande; Five Little Kachinas; Rhythym for Rain; The Rain Will Come; Field Mouse Goes to War.*

PUBLISHED WORKS: LaFarge (1956; 1960); Dockstader (1962); *International Studio* (March, 1922); *Travel* (1931); *Introduction to American Indian Art* (1931); *American Magazine of Art* (August, 1932); *Contemporary Arts of the South and Southwest* (November-December, 1932); *Cincinnati Art Museum Bulletin* (January, 1938); *Arizona Highways* (July, 1951); *Compton's Pictured Encyclopedia* (1957); *News Notes* (December, 1961); *Paintings by American Indians* (1962).

COMMISSIONS: Fred Harvey Company, murals, Painted Desert Inn; U.S. Government, Keams Canyon Agency; Hopi High School; Fort Sill Indian School.

ORGANIZATIONS: Federal Employees Association; Tiffany Foundation (trustee); Northern Arizona Society of Science, Art, Inc., (associate).

SPECIAL ACTIVITIES: Hopi Cultural Center; Delegate with Mrs. Kabotie, to Trade World Fair, New Delhi, India (1959-60) for U.S. Department of Commerce and Agriculture.

GLADYS TANTAQUIDGEON (MOHEGAN) ANTHROPOLOGIST

A descendant in the tenth generation from Uncas, immortalized in Cooper's *Last of the Mohicans*. Miss Tantaquidgeon is one of the first Indians to become an anthropologist. She is also descended from Samson Occum, the Mohegan who was instrumental in securing funds for the enlargement of the Indian school, which was at that time, the forerunner of Dartmouth College. She has been a community worker on the Yankton Reservation and a field worker for the Indian Arts and Crafts Board. She is now curator of the Tantaquidgeon Indian Museum, which she and her brother founded.

BIRTHPLACE: New London, Connecticut, June 15, 1899.
EDUCATION: University of Pennsylvania.
PROFESSIONAL PAPERS PUBLISHED: Nine, on Mohegan and Delaware crafts, medicine practices and folk beliefs.
ORGANIZATIONS: Connecticut Archaeological Society; Montville Historical Society.

HAROLD TANTAQUIDGEON (MOHEGAN) MUSEUM CURATOR

Chief Tantaquidgeon, with his sister, Gladys, owns and operates a museum of New England tribal artifacts. He lectures to visiting groups on the history and ethnology of the Mohegan and neighboring tribes.

It was a Tantaquidgeon who first put his hand on the shoulder of Miantonomo, the Narragansett chief, when Uncas ordered him to be taken prisoner. Since then, the hand symbol has been used as a crest by all male Tantaquidgeons.

Harold is especially adept in the reproduction of the artifacts of the New England region. He has taught stone and woodworking techniques to Scout and Camp groups.

A book, *Mohegan Chief: The Story of Harold Tantaquidgeon,* has been written about his life.

BIRTHPLACE: New London, Connecticut.
MILITARY SERVICE: U.S. Air Force, World War II, 1943-53 tail gunner on B-25 and Turret Gunner on P-61 Black Widow Night Fighter, in some of the fiercest fighting in the Pacific. (Purple Heart and Air Medal).

FRANK C. ESTES (DAKOTA-BRULE) SERVICE UNIT DIRECTOR, SIOUX SANITARIUM

A career man in the field of Indian health, Frank Estes has held varying positions of responsibility.

Among his many accomplishments are: assisting in the preparation of a health instruction unit for Hopi reservation schools; the organization, training and supervision of health study interviewers; and, initiation of the first mental health team on the Omaha reservation.

BIRTHPLACE: Fort Thompson, South Dakota, March 21, 1933.
MARRIED: Joann R. Stone. CHILDREN: Sheryl, Candice, Belva, Frank, Jr., Michael, Lonna.
EDUCATION: Reservation schools; South Dakota State University (B.S., M.S.); University of California (M.P.H.).
SCHOLARSHIPS: Tribal scholarship; John Hay Whitney Foundation Fellowship; Episcopal Church; Association on American Indian Affairs; Public Health traineeships.
HONORS: Scholastic Achievement Award, South Dakota State University.

ORGANIZATIONS: Arizona Public Health Association; American Public Health Association (fellow); Royal Society of Health, London; American School Health Association; National Institute for Applied Behavioral Sciences; Federal Hospital Institute Alumni Association; American Hospital Association; Federal Business Association; Dakota Tuberculosis and Health Association.
SPECIAL ACTIVITIES: Lower Brule Sioux Tribe (vice chairman).

SUE SILLAWAY LALLMANG (SENECA) AMERICAN INDIAN ADVISOR, HERITAGE GROUPS DIVISION, REPUBLICAN NATIONAL COMMITTEE

Mrs. Lallmang is an active worker in Republican politics.

As National Director of the American Indian Division for United Citizens for Nixon-Agnew, she gave Republicans across the country a better insight into the problems of Indians.

Mrs. Lallmang has lectured extensively on Indian customs and has recorded Indian songs for the archives of the Library of Congress. She also paints, illustrations of Indian Legends. In her platform appearances, Mrs. Lallmang is known as "Princess Silver Dawn."

She is a descendant of General Ely S. Parker who, as secretary to General Grant, penned the articles of surrender in the Civil War. Ely Parker was the first Indian to be appointed Commissioner of Indian Affairs.

BIRTHPLACE: Lancaster, New York, May 8, 1929.
MARRIED: Richard A. Lallmang. CHILDREN: Robin, Renee, Rex.
EDUCATION: Buffalo State Teachers College; State University of New York (Buffalo); George Washington University.
ORGANIZATIONS: Quota International; PAIR International (founder-president).

PABLITA VELARDE (PUEBLO-SANTA CLARA) ARTIST *

Pablita was first introduced to art by Tonita Pena, who was known as the "mother of Pueblo art." She was the only Indian woman painter of her generation and one of the truly greats.

There was a period in her childhood when Pablita was afflicted with a serious eye disease. When she regained her sight, she "wanted to see everything." She trained herself to remember what she saw, even to the smallest detail. She studied art under Dorothy Dunn, pioneer instructor of Indian artists and in 1938 began her professional career. She built her first studio at Santa Clara, doing everything herself but the most manual of labor.

From 1939-41, Pablita was employed to paint the murals for the Bandolier National Monument Museum. These composite pictures, portraying the daily life and crafts of the Rio Grande Pueblos, are considered among her greatest achievements.

In 1956, Pablita began her unique earth paintings, made from colored rocks that she grinds and mixes with other materials for a plastic effect. She has produced some outstanding abstracts in this technique of her ancestors, borrowing from pottery design forms and pictographs for her themes which are perfectly suited to the native earth color medium. Pablita contributes enormously to the field of ethnology as well as to art. One of her paintings -"Old Father Story Teller" - is predicted to go down in history as a great work because of its profound concept and illusion produced through ingenious composition. The painting is a new yet related version of the old life-linked legends and beliefs of all people. Never before reproduced in color, the painting appears in the book authored and illustrated by Pablita with her famous legend-paintings.

Pablita is considered to be the most outstanding Indian woman artist. Her work expresses a basic integrity and faithfulness to her culture and people. The artist sees great beauty in "yesterday" and says she cannot contribute thoughts of value unless she appreciates and understands the past. She sets down with conviction the deep, rich symbolism of Pueblo life, handling a variety of styles from naive realism to the most esoteric abstract. She is skilled in the use of casein, tempera and oil, painting always with poise and strength.

BIRTHPLACE: Santa Clara, New Mexico, September 19, 1918.
MARRIED: Herbert Hardin (div.). CHILDREN: Helen (also a noted artist); Herbert.
EDUCATION: Santa Fe Indian School.
HONORS: *Palmes d' Academiques,* French Government (1954); Special Recognition, Twentieth Century Art Club, St. Louis; *American Indian Painters; Southwest Indian Painting.*
EXHIBITIONS: More than 20 major exhibitions, several one-man shows; more than 15 permanent and many private collections.
AWARDS: One Grand Purchase Award among many.
COMMISSIONS: Corn Dance mural, Houston; Earth Painting Mural, Western Skies Hotel, Albuquerque; three interpretative Indian paintings of Nativity story, *New Mexico Magazine;* Buffalo Dance mural, First National Bank, Los Alamos.
AUTHOR/ILLUSTRATOR: *Old Father, the Story Teller.*
ORGANIZATIONS: National League of Pen Women.

✱ *See art section*

DENNIS E. FOX (MANDAN-HIDATSA) TEACHER-COACH

Dennis Fox is the grandson of Hannah Levings Fox, the Hidatsa woman who posed for the bronze statue representing Sakajawea which stands on the capitol grounds in Bismarck, North Dakota.

When Dennis started his education at the reservation school, he spoke little English. As he continued his schooling, his innate ability came to the fore and he was recognized by his teachers as a student of excellent quality.

In college, Dennis lettered in football for four years. He and his wife enrolled together and received their degrees together. They put themselves through school, working at part time jobs and with some scholarship assistance.

BIRTHPLACE: Elbowoods, North Dakota, September 8, 1943.
MARRIED: Sandra Harrell. CHILDREN: Dennis, Jr., Nancy.
EDUCATION: Federal Indian schools; Dickinson State College (B.S.); Northern Arizona University (M.S., pending).
SCHOLARSHIPS: Bureau of Indian Affairs; United Scholarship Service.
HONORS: William Danforth "I Dare You" Award.
ORGANIZATIONS: South Dakota High School Coaches Association; National High School Athletic Coaches Association; Dickinson State College Alumni Association; South Dakota Education Association.

B. FRANK BELVIN
(CHOCTAW) MINISTER

Dr. Belvin is general missionary to the Creek and Seminole Indians of Oklahoma. His father was the first fullblood Indian to qualify for the practice of law before the Supreme Court of the United States.

Graduating from high school at the peak of the depression of the 30's, Frank could not get work and was unable to enter college until a small scholarship and part-time employment came to his assistance. After teaching for a year, he hitchhiked east with a borrowed $5.00 - to begin religious training. He was ordained to the ministry in the church on the campus of his college. He later served this institution as Director of Christian Education. Later he entered graduate school, and toured many of the Indian mission fields to compile the material for his thesis.

BIRTHPLACE: Boswell, Oklahoma, January 23, 1914.

MARRIED: Wilma Mibek.

EDUCATION: Ottawa University (B.S.); Eastern Baptist Theological Seminary (MCE., DCE.).

MILITARY SERVICE: Oklahoma National Guard.

AUTHOR: *The Status of the American Indian Ministry; War Horse Along the Jesus Road; The Tribes Go up.*

ORGANIZATIONS: Inter-Tribal Council of Five Civilized Tribes (past secretary-treasurer; three-terms president); National Congress of American Indians (regional vice-president); Oklahoma Human Rights Commission (chairman).

FORREST J. GERARD (BLACKFEET). DIREC-TOR, OFFICE OF INDIAN AFFAIRS, DEPARTMENT OF HEALTH, EDUCA-TION AND WELFARE

Mr. Gerard's major interest has been in the field of health. His first positions were as executive secretary, Wyoming Tuberculosis and Health Association, and as staff member of the Montana Tuberculosis Association. For six years he was Tribal Relations Officer, Division of Indian Health, U.S. Public Health Service and then was chief of this division for four years. Before coming to his present post, he was legislative liaison officer for the Commissioner of Indian Affairs.

BIRTHPLACE: Browning, Montana, January 15, 1925.

MARRIED: Kay Pugh. CHILDREN: Patricia, Margaret, Stanley, Rebecca, Jennifer.

EDUCATION: Montana State University (B.A.); National Tuberculosis Association Training Institute; American Management Association.

MILITARY SERVICE: U.S. Air Force, World War II (35 combat missions).

HONORS: Congressional Fellowship (1966); Indian Council Fire Achievement Award and honorary life membership (1966).

SPECIAL ACTIVITIES: Surgeon General's Advisory Committee on Indian Health (executive secretary); Advisory Committee, Capitol Conference on Indian Poverty; National Indian Health Committee, Association on American Indian Affairs; Advisory Committee on Indian Health, National Congress of American Indians.

ORGANIZATIONS: American Political Science Association, National Congress of American Indians, Prince George's County, Maryland, PTA; American Public Health Association.

PATRICK HINDS (PUEBLO-TESUQUE) SILK SCREEN PAINTER, ARTIST

Although Patrick Hinds has lived most of his life in California, he usually spends his summers among his Tesuque people. He is a recognized artist, a silk screen processor, and a teacher of art.

BIRTHPLACE: Tesuque Pueblo, New Mexico, March 25, 1929.

MARRIED: Rita Ann Gunther. CHILDREN: Mark, Marita.

EDUCATION: Santa Fe Indian School; California College of Arts (B.A.); Mexico City College; Chicago Art Institute.

MILITARY SERVICE: U.S. Marine Corps, 1945-1946, 1950-1951, (Two purple hearts).

EXHIBITIONS: More than 25; several one-man shows; 30 private collections.

AWARDS: Grand Award and six first awards, among others.

ORGANIZATIONS: Oakland Art Association; Oakland Museum Association; California League for American Indians; American Indian Historical Society; East Bay Artists Association; Arts and Crafts Cooperative (chairman); American Indian Artists (chairman, painting committee).

ALFONSO ORTIZ (PUEBLO-SAN JUAN) PROFESSOR OF ANTHROPOLOGY, PRINCETON UNIVERSITY

Alfonso Ortiz is a relatively new type of social anthropologist. He comes from the very community that he studies and interprets. In this case it is the largest of the six surviving Tewa villages in New Mexico. It is also the most isolated of these pueblos, one of the least known, and long one of the most conservative.

Professionally, Dr. Ortiz is most interested in dual organizations, or societies which are divided into two opposing or contrasting halves and which usually perform reciprocal services. Such groups at one time made up at least 15 percent of all human societies, but few such groups survive today.

The Southwest is his primary area of research and interest, although he has studied other Indian tribes and is especially interested in the space and time concepts of the American Indian.

BIRTHPLACE: San Juan Pueblo, April 30, 1939.
MARRIED: Margaret Davisson. CHILDREN: Juliana, Elena, Antonio.
EDUCATION: University of New Mexico (A.B.); Arizona State University; University of Chicago (M.A., Ph.D.).
SCHOLARSHIPS: National Merit Scholarship; John Hay Whitney Foundation Fellowship (2); University of Chicago Fellowship; National Institutes of General Medical Sciences Fellowship.

HONORS: Roy D. Albert Prize, University of Chicago, for outstanding Master's thesis (1964).

AUTHOR: *The Tewa World,* University of Chicago Press (1969); Many professional articles, monographs and research papers.

ORGANIZATIONS: Association on American Indian Affairs, Inc. (executive committee); American Anthropological Association; National Advisory Council on Indian Leadership.

SPECIAL ACTIVITIES: Contemporary Indian affairs, especially education.

SPECIAL INTERESTS: Collection and restoration of antique furniture.

PAT PATTERSON (APACHE-SENECA) MUSEUM DIRECTOR

According to Pat Patterson, his father was a "frustrated artist" who rebelled at long hours of practice and ran away to join a circus. He became a balloon jumper and a wirewalker. Pat was born on the old Sells-Floto Circus circuit enroute to an Illinois engagement.

Pat's father decided that his son would become the artist he had never been, and so he made certain that Pat had as much training as possible.

The artist has painted more than 500 portraits and a number of church murals. He has made the Woolaroc Museum, Bartlesville, Oklahoma, for which he is director, one of the most unusual and imaginative museums in the country.

BIRTHPLACE: Centralia, Illinois, December 29, 1914.
MARRIED: Patricia Cain. CHILDREN: William, Patrick, Sally.
EDUCATION: University of Oklahoma, School of Art (B.F.A.).

CAROLINE ORR MAAS (COLVILLE) ARTIST

A descendant of Moses, a famous Wenatchee chief, Mrs. Maas has been actively engaged in painting her people in non-traditional Indian style for the past fourteen years. She has completed two collections of Indian portraits.

Mrs. Maas has been a staff member of the University of Washington art gallery; an assistant reader for a design class at the University of Washington; and staff artist for the Fort Okanogan Museum.

BIRTHPLACE: Republic, Washington, August 21, 1943.

MARRIED: Jonathan A. Maas.

EDUCATION: University of Washington (B.A.F.A.); University of Manitoba.

SCHOLARSHIPS: Colville Tribal Scholarship; University of Washington; federal grants.

HONORS: Lambda Rho (honorary art); University of Washington Honors Program.

EXHIBITIONS: More than 25 major exhibitions; more than 20 one-man shows.

COLLECTIONS: Eight public, 17 private.

AWARDS: Eight, including honorable mentions.

PUBLISHED WORK: *Omak Chronicle* (1964); *Spokesman Review* (1961); *Wenatchee World* (1952).

ILLUSTRATOR: *The Indian Side of the Story* (1961); *Black Robes and Indians on the Last Frontier* (1965);

EUGENE SEKAQUAPTE-WA (HOPI) EDUCATOR

Eugene Sekaquaptewa is Assistant Professor of Education at Arizona State University, teaching the Indian Education courses offered there. Previously he was training specialist for the ASU Indian Community Action Project.

His entire career has been spent in the educational field. At one time he taught at Sherman Institute. He has also been a recreation director on the Navajo reservation.

Mr. Sekaquaptewa enlisted in the Marines in World War II. He is one of the lucky ones who survived the bloody battle of Iwo Jima. He was among the 4th Division assault troops that surged across the beaches in the early morning hours of the day when the historic flag-raising took place on Mt. Suribachi.

He vividly recalls other "hairy" war experiences. In one, his patrol company set out to locate an enemy battallion in the hills. The enemy opened up with everything they had, and the patrol had 50 percent casualties. Trapped in the valley, Sekaquaptewa and the other survivors planned their escape. At dusk, they moved out, followed by gun fire - carrying a wounded soldier on a makeshift stretcher. When the group arrived at camp, he discovered that the heel of his left boot had been shot off and there were four bullet holes in the back of his shirt. As he ran at the end of the line, the wind from enemy crossfire blew out his shirt and saved him from being wounded.

BIRTHPLACE: Hotevilla, Arizona, July 7, 1925.

MARRIED: Rebecca Draper. CHILDREN: Yvonne, Lisa, Kristena, Denise.

EDUCATION: Arizona State University (BS.Ed., M.A.).

MILITARY SERVICE: U.S. Marines, World War II - four major combat operations including Marshall Islands, Saipan, Tinian Island, Iwo Jima; Also, Captain, United States Air Force Reserves.

PROFESSIONAL PAPERS: Two, on Hopi education and a curriculum guide.

DOROTHY W. DAVIDS (STOCKBRIDGE-MUNSEE) SPECIALIST IN HUMAN RELATIONS TRAINING

Miss Davids started out in life as a teacher in public schools. Becoming more and more involved in the affairs of Indian people, she directed a program for young people at the Chicago American Indian Center, and then became a recruiter for Mundelein College, working with minority groups. This led to her present position at the University of Wisconsin, Center of Community Leadership. Part of her work is to conduct educational seminars for minority groups and for those who work with them.

BIRTHPLACE: Gresham, Wisconsin. EDUCATION: Wisconsin State University (B.E.); University of Wisconsin (M.S.); special courses, Marquette University, University of Minnesota, University of Colorado and University of Chicago.

EDUCATION: Wisconsin State University (B.E.); University of Wisconsin (M.S.); special courses, Marquette University, University of Minnesota, University of Colorado and University of Chicago.

ORGANIZATIONS: Concerned Citizens-Community and University Affairs; Wisconsin Indian Student Movement; Equal Opportunities Education Committee; Great Lakes Inter-tribal Council (education committee); National Congress of American Indians (treasurer).

JOHN ECHOHAWK (PAW-NEE) ATTORNEY

John Echohawk is the first Indian to receive a law degree from the University of New Mexico after successfully completing the pre-law program for Indians - the only pre-law course of its kind in the nation. Demonstrating an aptitude for legal study, he received a scholarship from the University to continue study for his law degree.

John plans to work among Indians where there are specifically Indian problems. He hopes eventually to go to Washington in a policy-making or assisting position. In the meantime, he has accepted a Reginald Heber Smith Community Lawyer Fellowship to work with the California Indian Legal Services.

Raised as a "city Indian" young Echohawk was a star fullback on his high school team.

(A sister and brother begin their law studies this year).

BIRTHPLACE: Albuquerque, New Mexico, August 11, 1945.
MARRIED: Kathryn Martin. CHILDREN: Christopher.
EDUCATION: University of New Mexico (B.A.); University of New Mexico Law School (J.D.).
SCHOLARSHIPS: Santa Fe Foundation; Special Scholarship Program in Law for American Indians.
ORGANIZATIONS: Student Bar Association (past teasurer, president);

TED W. KEY (CHOCTAW) DENTIST

Dr. Key was orphaned at the age of eleven and raised in an orphanage. A football scholarship provided room, board and tuition at a junior college and he worked after school as a barber to pay for other necessities. He also worked his way through college, "swabbing the decks" of the State Capitol every night.

He entered dental school under the Navy war-time training program. When this ended, he played one year of football to earn the tuition for his final year and worked in a laboratory at night. After graduation, he served in the Navy for two years of active duty. During his tour of duty, he was head coach of the New Orleans Naval Station football team.

Dr. Key is a descendant of Tandy Walker, a chief of the Choctaws and a Confederate Army Officer.

BIRTHPLACE: Durant, Oklahoma, September 10, 1918.

MARRIED: Florence Schmitter.

EDUCATION: Murray State Junior College; Oklahoma City University; Central State College (B.S.); St. Louis University Dental School (D.D.S.); Washington University School of Dentistry.

MILITARY SERVICE: U.S. Naval Reserve, World War II, two years (total 27 years); Victory Medal, American Defense Medal, Naval Reserve Medal.

ORGANIZATIONS: American Dental Association; Missouri Dental Association; Greater St. Louis Dental Society (vice-president; President-elect); St. Louis Society of Dental Science; Navy League;

South St. Louis Dental Society (past president).
SPECIAL ACTIVITIES: Naval Reserve Research Unit (Commander).

DOLLY SMITH AKERS (ASSINIBOINE) TRIBAL LEADER

Mrs. Akers has a number of "firsts" to her credit. She is the first woman in the history of her tribe to be elected chairman of the tribal council, and one of the first Indian women in the country to hold such office. She is the only Indian woman to be elected to the Montana State Legislature, where she chaired the Federal Relations Committee. She was also delegated a personal representative by the Governor to appear in Washington on his behalf, to request that Montana Indians be included in all phases of the new public welfare act (1934).

When she was elected to the Legislature, many horses were given away in her honor by relatives and she was given the name of "Day Eagle Woman."

Before her marriage, Mrs. Akers was a welfare worker and at one time state-coordinator of all seven Indian reservations in Montana. With the death of her husband, she took on the management of their 1400-acre ranch.

BIRTHPLACE: Wolf Point, Montana, 1902.
MARRIED: George Cusker (Dec.) John Akers. CHILDREN: Alvina Cusker Welliver.
EDUCATION: Sherman Institute.
ORGANIZATIONS: National Congress of American Indians (past vice-president); Eastern Star.
SPECIAL ACTIVITIES: Montana State Chairman-Indians for Nixon (1968); Inter-Tribal Policy Board (past secretary); Governor's delegate to White House Conference on Children and Youth (1960).

WILFORD W. FRAZIER (DAKOTA-SANTEE) TRIBAL AFFAIRS OFFICER, INDIAN HEALTH SERVICE

Wilford Frazier is the son of Dr. George Frazier who won the Indian Council Fire Achievement Award in 1939. An uncle, Rev. Francis Philip Frazier won the same award in 1958. A great – grandfather, Ehnamani, was the first ordained Dakota Indian in the Congregational Church.

Dr. George Frazier instilled in his son a desire to help his people. Wilford planned to be a dentist, but his career was interrupted by military service in World War II. Upon discharge from the Marines, he set about continuing his education. Then, with a family to support, he accepted employment with the Bureau of Indian Affairs.

During the Korean Conflict, he was recalled to military duty and participated in the landings at Inchon and Wonson and in the historic march from the Chosin Reservoir.

Mr. Frazier joined the Indian Health Service in 1955 and is now stationed in Billings, Montana.

BIRTHPLACE: Santee, Nebraska, March 7, 1923.
MARRIED: Aileen Pickering. CHILDREN: Gregory, Scott.
EDUCATION: Earlham College; University of Oregon (B.S.); George Washington University; Southern Utah College.
MILITARY SERVICE: U.S. Marine Corps, World War II; Korea.
ORGANIZATIONS: Masons; National Congress of American Indians.

HAROLD W. SHUNK (DA-KOTA-YANKTON) GOVERNMENT ADMINISTRA-TOR, RETIRED

Mr. Shunk has served long years of constructive service as a public school teacher, athletic coach, and finally, as superintendent of three Indian agencies for the Bureau of Indian Affairs. His last position was at the Rosebud Agency.

Since his retirement he has been in great demand as a speaker. He is also engaged in historical writing.

BIRTHPLACE: Philip, South Dakota, July 25, 1907.
MARRIED: Delilah Wood. CHILDREN: Deloria Shunk Halone.
EDUCATION: Southern State College (B.S.); Colorado State College; South Dakota State University.
HONORS: Citation, Rosebud Tribal Council (1968); Meritorious Service Award, Department of Interior (1968).
MILITARY SERVICE: U.S. Army, World War II, 1943-45, Pacific Theatre.
ORGANIZATIONS: American Legion, Veterans of Foreign Wars (past commander); Lions (past president); Kiwanis; Masons; Shrine; Black Hills Girl Scouts (president). Boy Scouts (vice chairman); Commercial Club of Colome (honorary life member); 1200 Club of South Dakota; Minni Lusa Historical Society; State Historical Society of South Dakota (life member); Rushmore Coaches Club.

WILLIAM L. HENSLEY (ESKIMO) STATE REPRESENTATIVE

Mr. Hensley, who has served two terms as a representative in the Alaska Legislature is now campaigning for a Senate seat. If elected, his district will be over 150,000 square miles in size with a population of fifteen to twenty thousand people. At least 90 percent of these people are Eskimo, and some of them live quite close to Siberia.

Mr. Hensley has been active in Native organizations. In 1969 he presented a paper on the future of the Eskimos at an international meeting in Paris. Under a John F. Kennedy Memorial Award, given by Experiment in International Living, he travelled in Poland and Russia in order to study conditions in those countries.

BIRTHPLACE: Kotzebue, Alaska.

MARRIED: April Quisenberry. CHILDREN: Baker.

EDUCATION: University of Alaska (B.A., Polit. Sci.); George Washington University; University of New Mexico; University of California (Los Angeles).

ORGANIZATIONS: Northwest Alaska Native Association (past executive director); Alaska Federation of Natives (past vice-president; executive director); Bureau of Land Management.

SPECIAL ACTIVITIES: Alaska Village Electric Cooperative (board); Chairman, State Democratic Party.

FRANK CLARKE
(WALAPAI-MISSION)
PHYSICIAN

Frank Clarke entered a government school when he was ten and credits much of his success to the training received there. He decided to become a doctor when a severe eye condition threatened his sight. He was encouraged in this desire by the school physician.

His medical training was obtained with great difficulty. Because he was without funds, he worked as a field hand for clothing money. In school it was a struggle to survive until he was able to secure a janitor's job. Even then, food was meager.

Enlisting in the Navy, he was assigned to an attack transport engaged in the invasion of the Solomon Islands. After seven major engagements, Clarke was selected for Naval officer training and began his pre-medical education. With the termination of the Navy college program, funds were again short. He worked at night as a laboratory technician, and, in medical school at last, he prepared anatomy specimens and worked as a hospital extern. In debt for tuition, he saved every nickel, borrowed from every friend, but with the help of a grant was finally able to graduate.

Within two years, after opening his practice, he was appointed Chief of Medicine and then Chief of Staff and President of the Staff - the first time that both positions had been held by one person - at Memorial Hospital, Exeter, California. He also headed the Department of Obstetrics at that same hospital.

Dr. Clarke's great grandfather was "Walapai Charlie," the war chief of the Walapai's. Perhaps it is from this ancestor that he acquired his great determination and fortitude.

BIRTHPLACE: Blythe, California, November 11, 1921.

MARRIED: Pearl Tucker. CHILDREN: Michael, Timothy, Steven, Teressa, M. Robert.

EDUCATION: Sherman Institute; Los Angeles City College (Cum Laude); University of California at Los Angeles (B.S.); St. Louis University School of Medicine (M.D.).

HONORS: Fellowship, John Hay Whitney Foundation (1950); Indian Council Fire Achievement Award and honorary life membership, (1961); Boy Scouts of America Meritorious Service Award (1961); City of Woodlake Man of Year (1962); Tulare County Chapter, California Teachers Association, Lay Person of Year in Education (1964).

MILITARY SERVICE: U.S. Navy (12 years). World War II, Korea. Regimental Commander of Officer Candidates, San Diego Naval Training Station.

SPECIAL ACTIVITIES: Woodlake Union Elementary School District (president, Board of Trustees); Episcopal Church delegate to National Council of Churches, 1969-72; Physician-in-charge, Woodlake Well Baby Clinic; appearances before Congressional and State Legislative committees on Indian matters.

ORGANIZATIONS: American Academy of General Practice; American Medical Association; California Medical Society; Tulare County Medical Society; Flying Physicians Association; Rotary.

RAMON ROUBIDEAUX (DAKOTA-BRULE) COUNTY ATTORNEY

Ramon Roubideaux is among the first Indians who entered the legal profession. Admitted to practice in state and federal courts in 1950, he has been county attorney in his home state of South Dakota for the past fifteen years.

His decision to become an attorney stems from an incident when he was in the Air Force. He was evicted from a recreational spot because he was an Indian. Unable to hire a lawyer to prosecute the manager of the place, Mr. Roubideaux vowed to become one. He would see that Indians, and others, would not be discriminated against as he had been.

It was not easy for him to pursue his educational goals. At that time, there were almost no scholarship assistances for Indians, and he came from a poor family. The late Senator Case of South Dakota offered him part-time secretarial employment, and with GI money, he enrolled in school.

Somehow, his goal was accomplished and he opened private practice in Fort Pierre. Ability won him recognition and today he is prominent in legal and civic circles. He has held numerous city, county and state offices, and is active in Indian affairs.

BIRTHPLACE: Rosebud, South Dakota, November 15, 1924.
MARRIED: Cecilia Frank. CHILDREN: Michael, Marcus, Yvette.
EDUCATION: Haskell Institute; George Washington University (B.A., LLB).
HONORS: Phi Kappa Alpha; Delta Theta Phi.
ORGANIZATIONS: American Legion (past post commander); Veterans of Foreign Wars; Elks; Moose.

JODY DREADFULWATER (CHEROKEE) TEACHER-COUNSELOR; PRESIDENT, CHEROKEE FLOATS, INC.

Jody Dreadfulwater entered the Marine Corps as soon as he graduated from high school. After 4½ years in service, he enrolled in college. For six years after receiving his degree he taught school and then returned to school to secure a certificate in elementary teaching. He continued to add to his formal schooling by attending night classes and summer school. He says, "I wanted to get an education because I knew there was something better than eking out a living at a low level of existence."

Jody hitchhiked seven miles to college each day. His parents were not financially able to help him, which is really why he went into military service. The GI benefits would be useful in furthering his education. He borrowed funds from a local bank to attend college and repaid this loan from his GI benefits. He worked during the summer months at a funeral home to help get needed funds.

He is presently employed by the Indian Division, Oklahoma State Department of Education as Visiting Coordinator. He is assigned to two counties with predominantly Cherokee population. "Their problems are my problems," he says and he does what he can to help and encourage each student to complete his education.

A recognized leader among his people, Jody taught the first adult education class sponsored by the Bureau of Indian Affairs, among Cherokees.

In 1969, Jody embarked on an ambitious and unusual project. He organized, with the help of Oklahomans for Indian Opportunity, a Cherokee-owned corporation known as Cherokee Floats, Inc. The company was conceived by the Cherokee community at Briggs, Oklahoma, to give its young people needed employment. High school and college age students are employed as pilots of float boats along a 15-mile trip on the scenic Illinois River. The guides are trained in handling the floats and have an intimate knowledge of the river. They not only know where the good fishing is, but also are familiar with the history and legends of the countryside.

The boats hold two adults and a child and are operated daily throughout the year.

BIRTHPLACE: Tahlequah, Oklahoma.
MARRIED: Martha Holt. CHILDREN: Frank, Ruth.
EDUCATION: Northeastern State College (B.A., M.A., pending).
MILITARY SERVICE: U.S. Marine Corps, 4½ years, partly in Korea.

D'ARCY McNICKLE (FLATHEAD) PROFESSOR OF ANTHROPOLOGY, AUTHOR

Mr. McNickle is the author of a number of successful books on Indian subjects. He is one of the most highly educated of Indian people having attended both Oxford and Grenoble Universities. He financed his education through the sale of reservation holdings.

For several years, Mr. McNickle was employed by the Bureau of Indian Affairs as Director of Tribal Relations. He then was Executive Director of American Indian Development. He is currently Professor of Anthropology at the University of Saskatchewan.

BIRTHPLACE: St. Ignatius, Montana, January 18, 1904.
MARRIED: Viola Pfrommer. (Two daughters by a former marriage).
EDUCATION: University of Montana; Oxford University; Grenoble University.
HONORS: Honorary,Sc.D., University of Colorado.
AUTHOR: *The Surrounded* (1936); *They Came Here First* (1949); *Runner in the Sun* (1954); *Indians and Other Americans* (co-author 1959); *Indian Tribes of the United States* (1962) *Oliver LaFarge* a biography (in writing).
ORGANIZATIONS: National Congress of American Indians (a founder); American Anthropological Association (Fellow); Society for Applied Anthropology (Fellow).

GEORGE W. WALLER (SENECA-CHEROKEE) PHYSICIST

George Waller is an honor graduate of the University of California who has chosen astro-physics as his career. During his college years he maintained a 3.3 GPA (2=4), maintained a 3.5 GPA in his major, ranked in the upper 3 percent of the 1969 physics graduates. He plans to return to graduate school for further study in his chosen field.

George partly financed his way through college by working as a dormitory waiter; with a stage crew; and as a research assistant in the Department of Astronomy. At one point he was doing all these things to earn money. He also worked during summers as a science aide at the Air Force Weapons Laboratory, KAFB.

BIRTHPLACE: Evanston, Illinois, September 16, 1947.
EDUCATION: California Institute of Technology (B.S., Cum Laude)
HONORS: General Motors Scholar (1965-69); Presidential Scholar (1965); National Honor Scholar (1965); National Science Foundation Fellow (1969) (declined); Honor Certificate, senior year; Tau Beta Pi.
ORGANIZATIONS: American Astronomical Society; American Physical Society.

DILLON PLATERO
(NAVAJO) EDUCATOR

Dillon Platero has concentrated his activities in the field of Indian education since his graduation from college. As chairman of the Tribal Council Committee on Education, he worked to secure tribal funds for this purpose. He was so successful that the largest single appropriation by the Council at that time was a $10,000,000 perpetual fund for college scholarships.

Dillon believes that Indians should assume control of the education of their children, and this philosophy is put into practice at the Rough Rock Demonstration School where he serves as director. Thewschool has aroused much interest among educators.

Dillon is the founder and first editor of the *Navajo Times,* the tribal newspaper. He was a representative from the Tribe to India, sent to observe education and community development there. He has also been a field director for the Indian Community Action Program at Arizona State University. This assignment covered several states.

BIRTHPLACE: Canoncito, New Mexico, November 17, 1926.
MARRIED: Mary Rose. CHILDREN: (9).
EDUCATION: New Mexico Western College; University of New Mexico; Arizona State University.
SCHOLARSHIPS: Navajo Tribal Scholarship.
ORGANIZATIONS: Dine Biolta Association (president).
SPECIAL INTERESTS: National Advisory Committee on Bilingual Education (member); Leadership Training Institute for Career Opportunities (member).

LORETTA S. JENDRITZA (NAVAJO) NURSE, U.S. AIR FORCE

Major Jendritza is the first Navajo woman to attain the rank of Major while on active duty with the Air Force.

She has served as a surgical staff nurse and a medical evacuation flight nurse. Following a tour of duty at Cam Rahn Bay, Vietnam, she is now an operating-room supervisor at George, AFB.

Major Jendritza has represented American Indian Women in Military Service at special events, and frequently speaks before school and club groups.

BIRTHPLACE: Farmington, New Mexico.
MARRIED: Warren E. Jendritza.
EDUCATION: Ganado Mission School; Sage Memorial Hospital (R.N.)
SCHOLARSHIPS: D. A. R.
MILITARY SERVICE: U.S. Air Force, 1955 (Commendation Medal, for Vietnam duty; Vietnam Service Medal).
ORGANIZATIONS: Aerospace Medical Association; Association of Operating Room Nurses (past chairman of board, local chapter).

BUFORD MORRISON (CREEK) SUPERINTENDENT, MICCOSUKEE AGENCY

Mr. Morrison started as a $45.00 per month clerk with the Bureau of Indian Affairs at the Jicarilla Agency in New Mexico.

He rose through various positions at the Papago Agency, Haskell Institute, Anadarko Area Office, and the Potawatomi Agency where he was area field representative and superintendent for thirteen years.

Mr. Morrison can point with pride to many things in his carreer which have to do with Indian accomplishment. Modestly, he says that Indian people are 99½ percent responsible for any success they achieve and could achieve it without assistance.

Although he has had a measure of success without much formal education, Mr. Morrison advises Indian young people that his way was not easy and that it required much study and self-discipline. To young Indians, he says, "Get in there and make the most of every educational opportunity that becomes available."

BIRTHPLACE: Lenna, Oklahoma, November 24, 1919.
MARRIED: Barbara Jane Shepherd.
EDUCATION: Haskell Institute.
MILITARY SERVICE: U.S. Army, 1942-46, European Theatre.
ORGANIZATIONS: Kiwanis.

FRED W. GABOURIE (SENECA) ATTORNEY

Mr. Gabourie is a partner in a prominent California law firm specializing in Indian law and in the defense of Indians. The firm represents several reservations for the purpose of industrial development. It is also in the process of establishing a furniture manufacturing chain on reservations that will extend from coast to coast.

Raised on the Six Nations Reservation in Canada, Mr. Gabourie entered the movie industry in 1948 as a stunt man. He was a double for James Mason in *Twenty Thousand Leagues Under the Sea.* He has also been a professional racing car driver.

BIRTHPLACE: Los Angeles, California.

MARRIED: Frances. CHILDREN: Troy, Anne, Fred Jr., George,

EDUCATION: Loyola University (B.S.); University of Southern California; Van Norman University.

MILITARY SERVICE: U.S. Army.

ORGANIZATIONS: Urban Indian Development Association; Many Trails Indian Club; Drum and Feather Club (Board); California Indian Education Association (Board). California Indian Legal Services (Board); Este Muskegee Club; Federated Indian Tribes; Los Angeles Indian Center. American Bar Association; California State Bar Association; Los Angeles County Bar Association; San Fernando Valley Bar Association; San Fernando Valley Criminal Bar Association; American Judicature Society; U.S. Commission on Civil Rights; American Legion.

FRANK AUSTIN (NAVA-JO) TEXTILE ARTIST

Frank Austin has been interested in art for as long as he can remember, but it was not until 1954 that he began to express himself as a creative artist. His start in textile design was encouraged by Lloyd New, a top designer in this field.

The artist now offers his original, hand painted items exclusively through his own business, Nixhonie Fabrics, Inc. The name is a Navajo word meaning "elegant" or "beautiful."

BIRTHPLACE: Tsegi Canyon, Arizona, April 10, 1938.

MARRIED: Rose L. Adajie. CHILDREN: Camellia, Dwayne, Tanya.

EDUCATION: Phoenix Indian School; University of Arizona; Tempe College. (Part of his education was financed by the Rockefeller Foundation Fund for Indian Education).

HONORS: International Design Award, American Institute of Interior Designers (1962).

EXHIBITIONS: Many exhibits; several public and private collections.

AWARDS: One Grand Award among other awards.

ORGANIZATIONS: American Craftsmen's Council; Arizona Arts and Crafts Council.

AMANDA M. CROWE (CHEROKEE) WOOD SCULPTURE AND CARVING TEACHER

Amanda Crowe is a woodcarver of rare ability. She teaches her art on her home reservation and is dedicated to helping her people develop their natural skill in arts and crafts.

When she was in school, Amanda usually had a pocketknife and a piece of wood in her hands. She whittled extremely natural figures of the creatures of the woods - a squirrel gnawing on a nut, a frolicsome bear cub, or a mother bear - all brought to life with the magic of her hands.

When Amanda was orphaned in girlhood, she lived with friends in Chicago. She was encouraged to study art and many scholarships came in recognition of her ability. She earned her way through college with the sale of her work and by teaching during the summer months.

Seventeen years ago, she returned to her people to develop woodcarving as an important craft and an increasing source of revenue. She works with the beautiful native hardwoods of cherry, holly and walnut and her original pieces are in great demand. More important to her are the prizes won by her pupils, for these show the results of her devotion to the development of creativity.

BIRTHPLACE: Murphy, North Carolina, July 16, 1928.
EDUCATION: DePaul University (B.A.); Chicago Art Institute (B.F.A.).

54

SCHOLARSHIPS: Chicago Public Art Society (4 years); Past Graduate Scholarship; John Quincy Adams Fellowship for study in Mexico.

HONORS: Many prizes.

EXHIBITS: Many major exhibits, including travelling exhibits in Germany and Egypt; many permanent collections, including Blair House, Washington, D.C; and Queen Elizabeth's collections.

SPECIAL ACTIVITIES: (Qualla Arts and Crafts Mutual, Inc. (executive board).

MARVIN L. FRANKLIN (IOWA) BUSINESS EXECUTIVE; ATTORNEY

Marvin Franklin is Director of Special Cooperative Projects for Phillips Petroleum Company. He joined Phillips in 1947 after training combat pilots during World War II.

He started in the finance section of the company, and in 1951 transferred to the production department, handling regulatory matters before state, local and federal agencies. In 1964, he became associated with the chemical department, performing commercial evaluations relating to acquisition of companies in the Phillips diversification program.

In 1965, Mr. Franklin was appointed to his present position. It is his job to coordinate job availability potential of industry with government efforts toward developing industry in areas in which employment opportunities are desperately needed.

Particular emphasis is placed on programs, generated by the Bureau of Indian Affairs, aimed at accelerating industrial development in reservation areas. Feasibility data for funding such business enterprises is being developed in cooperation with the Department of Commerce, and with the Economic Development Administration and the Small Business Administration. Much has been accomplished in developing new industrial enterprises which will fulfill the goal of creating new, and exciting job opportunities for Indians.

At one time, Mr. Franklin organized and was an active officer in a life insurance company; an investment company; and a partner in a law firm.

He has worked with his tribe as a councilman and later as chairman of the general tribal council. He is presently vice-chairman of the tribal executive committee, and president of Indian Enterprises, Inc., founded by the four Indian tribes of northeastern Kansas to assist in bringing job opportunities to their tribal members.

The directors and stock holders of this group are representatives of these four tribes. The group functions to create opportunities for individual Indian business opportunities or tribally-owned businesses.

BIRTHPLACE: Ponca City, Oklahoma.
EDUCATION: Northern Oklahoma College; Oklahoma City University (LLB).
SPECIAL INTERESTS: Provesta Company (vice-president); Cherokee Nation Industries, Inc., (chairman, board; chief executive officer); Intertribe (chairman of board); Navajo Forest Products Industries (director); American Petroleum Institute (advisory committee, school materials); Navajo Forest Training and Scholarship Foundation (director; vice-president); Phillips Industrial Finance Committee (president); Indian Enterprises, Inc. (president); Eastern Navajo Indians, Inc. (director); Oklahoma Vocational Technical Foundation (president).

SAMUEL BILLISON (NA-VAJO) HIGH SCHOOL ADMINISTRATOR

Samuel Billison comes from a traditional Navajo family. Both of his parents are uneducated; his grandfather, Hosteen Gani, was a medicine man.

Mr. Billison, will be the first of his tribe to have a doctorate degree in education upon completion of his dissertation. Primarily trained as a high school administrator, he has been a high school principal in Oklahoma and in Texas. Returning to his reservation, as field worker for the Neighborhood Youth Corps, he planned and coordinated youth programs on all Arizona Indian reservations. He has been director of public services for the Navajo Tribe and is an elected member of the Navajo Tribal Council.

BIRTHPLACE: Ganado, Arizona, March 14, 1925.
MARRIED: Patsy Sells. CHILDREN: Samuel, Robert, John, Larry.
EDUCATION: Albuquerque Indian School; Bacone College (Dean's Distinguished Student; president, Student Council; East Central State College (B.A.); Oklahoma University (M.Ed.); University of Arizona (Ed.D. pending).
MILITARY SERVICE: U.S. Marines, World War II. (amphibious reconnaissance, radio-communication. Participated in landing on Iwo Jima and occupational duty in Japan).
ORGANIZATIONS: Arizona delegate to White House Youth Conference; Lions Club; Kinlichee School Board (chairman); Inter--agency School Board (chairman); Phi Delta Kappa; Veterans of Foreign Wars.

HAROLD S. JONES (DAKOTA-SANTEE) PRIEST, EPISCOPAL CHURCH

Harold Jones' grandfather was an Episcopal priest in charge of religious work on two reservations. When he died, Harold worked with a railroad section crew to help support his family. He worked his way through college until financial reverses forced him to stop. With whatever work he could get, with what he could save, and with some additional help from the government, he was able to complete both his college and seminary training.

Harold began his religious career on the Pine Ridge Reservation. He was ordained to the Diaconate at Pine Ridge by the Bishop of South Dakota who also ordained him to the priesthood. For a number of years he was in charge of the Trinity Mission and Director of Christian Education at Wahpeton Indian School, North Dakota. He is now vicar of the Good Shepherd Mission on the Navajo reservation. In 1969, he was instituted as Canon to the Ordinary by the Bishop of the Diocese of Arizona.

BIRTHPLACE: Mitchell, South Dakota, December 24, 1909.
MARRIED: Blossom Steele. CHILDREN: Norma Joy Jones Pederson.
EDUCATION: Southern State Teacher's College; Northern State Teacher's College (B.S.); Seabury-Western Theological Seminary (L.Th.).
ORGANIZATIONS: 32nd degree Scottish Rite Masons.

GEORGE P. LaVATTA (SHOSHONE-BANNOCK) GOVERNMENT EMPLOY-EE, RETIRED

Believing that work and organization are the salvation of any people, Mr. LaVatta dedicated himself to setting an example of industry and usefulness for his people.

As a youth, he persistently applied to the Union Pacific Railroad for work and was finally given a job as a laborer. He enrolled in night school to further his education, and his diligence brought him several promotions. In his later years with the railroad, he helped to organize safety, welfare and good-will programs, and organized work programs on his reservation, assisting many Indian young people to profitable employment.

As assistant guidance and placement officer for the Bureau of Indian Affairs he continued this activity. He was advanced to field agent, then to the superintendency of the Taholah jurisdiction comprised of ten reservations, and finally to Area Administration Officer, headquartered in Portland, Oregon.

BIRTHPLACE: Fort Hall Reservation, Idaho.
MARRIED: Viola Welch.
EDUCATION: Carlisle Indian School.
HONORS: Indian Council Fire Achievement Award and honorary life membership (1938); Citation for Distinguished Service, Department of Interior (1966).
ORGANIZATIONS: Optimist International; National Congress of American Indians.

JANE PABLO PENN (WANA-KIK-CAHUILLA) HISTORIAN, MUSEUM DIRECTOR

Mrs. Penn has lived most of her life on her home reservation. When she was a child, she heard tales of tribal history and became greatly interested in her cultural background.

Interest, enthusiasm and hard work helped her to establish the Malki Museum, the first public museum on a southern California Indian Reservation. The museum's initial collection of Indian artifacts belonged to her.

Some of this material includes mortars and an olla or pottery jar used in ancient times. A herb cooking pot used by Mrs. Penn's father to prepare herbs for medicinal purposes, is also in the collection.

BIRTHPLACE: Morongo Reservation, May 6, 1910.
MARRIED: Elmer Penn.
EDUCATION: Public school.
HONORS: Scope Award (first ever given by the Pacific Region, Soroptimist Federation of the Americas, for an older woman who started a new career (1968); Honorary Life Member, American Indian Historical Society (honored historian - 1968).
SPECIAL ACTIVITIES: Delegate from Morongo Reservation to Inter-Tribal Council of California.

WILLARD STONE (CHEROKEE) SCULPTOR, ARTIST *

With almost no artistic training, Willard Stone produces carvings of wood that are purely the result of genius and an inner urge to create. His works have an inner grace and great feeling for the use of wood grain - even a slender piece of wood is converted into captured beauty. His skill is all the more remarkable because he is without three fingers on his right hand.

Left fatherless in infancy, times were very rough for Willard and his mother. When an exploding dynamite cap blew off three fingers, he lost interest in school and worked at farming. As a pastime, he modeled some pieces with bits of clay and entered them in an exhibit. These won three blue ribbons and he was "discovered," and helped to enter college. He worked his way through school with the sales of his carvings, and today he can hardly meet the demand for his exquisite pieces.

BIRTHPLACE: Oktaha, Oklahoma.
MARRIED: Sophie Coger. CHILDREN: Sophie, Nettie, Jason, Danny, Evelyn, Lyda, Joyce, Dwight, Rocky, Michael.
EDUCATION: Bacone College.
EXHIBITIONS: More than ten major exhibits; many collections; many awards.
ORGANIZATIONS: Kiwanis; Masons.
SPECIAL ACTIVITIES: Gilcrease Museum; Museum of the Five Civilized Tribes.

*See art section

LIONEL H. deMONTIGNY (TURTLE MOUNTAIN CHIPPEWA) PHYSICIAN, RESEARCH AND DEVELOPMENT SPECIALIST

Dr. deMontigny joined the U.S. Public Health Service in 1962 as Field Medical Officer. He was the first appointee to the 3-year residency training program in preventive medicine established by the Division of Indian Health in cooperation with the University of Oklahoma School of Medicine and the Oklahoma State Health Department. He was next appointed deputy director of the PHS Portland Area Office. In this position he has initiated tribally operated health programs, and has tried to encourage Indian young people to enter medical school.

BIRTHPLACE: Belcourt, North Dakota, October 17, 1935.
MARRIED: Barbara Waupochick. CHILDREN: Suzy, Cindy, Cheri, Antoine.
EDUCATION: University of North Dakota (B.S., B.A.); University of Wisconsin (M.D.); University of Oklahoma (MSPH).
SCHOLARSHIPS: John Hay Whitney Fellow; Indian Health Scholarship.
HONORS: University of Oklahoma Honor Roll; Phi Eta Sigma (honorary fraternity).
ORGANIZATIONS: American Public Health Association, American Medical Association.

JAMES ATCITTY (NAVAJO) YOUTH CORP DIRECTOR

James Atcitty is one of the first two Navajos elected to the New Mexico House of Representatives. He entered politics because he believes that Indians of New Mexico are not fully aware of state legislation and that they should have a voice in matters affecting themselves. They are most properly represented by Indian people, he says.

Mr. Atcitty is currently Neighborhood Youth Corp Director at Fort Defiance, Arizona and Supervisor of the Board of Elections for the Navajo Tribe.

BIRTHPLACE: Shiprock, New Mexico, September 22, 1933.
MARRIED: Eleanor Henderson. CHILDREN: Charles, Shari, Renee, Shanan, Nicole.
EDUCATION: Navajo Methodist Mission School; University of New Mexico.
MILITARY SERVICE: U.S. Army, 1953-55.

Photo: Theodore B. Hetzel

EARL OLD PERSON (BLACKFEET) TRIBAL LEADER

Earl Old Person, chairman of the Blackfeet Tribal Council, is also president of the National Congress of American Indians. The organization represents two-thirds of the 650,000 Indian population from 118 tribes across the nation. Mr. Old Person was elected president during the largest convention ever held by the NCAI.

In his acceptance speech, Mr. Old Person called for the unification of all Indians and for an end to militancy. "I think we can solve our problems in an intelligent way," he said. "I've never advocated demonstrations to achieve our demands."

Under his leadership as tribal chairman, the Blackfeet have prepared a proposal for a 1½ million dollar recreational complex on tribal land. They have allocated funds to expand their museum so that it will be a research source. A modern housing development program is underway. They have also constructed several community centers and have set aside 67 acres for an industrial park.

"When I was a boy, my father told me I had the choice of a pencil or a spoon." Mr. Old Person says. "The pencil meant education, the spoon was a shovel. You used to be able to get a job with a shovel, but today, you need an education, even to dig a post hole. Education will be the Indians weapon," he says.

BIRTHPLACE: Browning, Montana.
MARRIED: Virginia Whitegrass.
EDUCATION: Public Schools.
HONORS: Selected as one of ten Indian leaders to participate in an exchange program with Maori leaders of New Zealand.
SPECIAL INTERESTS: Travel - has travelled through France, Belgium, Luxemburg and Switzerland.

WAYNE WOLF ROBE HUNT (PUEBLO-ACOMA) INTERPRETER OF INDIAN CULTURE

Wolf Robe grew up in the "sky city" of Acoma, which was built long before the Spaniards came to the Southwest. He was raised on a cradleboard. As a child he was trained to take part in the religious dances of his people. His father was chief of the "Delight Makers," the group which announces the dates of the tribal ceremonial calendar.

The State of New Mexico credits the elder Hunt as the one person most responsible for the growth of peaceful relationships between the Indians and the whites. He persuaded the people to permit the building of government day schools on the reservation and gave some of his own land for that purpose. He also effected on agreement permitting the Santa Fe Railroad to run tracks through the reservation.

Wolf Robe's mother was the daughter of a seven times governor of Acoma. She was an expert weaver and pottery maker.

A highly successful interpreter of Indian arts and customs, Wolf Robe is also an able artist. He has appeared before school audiences and educational bodies across the country, and for a time was interpreter of Pueblo material for the Smithsonian Institution. Since 1964, he has appeared in eleven foreign countries with the United States "America Weeks" promotions.

He owns and operates an Indian arts and crafts shop just outside of Tulsa where he offers only the best of authentic Indian wares.

BIRTHPLACE: Acoma, New Mexico.
MARRIED: Glenal Davis. CHILDREN: Lo-Way-Ne-Ma Hunt Craig.
EDUCATION: Albuquerque Indian School.
HONORS: Grand Award, Philbrook Art Center for painting, "Dancing With Snakes." (1967)
AUTHOR-ILLUSTRATOR: *The Dancing Horses of Acoma.* World, 1963.
ORGANIZATIONS: Scottish Rite Mason. Akdar Shrine.

KENNETH L. PAYTON (CHEROKEE) SUPERINTENDENT, SOUTHERN PUEBLOS INDIAN AGENCY

Mr. Payton has spent his life in working with Indian tribes and individuals in improving educational, social, and economic conditions.

"It appears that this is an era of opportunity for Indian people to make their own decisions and determine their own destinies in a manner never before possible," he says.

He has been superintendent at the Mescalero Indian Agency and Consolidated Ute Agency. His father was Indian Education Administrator on the Navajo reservation.

BIRTHPLACE: Picher, Oklahoma, August 3, 1926.
MARRIED: Dorothy Johnson. CHILDREN: Barbara, Janet, Cathi.
EDUCATION: Oklahoma State University (B.S.).
MILITARY SERVICE: U.S. Navy, 1944-46.
ORGANIZATIONS: Lions.

WOODROW SNEED (CHEROKEE) ATTOR-NEY

Woodrow Sneed, who has been on the faculty of the University of New Mexico Law School, was named a White House Fellow by President Nixon in 1970. In this capacity, he is special assistant to Vice President Agnew on the National Council of Indian Opportunity.

At one time, Mr. Sneed was legal aid adviser to the Navajo Tribe. He has also been a director of field training for VISTA; deputy director for the Office of Navajo Economic Opportunity; and, Director of Indian Services at the University of Utah.

Mr. Sneed is a descendant of Sequoyah, the inventor of the Cherokee alphabet who did so much to advance the progress of the tribe; of Tsali, who gave his life so that his people could remain in the Smoky Mountains; and of Swimmer, the keeper of legends.

BIRTHPLACE: Cherokee, North Carolina, April 21, 1937.
MARRIED: Rosemarie Dixon. CHILDREN: Woodrow, Lucianne, John, Matthew.
EDUCATION: Brigham Young University (B.S.); Harvard Law School (LL.B.).
SCHOLARSHIPS: Tuition scholarships; Bureau of Indian Affairs; John Hay Whitney Foundation Fellow.
ORGANIZATIONS: National Alliance of Indian Leaders (board); National Indian Training and Research Center (board).

GLADYS SKYE WALLACE (PEORIA) STOCKBROKER

Gladys Skye Wallace is one of not even a handful of Indian women in the world of finance. Her achievements in the financial field came after she had retired from an already successful career as an executive secretary and staff assistant with Sinclair and Gulf Oil Companies.

For the past fifteen years she has been in the securities business, working with women's investment clubs and handling mutual funds. She was the top producer of all the brokers in the Tulsa office of the company for which she once worked. Mrs. Wallace has carte blanche from many big investors to buy and sell for them at her discretion.

She is certified by the State and National Associations of Security Dealers and has passed the New York Stock Exchange examination and is a registered representative on the Exchange.

Mrs. Wallace's father was chief of the Peoria Indians.

BIRTHPLACE: Commerce, Oklahoma.
MARRIED: Grady Wallace.
EDUCATION: Haskell Institute.
HONORS: Outstanding Graduate Award, Haskell Institute (1970).
ORGANIZATIONS: Tulsa Council American Indians (public relations); Tulsa Chapter, Executive Secretaries (past president); Tulsa Country Club.

HORACE E. GLADSTONE (BLOOD) LIVESTOCK COORDINATOR, BLOOD AND PIEGAN RESERVES

Mr. Gladstone is the first member of his tribe to be appointed to the Senate of the University of Lethbridge.

Reservation born and raised, he is the son of Canada's only Indian Senator. For a number of years after his schooling, he was engaged in large scale, diversified farming and ranching. As the first Indian farm instructor for the Blood Reserve, the largest in Canada, he was responsible for the supervision of 85 grain farmers, and an area of 20,000 acres.

The next assignment was in northern Alberta to establish a new sub-agency among a group of Slavey Indians. Mr. Gladstone's work was outstanding, and the Indians have frequently requested his return. Immediately prior to his present situation, he was a general administrator on various Indian reserves in Alberta.

BIRTHPLACE: Cardston, Alberta, November 22, 1929.
MARRIED: Aileen Young Man. CHILDREN: Alexis, Rosie, Brenda, Rowena, Bernice.
ORGANIZATIONS: Lions; Elks; Lethbridge Chamber of Commerce Council.
SPECIAL INTERESTS: Art, music, Indian history.

THOMAS N. ALMOJUELA (SQUAMISH) ARMY OFFICER AND HELICOPTER PILOT

Captain Almojuela is the first Northwest Indian to graduate from West Point Military Academy, and one of very few Indians to attend the Academy. The enrollments of students are not kept by race so the exact number of Indians is not possible to obtain.

A brilliant student, he was a Congressional appointee to the Academy, one of two from his area chosen from the 1963 selection list.

At West Point, Almojuela was outstanding. Not only was his academic record brilliant, but he was a top ranking athlete.

Prior to service in Vietnam, Captain Almojuela commanded a tank company in Germany. In Vietnam he flew AHIG Cobra gunships and was also in ground combat.

BIRTHPLACE: Seattle, Washington, April 24, 1943.
EDUCATION: Olympic College; U.S. Military Academy. (B.S.)
HONORS: Phi Beta Kappa; Lettered in four sports; All-State Basketball (2 years); Dean's List at West Point.
MILITARY HONORS: Silver Star; Two Distinguished Flying Crosses; Bronze Star; Air Medal with 33 Oak Clusters; Army Commendation Medal; National Defense Medal; Vietnamese Campaign Medal; Combat Infantryman's Badge.

JAMES GLADSTONE (BLOOD) RANCHER; SENATOR, CANADIAN PARLIAMENT

James Gladstone is the first treaty Indian ever to be appointed to the Canadian Senate. (1958) Under the Conservative Government, he was named co-chairman of a Joint Committee set up to study the affairs of Canada's Indian population, then numbering 174,000.

Senator Gladstone owns and operates one of the finest ranches on his home reserve, building up its capacity and capabilities through modern ranching techniques. He was the first person on the reserve to use power machinery, chemical sprays and other new methods and equipment. His home was the first to be electrified.

During World War I, Mr. Gladstone was employed to put large areas into crops in support of the war effort. Then he was appointed stock man to teach his fellow tribesmen the proper care of their cattle. He has been noted for his devotion to the total Indian cause, and has worked for Indians on a national basis for nearly 60 years.

On several occasions, before his appointment to the Senate, he had been a delegate to Ottawa to discuss proposed changes in the Indian Act. During this time he travelled extensively to meet with the different tribes in the western provinces. He played a prominent role in the drive for better education, greater respect for Indian treaty rights, and participation of Indians in their own administration. Although reared in a mission church, he is also a supporter of native traditions and religious practices. Mr. Gladstone is a member of the ancient Crazy Dog Society.

In a statement made after his appointment to the Senate, Mr. Gladstone said: "My work will be aimed at improving the position of Canada's Indians, obtaining for them better conditions as they want them and are ready for them. I'm particularly interested in seeing more encouragement given to Indians for individual, rather than collective effort."

This continues to be his philosophy and throughout his more than twelve years in the Senate he has encouraged and promoted progress among the Indians of Canada so that they will become self-supporting.

BIRTHPLACE: Cardston, Alberta.

MARRIED: Janie Healy. CHILDREN: Lucy Gladstone Swite; Nora Gladstone Baldwin; Doreen Gladstone Hendra; Pauline Gladstone Dempsey; Horace. (Two daughters are registered nurses and one a social worker).

EDUCATION: Mission school; Calgary Industrial School.

HONORS: Outstanding Indian of the Year, All-American Indian Days (1960); Honorary Doctor of Laws degree, University of Lethbridge (1969); Indian Association of Alberta (honorary president 1958).

WALDO E. McINTOSH (CREEK) PRINCIPAL CHIEF, CREEK NATION

Chief McIntosh, better known as "Dode" came to Oklahoma with his family a few years before statehood. His father was superintendent of the Creek and Seminole schools.

"Dode's" career has been varied. He has taught a country school, been a city clerk, a lumber merchant, a real estate broker, a county assessor and a county treasurer. He is serving his fifth term as principal chief of the Creek Nation.

McIntosh County in Oklahoma is named for this illustrious family which is also related to the Clan McIntosh of Scotland. When visiting that country, Mr. McIntosh was honored by the McIntosh Clan. He has developed a plaid design for the Creeks which has been patented - the first patent of this type ever granted to an Indian tribe. The "Creek Indian Plaid" is to be manufactured on a mass production basis and a line of children's and women's wear is to be developed using it.

BIRTHPLACE: Carthage, Tennessee.
MARRIED: Lulu Vance. CHILDREN: William, Nocus, Chinnubbie, Wilfred McIntosh Lee.
EDUCATION: Tribal and public schools.
HONORS: Many, for civic services.
MILITARY SERVICE: World War I, six months.
ORGANIZATIONS: Inter-tribal Council, Five Civilized Tribes (president).

74

TRINIDAD J. DUPREE (PUEBLO-SAN JUAN) SCHOOL PRINCIPAL

Trinidad Dupree began his educational career on the Cherokee reservation in North Carolina. He is now principal of this reservation school. His 28-year career has been in federal Indian service as a shop teacher, a coach, a teacher-adviser and as a principal.

At Cherokee School, traditional educational programs are being evaluated in the light of educational needs of the present and future. A kindergarten program is being expanded and a Follow-Through program is under consideration. Other essentials in compensatory educational projects are to be put into effect.

Mr. Dupree has devoted himself to work with Indian young people and has an excellent record in this regard.

BIRTHPLACE: San Juan, New Mexico, October 28, 1916.
MARRIED: Betty Ann Craig. CHILDREN: David, Warren, Charmaine, Mark.
EDUCATION: Carson Indian School; University of Nevada; San Jose State College (B.A.); Northern Arizona Graduate School.
HONORS: Superior Service Award, Bureau of Indian Affairs (1960).
MILITARY SERVICE: U.S. Army Signal Corps, World War II, four years plus, South Pacific. (Two battle stars).
ORGANIZATIONS: National Congress of American Indians; Knights of Columbus (past recorder, Grand Knight); Cherokee Employees Association.

RAYMOND NAKAI (NAVAJO) CHAIRMAN, TRIBAL COUNCIL

At the time of his election to the chairmanship of the Navajo Tribal Council (1963) Raymond Nakai was a radio announcer and disk jockey. He also worked for a naval ordnance depot.

Nakai was virtually unknown outside the reservation when he made his bid for chairmanship. Today, he heads the 74-man council, administers a budget running into millions of dollars, and is known across the country.

Nakai is a shy, sensitive man, and an inveterate reader. His choice in books are those which have political thought, the Great Books, and the social encyclicals of the 20th century Popes.

It has been said that nowhere in the United States, and perhaps nowhere in the world, have a people faced challenge more energetically than have the Navajo in the past 100 years. The reservation is the largest in the country and is occupied by 118,000 Indians. Raymond Nakai has been very much a part of the accomplishments of recent times.

Navajo lands are producing coal, oil, gas, uranium, timber, crops and livestock. An irrigation system has transformed the once bleak land. There are tribally owned luxury hotels and motels; a thriving tourist business; nine tribal parks patrolled by Navajo rangers. Good roads span the once inaccessible reservation.

The tribe has its own public library and museum, and its own college. Ten years ago, thousands of Navajo children had no school to attend. Today, it would be hard to find a child not in school. The tribe has its own scholarship fund of $10 million and the young tribal leaders are well-educated and forward looking.

The Navajo Arts and Crafts Guild has restored the fine old crafts of weaving and silversmithing. Navajo language broadcasts are heard across the reservation. There are two industrial parks and a number of reservation-based industries. There are other vast tribal enterprises such as, a utility authority, a completely modern sawmill and a forest products industry. The Tribe has installed one of IBM's most advanced computers to manage its' million-dollar a month income and to handle the more than 125 distinct tribal projects and vast enterprises.

Mr. Nakai predicts the next 100 years will be a century of even greater achievement for his people. "We will not be content with modest achievements," he says, "we are on the threshold of great ones. Our goals are high."

BIRTHPLACE: Lukachukai, Arizona.
MARRIED: Ella Crawford. CHILDREN: Raymond Jr., Ursula, Michael, Richard, Laurinda.
EDUCATION: Fort Wingate and Shiprock Indian Schools.
MILITARY SERVICE: U.S. Navy, World War II, South Pacific.

RALPH A. FARROW (WALLA WALLA) PROFESSOR OF EDUCATION

A member of the faculty of Oregon College of Education, Ralph Farrow is especially interested in educational psychology, or learning and motivation.

Raised on the Umatilla reservation he has consistently pursued his educational interests.

BIRTHPLACE: Pendleton, Oregon, August 25, 1925.
MARRIED: Marian. CHILDREN: Daniel.
EDUCATION: Eastern Oregon College (B.S.); Colorado State College (M.A.); Stanford University (Ed.D.).
MILITARY SERVICE: U.S. Navy, World War II - 3 years.
ORGANIZATIONS: Phi Delta Kappa; Association for Student Teaching; Oregon Association for Student Teaching (past president); Oregon Education Association; National Education Association.

FRANK A. CALDER (NISHGA) PROVINCIAL REPRESENTATIVE; DISTRICT MANAGER, INVESTMENT COMPANY

Frank Calder is the first Indian to sit in a Canadian legislature. The son of an hereditary chief, he is credited with many major legislative actions. One of these important actions is the history making Nisgha land claim which is the first court case pertaining to Indian lands in Canada. It is expected to reach the Supreme Court of Canada, the United Nations and the International Court at the Hague.

As an outspoken champion for the franchise for Canadian Indians, he has advocated provincial rather than federal jurisdiction of Indian affairs.

Calder was first elected to the legislature in 1949. His far-flung political environs cover some of the most rugged territory in Canada and whites far outnumber his Indian constituents.

BIRTHPLACE: Nass Harbour, B.C., August 3, 1915.
EDUCATION: Anglican Theological College; University of British Columbia (L.Th.).
ORGANIZATIONS: B.C. Art and Welfare Society; B.C. Indian Affairs Branch (special advisory committee). Central Planning Committee for Western Canada; Nishga Tribal Council (founder-president); North American Brotherhood.

GERALD IVEY (ATHAB-ASCAN) NATIVE AF-FAIRS OFFICER, INDIAN HEALTH SERVICE

Well-known throughout the State of Alaska, Gerald Ivey has been very influential in furthering the interests of the Native people.

He has been especially interested in furthering the educational opportunities of the Alaskan Native Youth, working intensively on the development of the regional high school concept. At one time, he was principal of the elementary and high school at the Fort Wainwright Military Reservation.

In his present position, he is the coordinator of health programs with the Native people and with the involvement of Native leaders as advisors in the formation of new health program and planned program changes. He also relates to the health service the desires of the Native leaders and serves as the focal contact with BIA and State government agencies. He is concerned with some 50,000 Indian Eskimo and Aleut people and with nine hospitals varying in size from seven to 279 beds.

Among his goals are the formation of the Alaska Native Community Health Aide Training program and of Boards of Health composed of Native people.

BIRTHPLACE: McGrath, Alaska.
MARRIED: Rosalie Trejo. CHILDREN: Gerald, Clifford, Lou.
EDUCATION: Mt. Edgecumbe Indian School; Washington College

of Education; Western Washington College of Education; University of Alaska (B.A., M.A.).
ORGANIZATIONS: Fairbanks Native Association (past president); Alaska Federation of Natives (past board member); *Tundra Times* (past board); Alaska Education Association (past board member); Fort Wainwright Education Association (past president).

REX AHVAKANA (ESKIMO) AVIATION MECHANIC

Rex Ahvahana has been involved in aviation for 30 years. He lived in hunting, trapping and fishing camps until he was eleven - then decided to go to school when his family moved to Barrow.

"I felt pretty silly with all those little kids," he says, "but I was in the third grade by the end of the first year." He finished school at 16 and says proudly, "I was an 'on-time' student."

The next few years were spent in hunting, trapping and whaling. In 1935, when Will Rogers and Wiley Post crashed near Barrow, he had the unpleasant task of standing in three feet of water to saw the plane's metal in order to remove the bodies.

Ahvakana took his first plane ride in 1941 when he acted as guide to locate coal outcrops for the Bureau of Indian Affairs. Two years later, he was hired to do ground service and mechanical work for Wien Consolidated Airlines and has remained with the company except for a five-year period.

BIRTHPLACE: Barrow, Alaska.
MARRIED: Deva. CHILDREN: (5).
EDUCATION: Public School.

LOUIS B. MOFSIE (HOPI-WINNEBAGO) ART TEACHER

Louis Mofsie is an art teacher in the New York public schools. He also lectures on Indians and presents programs of Indian dancing.

Louis is one of the founders of the Thunderbird American Indian Dancers. With funds from programs given by this group, several scholarships for Indian students have been established. Through *Save the Children Federation* two Indian children are sponsored by this group.

Among other activities, Louis has choreographed two Indian dances for the Broadway shows, *Cherry* and *Operation Sidewinder*. He has helped produce an album of Indian songs distributed both here and abroad by Request Records. He has co-authored and illustrated a children's book about the Hopi tribe. He has introduced a Seminar for teachers at New York State University emphasizing the importance of Iroquois Indian culture in the history of the State and the nation.

Louis spends his summers visiting Indian reservations to learn the songs and dances of various tribes. He has also travelled extensively in Mexico and in seven European countries.

BIRTHPLACE: Brooklyn, New York, May 3, 1936.
EDUCATION: Public schools; State University of New York (B.S.); Hofstra University, Adelphi University, Long Island University.

SCHOLARSHIPS: D.A.R.; Arrow, Inc.; United Scholarship Service; Indian League of the Americas.

HONORS: Honorary degree in education. Hofstra University; Award for painting, Southwestern Association on Indian Affairs.

AUTHOR AND ILLUSTRATOR: *The Hopi Way* (Evans, 1969).

EXHIBITIONS: A number of museum exhibits.

ORGANIZATIONS: American Indian Community Center of New York (vice-president); Thunderbird American Indian Dancers; Indian League of the Americas of New York (past president); Folk Festival Council (treasurer, vice-president); Long Island Art Teachers Association (vice-chairman); New York State Teachers Association; National Education Association; Classroom Teachers Association.

WILLARD A. SCOTT (PUEBLO-LAGUNA) DIRECTOR, DIVISION OF INDIAN EDUCATION, NEW MEXICO DEPARTMENT OF EDUCATION

Mr. Scott began his educational career as guidance counselor and teacher in the Santa Fe Schools, and then as guidance specialist with the State Department of Education. In his present position, he is responsible for all educational matters affecting Indian school children and for the development of programs concerning them.

BIRTHPLACE: Albuquerque, New Mexico, June 28, 1930.

MARRIED: Lea Yandell. CHILDREN: Mark, Jeff, Carol.

EDUCATION: New Mexico State University (BA); University of New Mexico (MA).

SCHOLARSHIPS: Bureau of Indian Affairs; NDEA Fellowship.

MILITARY SERVICE: U.S. Army, Infantry, 2 years active service; 16 years, reserves.

ORGANIZATIONS: Kiwanis.

SPECIAL ACTIVITIES: Boy Scouts.

TE ATA (CHICKASAW) PLATFORM ARTIST

Te Ata's father was a member of the last council of the Chickasaws. In the course of her schooling, her unusual histrionic gifts were discovered and she went east for further training.

She first appeared on the New York stage as Andromache in *The Trojan Women.* Then came the fulfillment of her real destiny, the interpretation of Indian folklore. She has traveled far and wide in this country, and has appeared in several foreign lands, giving her program of legends, chants and rituals from a number of tribes. Her performance is a dramatic and striking presentation. She has appeared at the White House, and in Europe before the King and Queen of England. She is in great demand as a platform artist of rare skill.

BIRTHPLACE: Tishomingo, Oklahoma.

EDUCATION: Oklahoma College for Women (A.B.); Theatre School, Carnegie Institute of Technology; Columbia University; private teachers.

HONORS: Lake Te Ata, New York, named for her; Oklahoma Hall of Fame (1958); *Who's Who in America; Who's Who in East.*

ORGANIZATIONS: Society of Women Geographers; National Congress of American Indians; Oklahoma Historical Society; Zeta Phi Eta.

JACK R. RIDLEY (SHO-SHONE) CROP PHYSIOL-OGIST

Raised in an agricultural state, Jack Ridley naturally gravitated to a career in plant science. He is an assistant professor and assistant crop physiologist at the University of Idaho.

Aside from his regular duties of plant research and plant science teaching, Dr. Ridley is president of the newly formed Northwest Native American Graduate Program, Inc., which will be the first Indian planned, organized and executed graduate studies program in the country. The goal is self-improvement and self-determination through education for Native Americans. Management and leadership skills will be developed through the academic program, and better understanding between white and Indian culture will be advanced through cross-cultural comparisons.

BIRTHPLACE: Stewart, Nevada, June 16, 1933.
MARRIED: Sarah Kipp. CHILDREN: Jack, Jr., Jana, Jeffrey.
EDUCATION: Stewart Indian School; University of California (B.S., M.S., Ph.D.).
MILITARY SERVICE: U.S. Air Force, 1951-55.
PROFESSIONAL PAPERS: Eleven in scientific journals.
ORGANIZATIONS: Lions, American Society of Agronomy; Crop Science Society of America; American Society of Plant Physiologists; American Indian Historical Society.

GEORGE A. GILL (OMAHA) FACULTY ASSOCIATE, UNIVERSITY OF ARIZONA, COLLEGE OF EDUCATION

George Gill is the first Indian to receive a master's degree in Indian education. In addition to teaching at the University of Arizona, he directs the activities of the Indian Education Center. He has been a teacher in federal Indian schools and in public schools; a research assistant in the field of Indian education, and a director of workshops for instructional aides.

BIRTHPLACE: Sioux City, Iowa, July 25, 1925.

MARRIED: Frances Whitted. CHILDREN: Roger, Randy.

EDUCATION: University of Nebraska; Arizona State University (B.S., M.A.).

SCHOLARSHIPS: American Indian Foundation; National Congress of American Indians; Association on American Indian Affairs; American Missionary Association.

MILITARY SERVICE: U.S. Navy, 22 years, four months active and inactive - Europe, Mediterranean, Pacific, Korea. (Navy Good Conduct and Combat medals).

ORGANIZATIONS: American Legion Post 174 (past commander) American Legion Post No. 2 (past adjutant); Elks; National Congress of American Indians; Arizona Indian Association; national, state and local education associations.

SPECIAL ACTIVITIES: Annual Indian Education Conference (Conference Director); Editor, *Journal of Indian Education;* Arizona Indian delegate to 1960 White House Conference on Children and Youth.

86

LAURIE ARCHER CALK-IN (CHEROKEE) DANCER-ARTIST-ACTRESS

Mrs. Calkin has had a varied and successful career in the performing arts. She has studied modern dance, ballet, Spanish dance, Hindu dance, jazz, pantomime, acting and singing under distinguished teachers and has taught modern dancing and baton twirling. She has also designed the costumes for her own choreographic works and for other dance groups.

BIRTHPLACE:Corbin, Kentucky.

MARRIED: Brant C. Calkin.

EDUCATION: Colorado College (B.F.A.).

SCHOLARSHIPS: John Hay Whitney Fellow; Fulbright Fellow; Hanya Holm Scholarship; AMA Indian Affairs Scholarship; Louis Horst Scholarship; Jose Limon Scholarship; Colorado Springs Fine Arts Center Scholarship.

HONORS: Outstanding Art Student, Poetry prize, Drama Department Award, Colorado College (1959); Outstanding Actress, Lima (Peru) Theatre Workshop 1958; Columbia University Press Award 1952; National Scholastic Art Award (1949).

SPECIAL ACTIVITIES: Film animation; craft articles in various magazines.

BRANTLEY BLUE (LUMBEE) COMMISSIONER, INDIAN COURT OF CLAIMS

Brantley Blue is the first Indian to be appointed to the Indian Claims Commission. He was appointed by President Nixon in 1969.

An attorney, Mr. Blue practiced law in Tennessee for twenty years. He also served as city judge of Kingsport where he established his law practice.

Mr. Blue sees the work of the Claims Commission as one of the most important efforts ever made by this country to put its conscience on the table. "It is heartening to see the legislative branch willing to say to Indians, 'you were wronged by our predecessors and we want to make you whole'," he says.

BIRTHPLACE: Pembroke, North Carolina, October 11, 1925.
MARRIED: Dorothy Milam. CHILDREN: Janet, Patricia.
EDUCATION: Cumberland University (LL.B., supplemented by Doctor of Jurisprudence).
HONORS: Distinguished Alumnus Award, Pembroke State College (1969).
MILITARY SERVICE: U.S. Navy (1944-1946), European and Pacific Theatres.
ORGANIZATIONS: Hammond Post No. 3, American Legion (commander); Veterans of Foreign Wars.

WILL ANTELL (CHIPPEWA) DIRECTOR, INDIAN EDUCATION, STATE OF MINNESOTA

Will Antell has been a teacher of social science in high schools and a human relations consultant for the State of Minnesota. He has also taught courses on Indian culture and history, both historical and contemporary.

His primary interest is in Indian education. He has served on numerous, local and national committees and commissions dealing with Indian affairs. He testified before the United States Senate Subcommittee on Indian Education and has developed sensitivity training programs based upon his personal experiences as an Indian. He has been selected to represent Indian children and youth for the 1970 White House Conference on Children and Youth.

BIRTHPLACE: White Earth Reservation, Minnesota, October 2, 1935.

MARRIED: Mary Lou Ammerman. CHILDREN: Vicki, Ronald, Richard.

EDUCATION: Bemidji State College (B.S.); Mankato State College (M.S.); Northern Michigan University (NDEA Scholar); University of Minnesota (NDEA Scholar); St. Cloud State University; of Minnesota (post graduate studies, educational administration). Currently working on doctorate, University of Minnesota.

JOE MEDICINE CROW (CROW) ANTHROPOLOGIST

A cattleman; a real estate appraiser for the Bureau of Indian Affairs; and the author and director of the historical pageant *Custer's Last Stand,* presented each summer by the Crow Indians, Joe Medicine Crow is an avid student of Indian history. He is especially interested in the archeology and ethnology of his own tribe. He is well known as a master of ceremonies at various Indian events.

BIRTHPLACE: Lodge Grass, Montana, 1911.
EDUCATION: Bacone College; Litchfield College (B.S.); University of Southern California (M.S.)

FRED M. BRAY (CHOCTAW) AEROSPACE ENGINEER

As a boy, Fred Bray built and flew model airplanes and always hoped to be a pilot. He now has his degree in aerospace engineering and has entered the Air Force for a five-year tour of duty.

In college, Fred was an outstanding student. He was made a member of the Loyal Knights of Old Trust which engineering students consider the highest of honors. He was named a Knight of St. Pat, designating him as one of eleven outstanding senior engineers. He was tapped for Pe-et, the oldest honorary group for men at his university and was elected to membership in a number of honorary societies.

BIRTHPLACE: San Diego, California, November, 28, 1944.
MARRIED: Doris Jane Harris. CHILDREN: David, Jeffrey.
EDUCATION: University of Oklahoma (B.S., M.S.). (several scholarships).
HONORS: Air Force ROTC; Honor Cadet, Outstanding Cadet in Campus Activities, Outstanding Student Pilot, Distinguished Military Cadet, Distinguished Military Graduate, Commissioned Second Lieutenant, USAF Reserve; Outstanding Member Award and Student Lecture Award, American Institute of Aeronautics and Astronautics; Omicron Delta Kappa (past president); Outstanding Senior ROTC Engineering Student; Outstanding Senior, College of Engineering; Sigma Gamma Tau (past vice-president, president), one of six nationally to receive Honor Undergraduate Award; Sigma Tau (past historian), Tau Beta Pi (past vice-president); *Who's Who in American Universities and Colleges.*

ORGANIZATIONS: American Institute of Aeronautics and Astronautics (several offices and committees); Society of Automotive Engineers (past vice-president); Air Force ROTC (past Cadet Wind Comptroller and FIP Flight Commander).

RAY CHRISTIANSEN (ESKIMO) STATE LEGISLATOR

Ray Christiansen comes from a remote Eskimo village. To help with his schooling as a boy, he worked in the family trading post, fished and hunted. He went seal hunting often, and sometimes hunted baluga whales. He trapped beaver and mink with other Eskimo boys who were trained early in life to take part in such activities.

After service in World War II, Mr. Christiansen used his GI money and learned to fly at a commercial flying school. With his commercial flying license, he became a bush pilot for an airline company. Later he flew for Alaska Airlines and Wien Consolidated Airlines

Several years ago, Mr. Christiansen went into business for himself, operating an air taxi service out of the city of Bethel. He flies a "big door" Cessna 180.

Mr. Christiansen was elected to the Alaska House of Representatives in 1962. During his first two sessions he was a member of the Resources Committee. He later was chairman of this committee, the largest in the House.

BIRTHPLACE: Eek, Alaska.
MARRIED: Tillie. CHILDREN: Carol, Ray, Christine, David.
EDUCATION: Mission school.
MILITARY SERVICE: U.S. Army, World War II - special services on the Aleutians.

THOMAS RICHARDS (ES-KIMO) PILOT, WIEN CONSOLIDATED AIR-LINES

Captain Thomas Richards has climbed the ladder from bush pilot to Boeing 737 jets since he first joined Wien Alaska Airlines in 1948. In that time, he has accumulated more than 21,000 hours in the cockpit.

Capt. Richards began his career in aviation in 1943 after military service in the South Pacific. He partici-pated in the U.S. Navy-Marine landings in the Solomons and at Guadalcanal where he was wounded.

Shortly after he was hired as a bush pilot, he flew for a Hollywood movie crew in Alaska to produce the film, *Arctic Manhunt.* In 1952, the same producer returned to film *Arctic Flight* in which Richards both flew and acted.

"Flying is a way of life in Alaska," he says, "and Alaska is my life."

BIRTHPLACE: Kotzebue, Alaska, June 15, 1923.
EDUCATION: Haskell Institute; University of Kansas.
MILITARY SERVICE: U.S. Coast Guard, World War II, 1942-43, South Pacific.

CHRISTINE MORRIS (BLACKFEET) TEACHER OF SOCIOLOGY AND ANTHROPOLOGY

"I was raised in poverty," Mrs. Morris says, "but my father taught me a love of the land, a love of beauty, and a deep respect for all living things."

This background is the basic quality of her "Indianness." Mrs. Morris says, and it is this trait that she hopes will be preserved for Indian young people. "This is why I teach and why I chose to teach in my special fields."

Mrs. Morris worked her way through college as an assistant librarian, laboratory assistant, cook, waitress and in other work. She is a dedicated teacher and wants to see all Indian young people become educated.

BIRTHPLACE: Red Buttes, Wyoming, May 29, 1932.
MARRIED: Anthony G. Morris. CHILDREN: Stephan, David, Geneva.
EDUCATION: University of Wyoming (B.A.); Montana State University (M.S.).
ORGANIZATIONS: National Education Association; Washington Education Association; Indian Educators Association of the Northwest.

JOSEPH T. PROVOST (OMAHA) BOY SCOUT EXECUTIVE

Joe Provost, or "Injun Joe" as he is known in scouting circles, is the first Indian professional Boy Scout executive. He is Field Director for the Kit Carson Council in Albuquerque. He "grew up" in Scout work as an Indian, long before being Indian was the "in thing," he says.

"Injun Joe" has danced in full ceremonial dress, before thousands of Scouts and their leaders. He has been working with Indian Boy Scouts on the Navajo reservation since 1955 and with Indian leaders of Scouts. He seeks always to instill pride in Indian heritage - and the thought that Indians can do anything they choose in life if they are willing to work and train for it.

BIRTHPLACE: Walthill, Nebraska.
MARRIED: Inez Benham. CHILDREN: Monta Provost Blackwell, Julia Provost Rives, Joseph, Jr.
EDUCATION: Haskell Institute.
MILITARY SERVICE: U.S. Marine Corps, World War II, 1940-45.
ORGANIZATIONS: 32nd degree Mason; Shrine (past president); Alpha Phi Omega; Veterans of Foreign Wars (past post commander); Lions (past president, Tailtwister).

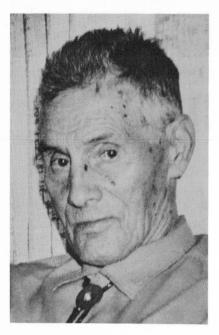

JARRETT BLYTHE (CHEROKEE) TRIBAL LEADER

For 24 years principal chief of the Eastern Cherokees, Jarrett Blythe has served in this capacity longer than any other Cherokee.

After completing his schooling on the reservation, he worked on a reclamation project in Montana. But the "call" of home was strong and he returned to his home to begin his long career of service.

Elected to the Tribal Council, Mr. Blythe was chosen chief in 1931 to serve four consecutive terms, and then was elected again in 1955 and in 1963. It would be impossible to detail his many accomplishments for his people. They are a living monument to his concern and compassion.

Mr. Blythe is a founder of the Cherokee Historical Association and an initiator of the Boundary Tree Enterprise, a luxury motel operated by the tribe. He was also instrumental in the start of the historical drama, *Unto These Hills,* which relates the story of the Cherokee removal. The pageant is produced nightly on the reservation during the summer months and attracts thousands of people. He also assisted in the establishment of the Oconaluftee Indian Village, a replica of a Cherokee village of early times.

Each of Jarrett Blythe's administrations has been a milestone in Cherokee history. Under his leadership ground has been purchased to build a modernistic, new high school and he has activiated other advances and progress. He initiated a loan fund available to those wishing to go into business for themselves. He has led in good farming and forestry practices and he has made valuable gifts of land to young couples to help them start a home.

Together with his wife he cared for many neglected children and has never failed to respond to the need of any Cherokee.

He succeeds a long line of ancestors who have also been distinguished in public service, among them: James Blythe, Indian agent at Cherokee and Nimrod Jarrett Smith who was principal chief and vice-chief and secretary of the Council. An uncle, David Blythe, was also principal chief.

BIRTHPLACE: Cherokee, North Carolina, May 30, 1886.
MARRIED: Mary Burgess.
EDUCATION: Hampton Institute, Haskell Institute.
HONORS: Indian Council Fire Achievement Award and honorary life membership (1956); Award of Merit, Steve Youngdeer Post of the American Legion (1967).
ORGANIZATIONS: Cherokee Fair Association (past president); Boundary Tree Tribal Enterprise (past chairman); Cherokee Historical Association (trustee).

EPHRAIM O. WHEELER (ESKIMO) AIRLINE RELIEF STATION MANAGER

"Eph" Wheeler comes from pioneer stock. His paternal grandfather came over the gold rush trail in 1898. His father was a trader-trapper and his mother was a member of an old Point Hope family.

"Eph" started his career as a Nome fire truck driver when he was fifteen. He became fire chief the following year and chief of police when he was nineteen. He had to get special legal dispensation to be on the streets at night in order to pursue his duties, because of a curfew law.

During World War II, "Eph" served in the Eskimo Scouts patrolling the Aleutians and the Arctic. While in service, he studied surveying, mapping and whatever other subjects he could get. After the war, he took up flying.

Wien Airlines hired Mr. Wheeler in 1951. For 36 months during the DEW line construction, he was coordinator for Wien, the Air Force, and Federal Electric across 2100 miles of the Arctic in Canada and Alaska. He had a crew of 21 men and seven aircraft working with him.

In 1960, Wheeler became station manager for Wien - DEW line at Point Barrow, and in 1968 he opened the station at Red Devil near the mercury mines. In February, 1970, he opened the Deadhorse station when the folding, prefabricated cargo building was put up in three hours at -58 degrees.

BIRTHPLACE: Kotzebue, Alaska.
MARRIED: Faye. CHILDREN: (9).
EDUCATION: Public Schools.
MILITARY SERVICE: U.S. Army, World War II.

EDWARD WAPP, Jr., (COMANCHE-SAC AND FOX) PIANIST

Edward Wapp began to study piano at the age of five, and made his debut when he was eight. He has played recitals in a number of states and has performed on both radio and television.

Edward who has been piano instructor at Intermountain Indian School, now teaches at the Institute For Indian Arts. Fluent in French and Spanish, he accompanied his mother on a study of artifacts in the museums of Europe and acted as her interpreter. His future plans include further piano study toward a doctorate in ethnomusicology, with emphasis on American Indian music..

BIRTHPLACE: Winfield, Kansas, May 13, 1943.
EDUCATION: University of Kansas (B.A.); Oklahoma State University; University of New Mexico; Utah State University.
HONORS: Featured, 1970 Indian Festival of Arts, La Grande, Oregon.
ORGANIZATIONS: Utah Music Teachers Association; National Guild of Piano Teachers.

LEON F. COOK (CHIP-PEWA) SENIOR REPRE-SENTATIVE, DEPART-MENT OF COMMERCE, OFFICE OF ECONOMIC DEVELOPMENT

Leon Cook describes himself as the "best paper boy the Red Lake reservation ever had." Without a family, work was necessary and he worked daily after school, on weekends, and summers. In addition, he had many "private contracts" for everything from cutting wood, hauling waste, and mowing lawns. With the money saved, he was able to enter Prep School. Completing college was so difficult financially that he dropped out to become the owner-operator of a structural restoration company. He later finished his college education.

A volunteer worker at Waite House in Minneapolis, Leon became seriously interested in Indian problems. He realized how fortunate he had been, even when he was unfortunate, he says. He had met with many friendly experiences, but he now discovered that Indians had many problems.

After a short stint with VISTA, he became consultant to the director of the Minneapolis OEO program and did the ground-work that eventually led to the establishment of the Minne-apolis Indian Center. He worked for OEO in Duluth and then for EDA in the same city before being transferred to Arizona.

BIRTHPLACE: Redlake, Minnesota, July 30, 1939.
MARRIED: Dane Lee Johnson. CHILDREN: Kristin, Tommy.

EDUCATION: St. Johns University (B.S.); University of Minnesota School of Social Work (M.S.).
MILITARY SERVICE: Army ROTC.
ORGANIZATIONS: Arizona Indian Association (chairman, social services committee); Phoenix Indian Center (board); Phoenix Forward Task Force Committee; Consumer's Council of Arizona; American Indians United; National Congress of American Indians.

WILLIAM ALCAIDA (CHEMEHUEVI) TRIBAL LEADER

Mr. Alcaida's achievements are numerous, but he is especially recognized for his endeavors to develop the potential of his reservation and the surrounding area. Through his work as a farmer (he owns a 500-acre farm) and as a tribal councilman, approximately 46,000 acres of reservation land have been brought under cultivation; about 6,000 acres a year are being developed. Through his efforts, the Tribe and residents of the nearby city of Parker have been brought closer together in mutual respect and cooperation.

BIRTHPLACE: Blythe, California.
MARRIED: Viola Burgoz. CHILDREN: William, Carolina, Beverly, James.
EDUCATION: Public Schools.
HONORS: Selected by Ford Foundation to visit New Zealand in an exchange program with Maori leaders, sponsored by the Citizens Crusade Against Poverty.
MILITARY SERVICE: U.S. Army, Infantry, 1942-45 (Staff Sergeant) - Purple Heart with two clusters.
ORGANIZATIONS: Parker Valley Grower's Association (past president); Conservation District (past president); Parker Chamber of Commerce (board); Parker Hustlers (past chairman); Veterans of Foreign Wars; American Legion; Elks.
SPECIAL ACTIVITIES: Colorado River Tribal Council (a total of 12 years - past treasurer; past vice chairman; past chairman).

FERRIS DOVE (NIANTIC) RESTAURANT OWNER

Ferris Dove is a direct descendant of Chief Ninigret who was prominent in early Colonial history. He is the first Rhode Island Indian to graduate from Bacone College when it was exclusively an Indian school. He is the owner of *Dovecrest*, the only Indian restaurant in Rhode Island.

Dovecrest is a beautiful old home set in landscaped grounds near Arcadia State Park. The restaurant specializes in Indian breads, serves luncheons and dinners, and has room for paying guests. It also sponsors special Indian events such as an art show.

BIRTHPLACE: Pawcatuck, Connecticut, August 1, 1915.
MARRIED: Eleanor F. Spears. CHILDREN: Mark, Paulla, Dawn, Lori.
EDUCATION: Bacone Junior College.
SPECIAL ACTIVITIES: Town Moderator, Town of Exeter; Chairman, Tax Assessment Board of Exeter.

ERMA HICKS WALZ (CHEROKEE) CHIEF OF TRIBAL RELATIONS, BUREAU OF INDIAN AFFAIRS

Mrs. Walz is in one of the highest ranking positions in the Bureau of Indian Affairs. She is responsible for the conduct of business affairs for 787 tribes, bands, villages, pueblos and other groups that are recognized as individual entities. Included are the Eskimos of Alaska.

Some of her work is concerned with arbitrating election disputes; another phase involves helping frame constitutions for those tribes that do not have them.

She came to Washington after finishing business school and started with the BIA as a stenographer. She reached her present status through a series of steady rises.

BIRTHPLACE: Hulbert, Oklahoma, October 10, 1915.
MARRIED: Peter F. Walz.
EDUCATION: Haskell Institute; George Washington University; Northwestern University.
HONORS: "Boss of the Year," L'Enfant Chapter, American Business Women's Association.
ORGANIZATIONS: National Congress of American Indians (secretary of first convention).

JOSEPH R. GARRY (COEUR d'ALENE) TRIBAL LEADER

Joseph Garry chose to stay with his people and serve them at a time when most Indians with his experience and ability were going into the outside world. Born in a tipi, Garry did not speak English until he was ten years old. As chairman of the tribal council, he dedicated his life in its service. Eventually, he became the only Indian ever to hold local, state, regional, and national offices at the same time.

Garry is the first Indian ever elected to the Idaho Legislature, first as representative and then as senator. He is a descendant of Chief Spokane Garry, for whom the city of Spokane was named and who founded the first school in Washington. He is the son of Chief Ignace Garry.

BIRTHPLACE: Coeur d'Alene reservation, Idaho, March 8, 1910.
MARRIED: Leona Trimble. CHILDREN: Ursula.
EDUCATION: Haskell Institute; Gonzaga; Butler University; St. Francis Xavier University; Washington State University.
MILITARY SERVICE: U.S. Army (Infantry), World War II; Combat Engineers, Korea.
HONORS: Outstanding American Indian Citizen, American Indian Exposition (1957); Boy Scouts of America Award (1957); Honorary Life Membership, Continental Federation of Adopted Indians; Outstanding Indian of North America, Indian Encampment of Pendleton (1959); "Apache Trophy" for outstanding work in Indian Affairs (1959). "Golden Deeds Award" for

outstanding public service (1961); "Outstanding American Indian," All American Indian Days (1961); Award of Merit, Coeur d'Alene tribe (1968); Special recognition, Otoe-Missouri Tribe, for special work on claims.

ORGANIZATIONS AND SPECIAL ACTIVITIES:Affiliated Tribes of Northwest Indians (past president); National Congress of American Indians (past president).

EMIL NOTTI (ATHABASCAN) ELECTRONIC DESIGN ENGINEER; ORGANIZATION EXECUTIVE

Emil Notti has long served his people in positions of leadership. In 1969, he received the first honorary doctorate ever awarded an Alaskan native by Alaska Methodist University and the first such degree to be given to an Athabascan Indian.

After receiving his degree in electronic engineering, Mr. Notti was employed as electronic design engineer with the Federal Aviation Agency. He now operates his own electronic systems firm. His activity in Native affairs brought him into organizational work and he was appointed field representative for the Alaska Human Rights Commission. He is presently Coordinator for the Alaska State Community Action Program, Inc.

BIRTHPLACE: Koyukuk, Alaska, March 11, 1933.

MARRIED LeNora. CHILDREN: John, Cindy, Joseph.

EDUCATION: Mount Edgecumbe Indian School; Northrop Institute of Technology (B.S.).

HONORS: Honorary Doctor of Humane Letters, Alaska Methodist University (1969).

MILITARY SERVICE: U.S. Navy, 1952-56.

ORGANIZATIONS: Cook Inlet Native Association (past president, two terms); Alaska Federation of Native Associations (past president); Alaska Conservation Society.

MAURICE W. BABBY (DAKOTA-OGLALA) SUPERINTENDENT, FORT BELKNAP AGENCY

Maurice Babby is especially interested in governments and in tribal governments in particular. As one of the younger Indian leaders, he believes that the need for highly educated and skilled young Indian people who can translate Indian problems - into meaningful approaches which benefit Indians is crucial. His entire career has been in administrative positions in the BIA.

BIRTHPLACE: Pine Ridge, South Dakota, January 25, 1934.
MARRIED: Bertha Laverdure. CHILDREN: Allen, Cynthia, Marty.
EDUCATION: Haskell Institute; Sacramento State College (B.A., 1965); Stanford University (Career Education Award, National Institute of Public Affairs); LaSalle Extension University (LLB, 1969).
MILITARY SERVICE: U.S. Army (1951-1952).
ORGANIZATIONS: Elks; National Congress of American Indians; Boy Scouts.
HONORS: Superior Performance Award, Sacramento Area Office, Bureau of Indian Affairs (1964); chosen one of Montana's five outstanding young men (1967), by State Junior Chamber Of Commerce.

RAY SATEPAUHOODLE (KIOWA) COUNSELOR

Ray Satepauhoodle is involved in a unique project for counseling Indian students in the Tulsa public schools. He calls this the "Indian to Indian" approach in dealing with youngsters who are, or who show signs of becoming, wayward students. The Tulsa program is thought to be the first such program in the country.

In his work, Mr. Satepauhoodle seeks out those youngsters who are academically weak and helps them to develop proper study habits and better attitudes. He says his approach is effective because he can personally follow-through with most of the cases he has. Previously he taught and counseled students in Indian and public school systems in Oklahoma, South Dakota, and Kansas.

BIRTHPLACE: Carnegie, Oklahoma.

MARRIED: Genevieve Jewell. CHILDREN: Angela, Clarissa, Siles, Craig.

EDUCATION: Panhandle A&M College (B.S.); Southwestern State Teachers College (M.Ed.).

SCHOLARSHIPS: Athletic scholarship (lettered 4 years in college); member, New Mexico All-Star Collegiate Team, (1954).

MILITARY SERVICE: U.S. Army, World War II, two years, Europe.

WILLIAM J. BENHAM, JR. (CREEK) EDUCATOR

Dr. Benham, Associate Commissioner for Education and Programs for the Bureau of Indian Affairs, brings to this assignment 19 years of professional education experience in the BIA. He has been a teacher, boarding school principal, education specialist and director of schools in the Navajo area. His interest in Indian education has perhaps come down from his great-great grandfather who was superintendent of the Creek Nation schools following the Civil War.

Dr. Benham's first position in the Indian Service was as a teacher in a one-teacher school on the Navajo reservation. From there, his rise has been meteoric. He was instrumental in the establishment of Rough Rock Demonstration School, which is attracting considerable educational interest; and, he encouraged the development of Navajo Community College, the first school of higher learning to be established on an Indian reservation.

Under Dr. Benham's leadership the Navajo area took the lead in starting innovative educational programs, and the Navajo people have become directly involved in education. Among some of the innovations are the formation of a Navajo Education Committee; a method of teaching English to non-English speaking beginners which exists in every federal school on the reservation; Indian school boards; Navajo social studies to acquaint Navajo students with their own culture; and

108

bi-lingual, bi-cultural, kindergartens opened for the first time; and many other exciting programs.

BIRTHPLACE: Lamar, Oklahoma, June 4, 1928.

MARRIED: Bobbye Meek. CHILDREN: William, III, Bruce, Melinda.

EDUCATION: East Central State College (B.A.); University of Oklahoma (M.A., D.Ed.).

HONORS: Outstanding Achievement Award (3), Bureau of Indian Affairs; Silver Beaver Award, Boy Scouts of America (1969); Phi Delta Kappa.

ORGANIZATIONS: Southwest Curriculum Laboratory (regional board of directors); American Association of School Administrators.

SPECIAL ACTIVITIES: Journal of American Indian Education (editorial board).

WILBERT C. BEGAY (NAVAJO) STATE REPRESENTATIVE

Mr. Begay is one of several Navajos serving in the State Legislature. He was elected in 1967 as a Republican and immediately asked that English-speaking Navajos be appointed to some state and county positions. In the House, he is a member of the Natural Resources and Transportation Committees.

BIRTHPLACE: Shiprock, New Mexico, March 22, 1939.

MARRIED: Marietta Simpson. CHILDREN: Warren, Darren.

EDUCATION: Fort Lewis College; Utah State University.

SCHOLARSHIPS: Navajo Tribal Scholarship.

MILITARY SERVICE: U.S. Army, 1963-65, Germany.

MOSE PARRIS (CHERO-KEE) ASSISTANT DIRECTOR, OFFICE OF TRIBAL AFFAIRS, INDIAN HEALTH SERVICE

Mose Parris is a great grandson of Wahillau Eagle, noted Cherokee Civil War leader, and a great-great--grandson of Chief John Ross, the principal chief at the time of the Cherokee removal.

After graduation from high school, he enlisted in the Navy. With no skilled vocation after military service, he worked for a time in the oil fields. Then he decided to enter college and complete the requirements for his bachelor's degree.

Mr. Parris taught school for a time. He served as a guidance counselor for the Bureau of Indian Affairs while continuing his education. He then became a principal of BIA schools and, just prior to going with the Indian Health Service, acted as education specialist in charge of college scholarships for Indians.

BIRTHPLACE: Park Hill, Oklahoma, February 26, 1922.
MARRIED: Dorothy Thayer. CHILDREN: Michael, Alan, Jeffrey.
EDUCATION: Chilocco Indian School; Bacone College; Northeastern State College (BA): Oklahoma State University (MS).
MILITARY SERVICE: U.S. Navy, World War II, Asiatic-Pacific Theater.
ORGANIZATIONS: Lions; Masons.

DAVID L. BALDWIN (OSAGE-KAW) SUPERINTENDENT, YANKTON INDIAN AGENCY

David Baldwin has spent his career in government administration, community service, and in education. He has been an education specialist, grade school principal and high school teacher.

Mr. Baldwin says that the future of the Amerindian rests within himself. "It doesn't really matter where we originated," he states. "What is important is that the Indian was created with all the faculties of any other race of man. He created and built a civilization long before the coming of the white man. We are a very proud people for we have many, many reasons to be proud of being Indian. We have a 25,000 year old heritage of customs, beliefs and teachings that have sustained us longer than any other ethnic group known."

"Some day soon we will again be the givers and not the takers. Each day we become more and more aware of the beauty of being an Indian," Mr. Baldwin emphasizes.

BIRTHPLACE: Ponca City, Oklahoma, August 29, 1933.
MARRIED: Carolyn Mathews. CHILDREN: George, Robert, Marcelyn.
EDUCATION: Washburn University (B.A.); University of Kansas (M.Ed., pending).

FRANK MEDINA (CHEROKEE) ATHLETIC TRAINER

Frank Medina, Head Athletic Trainer at the University of Texas for the past twenty years, is nationally and internationally recognized.

His dedication to his profession has taken him to many far-off places. With East-West Shrine Game in San Francisco, as a starting point, he went on to the 1948 Olympics in London and, a decade later, made a sojourn into the Soviet Union for the first confrontation in athletic competition in Moscow. Subsequent competition in Poland, Hungary and Greece was followed by an assignment for the International Games (Deaf Olympics) in Helsinski, Finland. In 1963, he was back in the Soviet Union, Poland, West Germany and Great Britain.

In 1964, his first of five assignments as a "one-man mission to the Middle East" had but one purpose-to improve the American image. In 1965, he once again served the International Games in Washington, D.C.; in 1968, he was trainer for the Turkish Olympic Team in Mexico City; and in 1969, for the third time, he served as Head Trainer at the International Games for the Deaf in Belgrade. There, he was honored in the closing ceremonies of the Games by American athletes and officials for his contribution to international good-will and brotherhood. He was also presented the gold medal for his contribution to all visiting athletes by the *"CISS" Comite International des Sports Silencieux"* - the only non-athlete to receive such an award which is emblematic of first place or world champion.

The president of the Turkish Federation of Amateur Athletics has written of Mr. Medina that his "character, qualifications . . . considerate and generous deeds are leaving indelible impressions on our youth . . . we have never had the equal of Mr. Medina's qualifications, nor have we had anyone merit the love, the trust and confidence that Mr. Medina has achieved through his diligence and sincerity . . . We here in Turkey acknowledge (him) as an INternational Father . . . his candor and his compassion for the youth of today are unequalled."

Mr. Medina's love and interest in youth is further displayed by his adoption of eleven children from various countries and races. He has raised these young people, given them a good education, and seen them return to their homelands as useful citizens.

BIRTHPLACE: Lincoln, Nebraska.

MARRIED: Fernne Adams.

EDUCATION: Haskell Institute; Arizona State University; St. Mary's College (B.A.).

HONORS: Olympic gold medals from London and Mexico City games; "Trainer of Year" Award, Rockne Club (1957-1961 - only one to receive); Helms Hall of Fame Inductee (1965); First Distinguished Service Alumni Award, Haskell Institute (1965); *Sport Magazine* "Service Award" (1968); First Recipient, University of Texas Ex-Students Association "Distinguished Service Award: (1969); Lane Bryant International Volunteer Award (1969).

ORGANIZATIONS: National Athletic Trainers Association (charter member); Association of Overseas Educators; Southeast Trainers Association (first president).

ALBERT STEWART (CHICKASAW) CONCERT SINGER

A successful platform and concert artist, Albert Stewart is known to thousands across the country. He has appeared before more than 5,000 schools and colleges, many clubs and other organizations.

A grand-nephew of Robert Harris, a former governor of the Chickasaw Nation; of Ton-Tubbee, chief of the Chickasaw; and of Moshala Tubbee, chief of the Choctaw, he is also a descendant of Frances Folsom, the wife of President Cleveland.

Gifted with a rich bass-baritone voice of remarkable range and power, Albert earned his way through college largely by his singing. He has been the featured singer at the Stand Rock Indian Ceremonials, Wisconsin Dells, for the past ten years, and he was the leading singer-actor at the Chicago Railroad Fair (1948-50). He has been featured on major TV programs for children and in the film *Rhythm,* produced by Encyclopedia Britannica films for school distribution.

BIRTHPLACE: Wynnewood, Oklahoma, July 19, 1909.
MARRIED: Eula Bryant. CHILDREN: Romula.
EDUCATION: Chicago Musical College; Roosevelt University; private voice teachers.
HONORS: Chicago Music Festival winner (1939); offered contract, New York City Opera Company (1950).
ORGANIZATIONS: Chicago Program Service (past director); Indian Council Fire (president, two terms); International Platform Association of Lecturers and Concert Artists.

IOLA POHOCSUCUT HAYDEN (COMANCHE) EXECUTIVE

A former teacher at Intermountain School and home demonstration agent for Oklahoma State University Extension Department, Mrs. Hayden was instrumental in starting the Indian Education Center in Oklahoma and initiating the Community Action Program in Lawton.

She is presently director of Oklahomans for Indian Opportunity, an educational and self-help project.

She was recently appointed to the Oklahoma State Advisory Committee to the U.S. Commission on Civil Rights. The State Advisory Committee is one of 51 such units whose members serve to provide the Commission with information concerning civil rights activities in their communities.

BIRTHPLACE: Lawton, Oklahoma, September 5, 1934.
MARRIED: William G. Hayden. CHILDREN: John, Marcia, Sarah.
EDUCATION: Fort Sill Indian School; Oklahoma State University (B.S.); University of Oklahoma (M.A., pending).
SPECIAL ACTIVITIES: State Advisory Committee to U.S. Commission on Human Rights; Americans for Indian Opportunity (board).

ADA DEER (MENOMI-NEE) SOCIAL WORKER

Reservation born, Ada Dear lived in a one-room log cabin without any "modernization." Deciding early in her life that education had to be "the way," she now has a master's degree, a long list of a-chievements and a position that enables her to con-structively help Indian young people. Her level of education and experience ranks among the highest ever achieved by a member of her tribe.

Miss Deer has great "sympatico" for her people and her approach to Indian problems has been widened by service as a social worker in the Minneapolis schools, coordinator of Indian affairs in the University of Minnesota's Training Center for Community Development, and social worker for private organizations.

Currently director of the Upward Bound Project at Stevens Point (Wis.) State University, she hopes to instill a pride of heritage in Indian teen-agers, encourage them to get a good education and to lead lives of purpose and significance.

After study and experience with numerous minority groups, Miss Deer concludes that Indians cannot succeed without this pride and the recapture of their own spirit. "only then will they develop dignity and self-worth," she says.

BIRTHPLACE: Menominee Reservation, August 7, 1935.

EDUCATION: Public high school (top ten of class); University of Wisconsin (B.A.); Columbia University (M.A.).

SCHOLARSHIPS: Menominee Tribal Scholarship (3 years); King Christian Brotherhood Award, University of Wisconsin; John Hay Whitney Fellowship, Delta Gamma Foundation Memorial Fellowship.

HONORS:Outstanding Young Woman of America (1966).

ORGANIZATIONS: Joint Commission on Mental Health of Children, Inc. (board); Girl Scouts of America (board); Americans for Indian Opportunity (board).

WILLIAM A. MEHOJAH (KAW) SUPERINTENDENT, FORT HALL INDIAN AGENCY

Mr. Mehojah has spent his career in administrative work, first with the Veterans Administration as a claims examiner, and then with the Bureau of Indian Affairs.

His first position with the BIA was as a supervisory procurement clerk at the Billings Area Office. Other administrative positions followed. Just before coming to Fort Hall, he was agency superintendent at Turtle Mountain.

BIRTHPLACE: Washunga, Oklahoma, August 6, 1917.

MARRIED: Frederica Gray. CHILDREN: Sandra Mehojah Loh, William Jr., Frederica.

EDUCATION: Haskell Institute; Muskogee College; Idaho State University.

MILITARY SERVICE: U.S. Army, World War II - three years plus 28 months overseas.

ORGANIZATIONS: Upper Snake River Federal Executives Association; 32nd degree Mason; Lions.

THOMAS TOMMANEY (CREEK) EDUCATIONAL ADMINISTRATOR

Mr. Tommaney began a long career with the Bureau of Indian Affairs in 1938. He was assistant Boy's Adviser at the Cheyenne River Boarding School.

Since then, he has held a number of challenging positions including the superintendencies of Intermountain School, Haskell Institute, and director of schools on the Navajo reservation.

As Assistant Area Director (Education) for the Bureau in Oklahoma, he is now climaxing a lifetime of service built on doing good for his people.

"Today's Indian youth need to speak out," Mr. Tommaney says, "but they need to speak intelligently. This can only come through educational opportunities, wisely used." In no small measure, he has helped Indian youth in the educational quest.

BIRTHPLACE: Eufaula, Oklahoma, June 12, 1913.
MARRIED: Grace Henry. CHILDREN: Frances Tommaney Holt; Theresa Tommaney Coons.
EDUCATION: University of Kansas (A.B.); Oklahoma University (M.A.).
MILITARY SERVICE: U.S. Army Air Force, 1944-46. (Good Conduct Medal).
ORGANIZATIONS: American Association of School Administrators.

118

SISTER GLORIA. ANN DAVIS (NAVAJO-CHOCTAW) TEACHER

Sister Gloria has been a nun for the past 17 years, serving as an elementary teacher. When she entered the Order of the Blessed Sacrament in 1932, she was the only Indian in the Congregation. Her training period was very difficult, but her desire to go back to her people in terms of service was very strong.

After 2½ years, Sister Gloria was missioned to a small town in Louisiana where she taught third-graders. It was shocking to see how hard these children worked in the cotton fields. Her next mission assignment was in New Orleans and the following year she was sent to Arizona where she spent six years teaching Navajo children. While there, she broadcast a regular program in the Navajo language over KGAK.

The next transfer was to a "disturbed district" in Philadelphia for three years. Now, she is again stationed among her people at St. Michael's School for Girls. Her goal is to help Indian young people value their traditions and to acquire a sense of security "to meet the fact of change in the world about."

BIRTHPLACE: Fort Defiance, Arizona, September 5, 1933.
EDUCATION: Xavier University (B.A.).
HONORS: National Honor Society.
ORGANIZATIONS: Catholic Youth Organization.

LOUISE ABEITA CHEWIWI (PUEBLO-LAGUNA) AUTHOR-TEACHER

When she was thirteen years old, Mrs. Chewiwi wrote a book which is a classic in children's literature.

Although she had intended to become a social worker, she was diverted to teaching. She has taught primary grades and has counselled high school and college students, and assisted adults find employment.

"Indian young people should not be allowed to settle for just anything simply because they become discouraged," she says. Because she was improperly counseled when in college and did not have the right credits for her planned career, she strongly believes that Indian students should be directed toward professional fields. She plans to make guidance and counseling her life's work.

BIRTHPLACE: Laguna, New Mexico, September 9, 1926.
MARRIED: Steven Chewiwi. CHILDREN: Linda, Susan.
EDUCATION: University of New Mexico (first Robert P. Goodkin award for work in sociology).
AUTHOR: *I Am a Pueblo Girl.* (Morrow, 1939).

KENT FITZGERALD (CHIPPEWA) EXECUTIVE

Kent Fitzgerald began a career in government service on his mother's home reservation in Minnesota. Promotions eventually took him to Washington as a member of a team responsible for a research program designed to develop procedures related to the Indian Reorganization Act.

From here he was placed in a position to direct a major revamping of the position structure of the Bureau of Indian Affairs. This resulted in the upgrading of Bureau positions and in higher job qualification standards. Later he designed the initial organization and staffing pattern for the Relocation Program, now the Employment Assistance Program, which assists Indians in finding work in urban areas. Later, as area relocation officer, he supervised the relocation program in the mid-West.

Returning to Washington, he provided professional supervision and guidance to the Mississippi Choctaws, to Oklahoma and Southwestern tribes, and to Indians in Chicago, Los Angeles and the San Francisco Bay area. He played an important part in developing counseling procedures for reservations and relocation cities.

As agency relocation officer on the Navajo reservation, Fitzgerald established the Tribal Council Relocation Committee to develop Navajo involvement in the planning, directing and evaluation of the relocation program. He next became superintendent of the Crownpoint Subagency on the Navajo reservation. His jurisdiction covered 25,000 Navajos living in the off-reservation "checkerboard" area of northwestern New Mexico. He then served as community development officer for the Navajo area.

After 33 years in government service, Mr. Fitzgerald was appointed Executive Officer for Indian Affairs for the Executive Council of the Episcopal Church. With this appointment, an Indian Desk was established with title and responsibility for Indian work, a national committee on Indian work within the Church was assured, and a fund was established for Indian programs.

BIRTHPLACE: Chicago, Illinois, September 9, 1911.
EDUCATION: Northwestern University (A.B., M.A.)

JOE JIMENEZ (PUEBLO-NAMBE) CLINICAL PSYCHOLO-GIST

Joe Jimenez has been employed as a clinical psychologist on the Navajo Reservation; by the Bureau of Indian Affairs; the New Mexico Department of Public Health; and by Philco-Ford.

In addition to his college training, he has received private instruction in his speciality from two psychiatrists.

He is presently Executive Dean of the million dollar Career Center, aimed at combating unemployment on the Gila River Indian Reservation. The initial Career Center complex houses vocational-technical instruction and laboratories. The multi-complex campus is to be finished by December, 1970.

Professionals at the Center will train Pima and Maricopa

Indians in a variety of skills so they may become part of the area's work force. A cooperative effort with area industry is also planned. Construction and operational funds are provided by federal grants. Central Arizona College staffs the program and students will attend tuition-free. Non-Indians may also particpate in the six areas of training.

BIRTHPLACE: Nambe, New Mexico.
MARRIED: Jennie Dodge. CHILDREN: Matthew, Eric.
EDUCATION: New Mexico Highlands University (B.S.); Brigham Young University; Easlen Institutes.
HONORS: Psi Chi (National honorary psychology).

ALICE NARCHO PAUL (PAPAGO) ASSISTANT COORDINATOR OF TRAINING, UNIVERSITY OF ARIZONA EARLY CHILDHOOD LABORATORY

Mrs. Paul would have continued in the teaching career for which she had prepared, but she became involved in a cooperative experimental project conducted by the Tucson schools and the Early Childhood Laboratory at the University of Arizona. After working in this project for a year, she was asked to join the staff as field representative.

In this capacity, Mrs. Paul travels monthly to Alaska to work with the Tlingit Indians. She also goes to Philadelphia, Mississippi, to work with the Choctaw and to the Appalachian area to work with a unit used as a model for the Office of Education Follow Through Program.

Mrs. Paul's own education was interrupted while she served in the U.S. Navy Waves. She returned to school to get her degree once she had her own family started. As she gains more experience as a trainer of teachers, she hopes to make some contribution toward helping Indians find their "keys to fulfillment."

BIRTHPLACE: Tucson, Arizona.
MARRIED: Richard · A. Paul. CHILDREN: Deborah, Kathryn, Bert, Lisa.
EDUCATION: University of Arizona (B.A., M.Ed.).
MILITARY SERVICE: U.S. Navy Waves, 1951-52.
ORGANIZATIONS: Alpha Delta Kappa; Arizona Bilingual Council; Association For Childhood Education International; Teachers of English and Other Languages.

ALLEN C. HOUSER (APACHE) ARTIST/SCULPTOR ✻

Allen Houser's parents were taken to Fort Sill and held prisoners along with the war leader Geronimo and his band. At Fort Sill, the Apaches began to farm and Allen helped his father. He went to school only intermittently, and his childhood held many hardships. This did not deter him from an outstanding career and a firm reputation in the art field. He is rated highly as both artist and sculptor.

He had intended to become a professional athlete, but an illness diverted his attention to drawing. For his outstanding art work he received a trophy the year before he graduated from high school. Following several one-man shows he was commissioned to paint some of the murals in the Department of the Interior Building in Washington. His paintings were also exhibited at the New York and San Francisco World Fairs, and in Geneva, Switzerland. At one time, he was asked to demonstrate his work to art students in China.

For a period, Houser was instructor in arts and crafts at

Intermountain Indian School. He is now instructor in painting and sculpture at the Institute of American Indian Art. He is a popular illustrator of books, both adult and juvenile. One of his first pieces of sculpture, a marble statue, is a memorial to Haskell Institute Indian students who lost their lives in World War II.

Allen Houser's paintings are typified by splendid action. There is vitality and vigor, but the lines are simple. He paints primarily in the Indian two-dimension form with broad flat brush strokes which are both clean and definite.

BIRTHPLACE: Apache, Oklahoma, June 30, 1915.

MARRIED: Anna Marie Callegos. CHILDREN: Roy, Lonnie, Robert, Stephen.

EDUCATION: Fort Sill Indian School; Chilocco Indian School; Haskell Institute; Santa Fe Indian School.

HONORS: Guggenheim Scholarship for Sculpture and Painting (1948); Palmes D'Academiques, French Government (1954); Certificate of Appreciation, Indian Arts and Crafts Board (1967).

EXHIBITIONS: More than 20 major exhibits; six one-man shows; 25 public and private collections.

AWARDS: Five Grand Awards among many others.

WORKS PUBLISHED: Jacobson and D'Ucel (1950); Carter (1954); Dockstader (1961); Jacobson (1964); Arizona Highways (February, 1950, November, 1962); *Oklahoma Today* (1965); *Sunday Bonanza, San Francisco Chronicle* (1958); *Indians From Oklahoma,* BIA (1966); Compton's Pictured Encyclopedia (1957).

* *See art section*

JAY SILVERHEELS (MO-HAWK) ACTOR

Jay Silverheels is "Tonto" of the Lone Ranger TV series. His non-professional name is Harry Smith.

Jay's father, Captain A.G.E. Smith, was said to have been the most decorated Canadian Indian soldier of World War I. Several of Jay's brothers are steel construction workers and have worked on many of the largest buildings in New York City.

Before entering the theatrical world, Jay was a star lacrosse player. He was also a "name" in hockey, football and track and won honors in boxing and wrestling.

Jay was discovered by Joe E. Brown who got him his start in Hollywood. He has played opposite Tyrone Power, Elizabeth Taylor, Errol Flynn and other noted stars. He accepted the part of Tonto in 1949 a name which became nationally known and respected.

A sports center in honor of Silverheels has been erected on his home reservation. Ten acres of land were donated for the project by his mother.

Jay Silverheels is helping other Indians get a start in Hollywood. He has opened an actor's workshop in Los Angeles and has done much to further the progress of Indians in movie and TV roles.

126

JOHN L. PAPPAN (KAW) SUPERINTENDENT, OSAGE INDIAN AGENCY

Mr. Pappan is related to Charles Curtis, who was Vice-President of the United States, the only Indian to hold this high office. Mr. Curtis was a senator for many years.

Mr. Pappan is a specialist in agricultural economics. He has been land use planner, Tribal Operations Officer and Loan Examiner, with a number of tribes. His first position was as agency superintendent at Fort Hall, Idaho.

BIRTHPLACE: Newkirk, Oklahoma, March 8, 1927.
MARRIED: Barbara Wilson.
EDUCATION: Oklahoma State University (B.S.).
MILITARY SERVICE: U.S. Navy.
ORGANIZATIONS: Masons; Lions; Pawhuska Chamber of Commerce (community development committee); American Legion.
SPECIAL ACTIVITIES: Pawhuska Housing Development Committee; United Presbyterian Church (board of deacons).
SPECIAL INTERESTS: Study of Indian heritage and culture.

LOUIS R. BRUCE (MOHAWK-DAKOTA) COMMISSIONER OF INDIAN AFFAIRS. (1969 -   )

Mr. Bruce is the third Indian Commissioner of Indian Affairs since Ely S. Parker, a Seneca civil engineer and Brigadier General on General Grant's staff was named to that post after the Civil War.

His father, Louis Bruce, was a professional ball player, one of the first Indians to practice dentistry, and a long-time Methodist missionary among the Onondagas and Mohawks.

Louis Bruce, Jr., worked his way through high school, college preparatory and business administration college. He starred in pole vaulting in college and won a Track Scholarship.

Mr. Bruce was appointed New York State Director of Indians under the National Youth Administration in 1935. Under his direction, work projects were started on every reservation, special emphasis was given to Indian lore and crafts, and committees were established in surrounding communities to work with Indian groups for the promotion of good will. A number of community centers were built on Indian reservations with Indian labor.

Bruce, Jr., was instrumental, too, in establishing a section devoted to Indian Welfare in the New York State Conference.

His absorbing interest in youth has remained and he is giving emphasis to this interest by bringing young Indian people into top positions within the Bureau of Indian Affairs.

The owner and operator of a 480-acre dairy farm, Mr. Bruce has been active in farm organizations and has stimulated interest in his state in the need for programs for rural youth. He assisted in organizing the New York State Youth Council Program and the State Council of Rural Youth Organizations. As president of the Dairymen's League, he organized young farm people in various communities. As Youth Director of the

Dairymen's League Cooperative Association, he supervised the only youth program of its kind in the country. Under his leadership, the first National American Indian Youth Conference was held in Washington with many prominent people in attendance (1957).

Throughout his career, Louis Bruce has won many honors. In 1949, his article on *What America Means to Me* was published in the *American Magazine* and reprinted in *Reader's Digest* in sixteen languages throughout the world. It is still worthwhile reading.

Among others of his achievements, he has been an executive for a national advertising agency, special assistant commissioner for cooperative housing, FHA; public relations director for a chain of 23 cooperative super markets; executive director and chairman of the Board of Trustees for Zeta Psi Educational Foundation and Fraternity of North America.

BIRTHPLACE: Onondaga Reservation, December 30, 1906.
MARRIED: Anna Wikoff. CHILDREN: Charles, Katherine, Bruce, Berry, Donald.
EDUCATION: Reservation schools; Cazenovia Seminary; Syracuse University (AB).
HONORS: Freedom Foundation Award (1949) (Presented at Valley Forge by President Eisenhower). Indian Council Fire Achievement Award and honorary life membership (1953); Sigma Delta Chi (honorary Journalistic Fraternity).
ORGANIZATIONS: Rotary; Masons; Arrow (board); Yale Broadcasting Company, Ivy League Network (board); Association of American Indian Affairs; Columbia University Club; Syracuse University Alumni Association (New York board); Farm Bureau Federation; Boy Scouts of America; College Editors and Fraternity Secretaries Associations; New York State Indian Villages Associations; Cooperative Institute Association.

KERMIT C. SMITH (ASSINIBOINE) OSTEOPATHIC PHYSICIAN AND SURGEON

Dr. Smith may be the only Indian doctor in the field of osteopathy in the country. He entered private practice in 1967 and has a successful business in a Chicago suburb.

When he was a boy, he traveled to a number of Indian reservations and to various ceremonials. He has been an instructor in Indian lore at summer camps and frequently speaks on this subject now before grade school assemblies and service organizations.

BIRTHPLACE: Poplar, Montana, February 21, 1940.
MARRIED: Mary Larson. CHILDREN: Vincent, Matthew.
EDUCATION: St. Olaf College (BA); Chicago College of Osteopathy (OD).
ORGANIZATIONS: Chicago American Indian Center.
SPECIAL ACTIVITIES: Indian Guides, YMCA.

GRACE MARSH CALIFANO (PISCATAWAY) ENTERTAINER

Mrs. Califano also uses the name of Princess Grace Fair Cloud. She is a descendant of Chief Wahacasso whom the Maryland colonists called "Emperor."

In show business since the early 1920's, she has appeared on a long list of major TV shows and commercials, and in stage appearances. She is also influential in referring work in these fields to other Indians.

In her private life, Mrs. Califano works actively as a volunteer in various welfare campaigns and in giving direct service to the needy. She has been instrumental in arranging the donation of a parcel of land in Maryland, originally owned by the Piscataway's to the Secretary of the Interior for a public park.

BIRTHPLACE: Cumberland, Maryland.
MARRIED: Michael A. Califano.
CHILDREN: Hiawathia Califano Wittson; Dante Michael, Yolanda Califano D'amico, Theodore, Gregory.
EDUCATION: Public high school; New York University; Abilene Theatre School.
HONORS: Honorary certificates and plaques from several national health and welfare groups; *Who's Who of American Women* (1969).
ORGANIZATIONS: National Congress of American Indians; Indian League of Americas (past treasurer); American Federation of TV and Radio Artists (charter member); Screen Actors Guild;

International Platform Association; National Geographic Society.

JOANNE GREEN LABIN (MOHAWK-SENECA) INSTRUC-TOR OF NURSING

Mrs. Labin is the first member of her family to secure a college education. Her father was a champion Lacrosse player, and her grandfather was a chief of the Iroquois, or Six Nations Indians.

In her various positions since receiving her R.N., Mrs. Labin has been a staff nurse, a supervisor at Buffalo Columbus Hospital, and an instructor of nursing at D'Youville College. Although presently raising a daughter, she intends to continue with postgraduate training in the future.

BIRTHPLACE: Rochester, New York, September 26, 1942.
MARRIED: Thomas S. Labin. CHILDREN: Tracy Anne.
EDUCATION: D'Youville College (B.S.); University of Buffalo.
ORGANIZATIONS: Woman's Auxiliary, Erie County Bar Association; German Shepherd Dog Club of Western New York; Western Lakes Training Club.

LOUISE TIGER SHUNATONA (CREEK) CLASSROOM TEACHER, OKLAHOMA PUBLIC SCHOOLS

Mrs. Shunatona is the granddaughter of a former principal chief of the Creek Nation. She has been a classroom teacher in Oklahoma public schools for more than thirty years. She is very active in tribal affairs and is considered one of the most distinguished women in Oklahoma. She is also active in church affairs, and raises "show" gladiolas.

BIRTHPLACE: Wetumka, Indian Territory (now Oklahoma) May 5, 1905.

MARRIED: Baptiste Shunatona -first fullblood Indian to graduate from the University of Oklahoma Law School. An Otoe, he is Commissioner of Indian Affairs in Oklahoma.

CHILDREN: Baptiste, Jr. (graduate of the University of Oklahoma Engineering School with double degree in Petroleum and Geological Engineering); Richard.

EDUCATION: Stephens College (A.A.); University of Oklahoma (B.S., M.Ed.).

HONORS: Kappa Delta Phi (honorary education).

ORGANIZATIONS: American Association of University Women (twice president, local branch); Classroom Teachers Association (secretary).

SPECIAL ACTIVITIES: Creek Tribal Council (education committee).

JAMES P. HOWELL (CHEROKEE) SUPERINTENDENT, TUBA CITY AGENCY

Mr. Howell is superintendent of the largest field unit in the Bureau of Indian Affairs. The Tuba City Agency has 950 regular employees, and serves the needs of 24,000 Indians.

Howell has spent his entire career in government service. Beginning as a clerk, he has progressed through increasingly responsible positions, first as assistant area personnel officer, then, to superintendent at various agencies.

BIRTHPLACE: Fort Gibson, Oklahoma, April 1, 1921.

MARRIED: Norma Green. CHILDREN: June Howell Burger, Patricia, Janet, James, Jr.

EDUCATION: Haskell Institute; Kansas University; Everett Junior College; George Washington University.

MILITARY SERVICE: U.S. Army Air Force, World War II -four years; flew twenty combat missions over Japan as a Bombardier. (Air Medal, one oak leaf cluster; Asiatic-Pacific Theater, Unit Citation).

ORGANIZATIONS: Boy Scouts; Atsa Flying Club (founder); Lions (Board).

SPECIAL ACTIVITIES: American Indian Leaders Conference on Scouting (public relations chairman).

GEORGE BLUE SPRUCE, Jr., (PUEBLO-SAN JUAN-LAGUNA) DENTIST

Dr. Blue Spruce is the first and only Pueblo Indian dentist, and the only Indian dentist in the Commissioned Corps of the U.S. Public Health Service. At this time, his rank is equivalent to that of Navy Commander.

Dental training was launched when George won a contest for outstanding high school students in New Mexico. He is now Branch Chief, Dental Manpower Development, Division of Dental Health in the Public Health Service. He has been dental consultant for the Pan American Health Association and Chief Dental officer of the American Health Organization.

His scholastic abilities were demonstrated early. From third grade on and through high school, he never missed the honor roll award. In high school, he was class president in both his junior and senior years, and was class valedictorian.

Dr. Blue Spruce has recently been promoted to the rank of Dental Director in the commissioned corps of the U.S. Public Health Service. (equivalent to rank of Army Colonel). In addition to this new duty, Dr. Spruce has been assigned to the Manpower Development Branch, N.I.H., Bethesda, Md. He will be responsible for the Division's activities in administering federal grants and technical assistance to schools of dentistry throughout the country that are participating in the training of dental students to efficiently utilize dental assistants. Dr. Spruce will also be responsible for the support of studies and projects directed toward improving utilization and effectiveness of dentists and allied dental personnel, and in promoting activities concerned with developing new careers within the dental and allied dental profession.

BIRTHPLACE: Santa Fe, New Mexico, January 16, 1931.

MARRIED: Darlene Hogan. CHILDREN: three.

EDUCATION: Creighton University and School of Dentistry (D.D.S.); University of California (Berkeley) (M.P.H.).

SCHOLARSHIP: New Mexico State Elks Association.

MILITARY SERVICE: U.S. Navy, 2 years (Lieutenant in dental corps).

HONORS: U.S. Public Health Service Award for best scientific paper at annual meeting (1961).

PROFESSIONAL PAPERS: Several on dental subjects.

ORGANIZATIONS: American Dental Association; New Mexico State Dental Association; Commissioned Officers Association, USPHS; American Public Health Association; Middle Atlantic Tennis Association; U.S. Lawn Tennis Association; Delta Sigma Delta.

BERYL BLUE SPRUCE (PUEBLO-SAN JUAN-LAGUNA) PHYSICIAN

Dr. Blue Spruce is the only Pueblo Indian physician and the brother of the only Pueblo Indian dentist.

His interests center around the areas of Indian health and education. He is especially concerned with the health of the Indian woman, and with the use of indigenous health assistants and the cultural and personal determinates of the health behavior of Indian people.

Dr. Blue Spruce is presently attempting to organize Indian health professionals who can act as consultants to their own people and who will provide role models, financial assistance, and emotional encouragement to Indian young people interested in health careers.

BIRTHPLACE: Santa Fe, New Mexico, November 24, 1934.
MARRIED: Ernestine Rodriguez. CHILDREN: Roxane, Shawn.
EDUCATION: Stanford University (B.S.); University of New Mexico; University of Southern California School of Medicine (M.D.); University of Michigan (M.P.H.).
SCHOLARSHIPS: Daughters of American Revolution; California Federation of Women's Clubs; United Scholarships, Inc., John Hay Whitney Fellowship.
HONORS:Mead Johnson Postgraduate Award in Obstetrics and Gynecology (1967-1968); Children's Bureau Fellow in Maternal and Child Health (1968-1969); Phi Rho Sigma Medical Fraternity.
ORGANIZATIONS: American College of Obstetrics and Gynecolo-

gy (junior fellow); Washtenaw County Medical Society; American Public Health Association; National Board of Medical Examiners (diplomate).

SPECIAL ACTIVITIES: Instructor, University of Michigan School of Medicine; Department of Obstetrics and Gynecology; Consulting Gynecologist, Student Health Service, University of Michigan; Committee on Indian Health, College of Obstetrics and Gynecology (chairman), University of Michigan.

PAUL LITTLE CHIEF (KIOWA-COMANCHE) ENTERTAINER AND BAND DIRECTOR

Paul Little Chief is the highly popular director of a seven-person musical troupe. His first experience in show business was in 1950 when he played a steel guitar with two others on a TV program. He later played with a swing band, and then formed his own band, playing mostly in Southern California.

As interest in the group built up, Little Chief was offered an Asian tour. The group first played to civilian audiences in Tokyo night clubs, including the exclusive Copa Cabana and Ginza. The band was in Okinawa for a time, and then entertained American troops in Vietnam. They toured village after village, performing variety shows for troops whether they were on duty or were recuperating in hospitals. They even played Bien Dein, the home town of Ho Chi Minh.

Once they were fired on by snipers, and once the enemy fired on a building not 500 yards from where they were resting. Two of the V-C's were killed in that exchange of rifle fire.

After returning to America, Little Chief was honored by the Kiowa Tia-Piah Society, made up of descendants of chiefs. He was formally initiated into the society, and gifts were given by his parents to honor him.

139

BIRTHPLACE: Lawton, Oklahoma.
MARRIED: Rae Cornell.
EDUCATION: Public Schools.

JACK TONNY BOWMAN (NAVAJO) INDIAN COUNSELOR

Following graduation, Jack Bowman stepped into the newly created post of Indian Counselor at the University of Utah. The University initiated a new program for its Indian students with benefits not heretofore before available.

Mr. Bowman helps with the unique needs of these students. He recruits students; assists with financial problems; promotes social life; and advises on personal and academic problems of the twenty Indians now attending the University.

"Having a friend can make the difference between fulfillment of purpose and discouraged resignation," he says.

Eventually, Bowman intends to go into the engineering field for which he is trained. At the moment, he wants to help Indian students get the most from their educational opportunities. He has had wide inter-cultural experience, particularly in migrant agricultural work. He has also worked in the aircraft industry.

BIRTHPLACE: Navajo Reservation.
EDUCATION: Fort Wingate Indian School; Intermountain Indian School; Technical Engineering Institute; University of Utah (B.Eng.).
MILITARY SERVICE: U.S. Army, Korea.

BUFFY SAINTE-MARIE (CREE) FOLK SINGER

Orphaned when she was a baby, Buffy was adopted by a Micmac Indian couple and raised in Massachusetts. With the help of a government loan, she entered the university and studied Oriental philosophy. She graduated an honor student, and toyed with the idea of going to India and trying her luck at singing songs.

When her father gave her a guitar for her sixteenth birthday she taught herself to play. She composed her own songs and people seemed to like to listen to her. So she went to New York City, sang at a Greenwich Village "hootenanny," and was at once offered a recording contract and nightclub dates.

In a very short time she was singing professionally and today she commands up to $2,500 for a single concert. Many of her songs are based on Indian themes. She has written more than 200 -"not for any reason except that there's a song in my mind. I don't know where my songs come from."

Recently, Buffy has appeared in major TV shows, such as *The Virginian*. When she accepts a contract, she insists that all Indian roles be played by Indians, and in this way has opened doors for other Indian performers.

VAN H. DYER (CHOC-TAW) CHIEF, OFFICE OF TRIBAL AFFAIRS NAVA-JO AREA INDIAN HEALTH SERVICE

Van Dyer obtained all of his formal education in government Indian schools. He has been a government employee since his graduation. His first job was on the Navajo reservation.

During the ensuing years he has been given increased responsibility for working directly with the Navajos. In 1955, the health responsibilities for Indians were transferred from the Bureau of Indian Affairs to the Public Health Service. Mr. Dyer was, at that time, an administrative assistant under the BIA. He became the liaison person between the Service and the Navajo Tribe. Presently, he promotes, plans and coordinates all health services for the Navajo people.

BIRTHPLACE: Eagletown, Oklahoma, May 24, 1912.
MARRIED: Elsie Steward. CHILDREN: Vernon (M.S. in zoology, third year medical student); Darlene Dyer Stanhoff, Lenora Kyer Hotema.
EDUCATION: Sequoyah Indian School; Haskell Institute.

JOHN DERBY (DAKOTA-SISSETON) TEACHER, COACH

John Derby has been a teacher at the Fort Totten Indian School. An excellent athlete in high school, he was offered the opportunity to sign as pitcher, with the St. Louis Cardinals or Chicago White Sox. Deciding that it was more important to continue with his education, he entered college under a baseball scholarship.

For a time he taught swimming and physical education to blind students at the Minnesota Braille and Sightsaving School. He was a staff member of the swimming and camping program conducted for mentally retarded children by the Faribault State Hospital and camp director for a day camp for handicapped children.

"Indians cannot blame the government forever for their difficulties," he says. "The government can only deal with the effects and not with the causes of our problems. Changes are going to have to be made, beginning with the home and family."

He is currently a graduate student at the University of South Dakota, working toward his Master's degree.

BIRTHPLACE: Browns Valley, Minnesota, March 14, 1943.
MARRIED: Cynthia Moses. CHILDREN: Dean, Beth Ann.
EDUCATION: Buena Vista College; University of South Dakota (BS. Ed.).

143

ALLIE P. REYNOLDS (CREEK) EXECUTIVE; FAMOUS BASEBALL PLAYER

Mr. Reynolds is one of the most noted of present-day athletes. As pitcher for the New York Yankees, his name was a household word among sports fans who still remember him.

Starting his athletic career in high school. Reynolds was on football, track and baseball teams. When he captained the baseball team he pitched a no-hit game.

Reynolds entered professional baseball in the Major Leagues, in 1939. In 1942, he moved up to the Major leagues, first with the Cleveland Indians and then with the Yankees. Among his achievements, he led the American League in strikeouts (1943, 1952); had the best earned run average in that League (1952) and pitched the most shutouts for two years (1945, 1952). He pitched two no-hit games, the first in the history of the American League (1951) and he was the second among modern players to have 37 shutouts. He had seven World Series wins, tieing the World's record at that time.

Mr. Reynolds retired from professional play in 1954 and is now president of the Atlas Mud Company. He is also president of the American Association of Professional Baseball Clubs.

BIRTHPLACE: Bethany, Oklahoma, February 10, 1917.
MARRIED: Dale Jones. CHILDREN: Allie, Bobbye, James.

EDUCATION: Oklahoma State University (B.S.) (Dean's Honor Roll).

HONORS: Oklahoma State University Hall of Fame (1958); Sid Mercer Player of Year Award, New York Sports Writers (1951); *Los Angeles Times* Sports Award (1951); Art Griggs Award (four times); All American All Professional (1952); Professional Athlete of Year, Hickok (1951); Oklahoma Outstanding Athlete (1951-52); Oklahoma Sportsman of Year, Quarterback Club (1951); Oklahoma Baseball Hall of Fame (1966); Metropolitan Council B'Nai B'rith Award (1950); Page One Award, New York Newspaper Guild (1952); Achievement Award, Creek Nation (1954-first to be awarded by the tribe and presented with impressive rites in the House of Warriors, Creek Tribal Council House); National Baseball Players Golf Tournament (champion, 1952); Player Representative, New York Yankees (1952-53-54); American League All-Star Team (six years).

ORGANIZATIONS: Oklahoma City and Country Club; Independent Producers Association; Petroleum Club; 33rd degree Mason.

WILLIAM D. ENGLISH (ESKIMO) COMMERCIAL AIRLINE PILOT

William English has been a pilot with Wien Airlines since 1946. He flies B-737 jets and is also a member of the company's board of directors.

English, as a little boy, decided to be a pilot when he grew up. He spent two years in the U.S. Air Force after college and was chosen to attend the Military Academy at West Point. Though appreciating the honor, he declined because his goal was to become a commercial pilot.

His flying career began in 1945 and he got his commercial license the following year. In 1947 he was flying a Cessna 140 on a gravity meter job for oil exploration. He continued his flying in many types of aircraft and became one of the first F-27 pilots when his company acquired them. He has since logged 20,000 flying hours.

For three years, English served as American Airline Transport Pilot examiner for the F.A.A. An interest in speech and radio has led him into many community activities. He was aerial radio announcer for KFAR for several seasons of the North American Sled Dog Championship races; and was "emcee" for the Eskimo Olympics for many seasons. He is vice-president and a director of Northern Television with stations in Anchorage and Fairbanks.

In 1954, he went into partnership to build the riverboat "Discovery" which provides sightseeing cruises on the Chena and Tanana River.

In 1960, he decided to complete his education by working toward a degree in business administration at the University of Washington. He is within a few credits of this goal.

BIRTHPLACE: Wiseman, Alaska.
MARRIED: Shirley. CHILDREN: Sharon (attending college in Austria); William, Jr., Tamara.
MILITARY SERVICE: U.S. Air Force, 1943-45.

PETER MacDONALD (NAVAJO) EXECUTIVE

Peter McDonald, who has been executive director of the Office of Navajo Economic Opportunity, is currently campaigning for the office of chairman of the Tribal Council.

In his youth, Peter was beset with feelings of inferiority and discouragement. He struggled with poverty, dropped out of school and then returned so that he could go to college. Coming from a traditionalist home, he had an additional battle in trying to reconcile two cultures.

He overcame his feelings of inferiority and lack of self-confidence by learning that other races did not have superior cultures. He studied about the European Dark Ages in college and learned that "these people of the white races had been just as uneducated, uncivilized, and savage as any primitive Indians."

Known throughout the country as one of the outstanding Indian leaders, MacDonald gave up an $18,000 a year job as project engineer with Hughes Aircraft Company to return to his people. This represented a considerable drop in income and future financial opportunity.

"I needed to achieve that success which only comes with applying your talents for the benefit of those less fortunate," MacDonald says. "I do not regret the decision I made. Success is not money. It is not position. It is education and awareness so that you see and recognize the means to develop your character and enrich this by serving other than your narrow self-interest."

BIRTHPLACE: Teecnospos, Arizona, December 16, 1928.

MARRIED: Rubye Wallace. CHILDREN: Peter Jr., Linda.

EDUCATION: Bacone Junior College; University of Oklahoma; University of California (Los Angeles).

SCHOLARSHIPS: University of Oklahoma Alumni Fund; Navajo Tribal Scholarship.

HONORS: "Distinguished American" award, National Institute for Cooperative and Economic Development for 14 national leaders (Only Community Action Agency Director to receive this award); Hughes Aircraft Company Outstanding Achievement Award for Cost Improvement Program; *Who's Who in the West; Outstanding Personalities of the Midwest.*

MILITARY SERVICE: U.S. Marine Corps, 1944-46, Pacific and China (Corporal).

ORGANIZATIONS: Arizona Community Action Association; National Association for Community Development; National Congress of American Indians; Kit Carson Council; Boy Scouts of America.

SPECIAL ACTIVITIES: Working with young people; New Mexico Governor's Economic Development Board; Navajo Reservation Development Committee. Testified before House Sub-Committee on Urban Small Business Committee; Senate Sub-Committee on Indian Education; National Advisory Committee on Rural Poverty; U.S. Senate Sub-Committee hearings on Employment, Manpower, and Poverty.

JOHN LOUIS CLARKE (BLACKFEET) CARVER, ARTIST

When John Clarke was a child, he became permanently mute because of scarlet fever. Unable to converse, he roamed the mountains and came to know the native animals intimately. Because he has had to contend all of his life with this physical handicap, his achievements of success and self-expression have more than simple artistic interest.

After special schooling in training schools for the deaf, he worked for awhile doing carving for furniture factories and for church altars. Realizing that this was something he liked to do, he returned to Montana and established a studio in East Glacier Park. Here he began to make life-like reproductions of the mountain animals he knew so well. Without any training, he carved figures of worth and beauty from any bit of wood, especially stumps.

His wild animal carvings have brought him many awards, among them a gold medal for a mountain lion carved from cottonwood, and a silver medal for a mother bear and cub. The bear is his specialty, though his other animal figures are equally remarkable for their naturalness of expression and attitude.

His works have been widely exhibited at leading galleries and are sought after by collectors and connoisseurs. He is one of Montana's most notable artists.

BIRTHPLACE: Highwood, Montana.
EDUCATION: Fort Shaw Indian School; North Dakota School for the Deaf; Montana School for the Deaf and Blind; St. John School for the Deaf.
HONORS: Gold medal, Philadelphia Academy of Fine Arts (1919); silver medal, Spokane Art Association (1928); *American Indian Painters.*

RAYMOND L. RODGERS (SENECA) HOSPITAL ADMINISTRATOR

Raymond Rodgers has been associate administrator in charge of general services at Archbishop Bergan Mercy Hospital, Omaha. So far as is known, he is the only Indian hospital administrator in a city situation.

Rodgers started out as an X-ray technologist. He completed his administrative residency at a Veteran's Administration Hospital and then was a hospital administration officer with the U.S. Public Health Service.

Mr. Rodgers joined St. John's Hospital and School of Nursing, in March 1969, as Associate Administrator.

BIRTHPLACE: Miami, Oklahoma, 1932.
MARRIED: Helen Henry. CHILDREN: Terry, Ray II, Kateri, Ahwenhatagi.
EDUCATION: Chilocco Indian School; Oklahoma University, R.T., B.Sc.); State University of Iowa (M.A.).
MILITARY SERVICE: U.S. Army, 1950-52, Korea (S/Sgt.); Oklahoma National Guard; Army Reserves (First Lt., MSC).
ORGANIZATIONS: American College of Hospital Administrators. National Association for Hospital Development; American Registry of Radiologic Technologists; Tulsa Areawide Health and Hospital Planning Council (board); Tulsa Chamber of Commerce; American Indian Development Center.

WESLEY BONITO (WHITE MOUNTAIN APACHE) EDUCATION COORDINATOR

Wesley Bonito is a great--great grandson of Chief Bonito. He has worked for his tribe for the past ten years as athletic director, recreation director, and in his present position of education coordinator.

He has also had his own exterior and interior painting and contracting business - the first of its kind for an Apache.

Mr. Bonito is especially interested in helping obtain scholarships for Indian young people. In the past three years he has assisted 200 students enter college and all have stayed. This is a record number. He has also initiated and implemented the first Phoenix Area Intertribal School Board. As an instructor for the National Indian Education Workshop, he drafted the proposal and implemented education coordinator positions across the United States and Alaska.

BIRTHPLACE: Whiteriver, Arizona, January 17, 1937.
MARRIED: Alethia Carroll. CHILDREN: Joan, Orville, Kearney, Keith, Jennifer.
EDUCATION: Arizona State College; Arizona State University.
SCHOLARSHIPS: Southwest Forest Industries.
HONORS: National Indian Education Institute (2).

ARTHUR S. JUNALUSKA (CHEROKEE) PLAY-WRIGHT-DIRECTOR, PROFESSIONAL THEATRE

The descendent of two great chiefs and sages - Junaluska and Yonaguska - Arthur Junaluska is a playwright-director, choreographer-actor, and lecturer. He is the founder of the American Indian Society of Creative Arts and the only Indian to have played in a Shakespearean Repertory Company.

In 1956, he organized the first American Indian Drama Company to present the performing arts of the American Indian in the professional theatre. He used only Indian talent in these productions. He has since produced and directed other plays unrelated to Indians. He has written plays for, and appeared in dramatic roles on radio, television, the stage, and the screen. One of his "tours de force" is an evening with Edgar Allen Poe.

Among his many activities, Junaluska directed the drama workshop at South Dakota Wesleyan University and staged an historical drama about the people of the plains. As director and coordinator of the Indian Village, Freedomland, in New York City, he presented Indians in tribal dances, songs and legends. He has presented his own American Indian ballet production, Dance of the Twelve Moons, in a number of places including the Indian Festival at LaGrande, Oregon. He has been director of dramatic art for the Indian Circle Program for Indian youth in Minnesota, and for two Indian Circle Programs at Bacone College and at the Indian Arts

Institute. He has been a consultant for many stage plays, motion pictures and radio and TV productions.

Before going into theatrical work, Junaluska considered a medical career. At one time, he was engaged in medical research in England where he is credited with modifying a quick serological test now in use by commercial blood banks.

BIRTHPLACE: Cherokee, North Carolina.
MARRIED: Betty Wright.
EDUCATION: Cherokee Indian School; Okmulgee Junior College; Maryville College; Western Carolina Teachers College; London School of Medicine.
MILITARY SERVICE: U.S. Army, World War II.
AUTHOR: *The Medicine Woman* (drama); *The Spirit of Wallowa; The Man in Black* (drama); *Shackled* (documentary); *Hell-cat of the Plains* (drama); *Spectre in the Forest* (drama) *Grand Council of Indian Circle* (drama-pageant).
ORGANIZATIONS: Actors Equity; AFTRA: Screen Actors Guild.

HAROLD GRAY (BLACKFEET-CREE) EDUCATOR

Harold Gray is special projects coordinator for the Indian Community Action Project at the University of Montana.

Specifically interested in the development of educational programs and opportunities for Indians, he worked entirely in this field as a teacher, reservation Head Start director, and Area Tribal Affairs assistant with the Bureau of Indian Affairs.

Indians must be given the initiative in planning their own goals, Mr. Gray believes. He so definitely advocates Indian self-determination that he would like to see Indian tribes become independent nations within the republic.

BIRTHPLACE: Browning, Montana, November 9, 1941.
MARRIED: Susan Brown. CHILDREN: Nicole, Ernest, Elizabeth.
EDUCATION: University of Montana (B.A., M.A.).
SCHOLARSHIPS: Tribal grants; Bureau of Indian Affairs; John
Hay Whitney Foundation fellowship.

JAMES JACKSON (QUINAULT) TRIBAL LEADER

James Jackson, president of the Quinault Tribal Council, has
made headlines around the country on two different occasions. Concerned about a possible high mortality of Quinault salmon due to irresponsible fishing and the wanton use of
outboard motors over spawning grounds, he first closed the
reservation and Lake Quinault to all hunting and fishing. The
ban applied to everyone including tribal members. The action
was taken by the Tribal Council, but Jackson's spirit was
behind the move.

On the second occasion, he closed 25 miles of Pacific coast
on the western boundary of the reservation to non-Indians.
He said that the beach was being littered and rocks sacred to
the Indians were being defaced. This action was upheld by the
State of Washington.

Mr. Jackson is a "self made" man. He grew up on the
reservation and at the age of 20 went into the shingle
business. He now has a fine modern plant which operates with
a crew of 17 men to a shift.

As a tribal leader, Mr. Jackson brought about the Quinault
National fish hatchery; a new law and order facility; a new
public health clinic; a mutual self-help housing program;
advanced education at both vocational and college levels; plus
various pilot programs for the benefit of his people.

154

Mr. Jackson takes great pride in the Taholah school which is a cooperative effort between the Quinaults and the school district. There is a nursery school for which the tribe provides two teachers, and a special course on the Quinault language and culture. The Council provides free school lunches.

The Quinault mutual self-help housing project also provides education. Each owner of the units under construction must build his own and a special school has been started for tribal members on blueprint reading, plumbing, electrical work and the use of all tools.

"Our people are forward looking, and even though we study our culture and preserve the best of our traditions, our people will not be petrified to some era of the past," Mr. Jackson states. He stresses that the Quinaults will adopt and adapt themselves to every modern advance compatible with their traditions, culture and ideals.

BIRTHPLACE: Quinault Reservation.
MARRIED: Mary. CHILDREN: James, Michael, Glenn, Georginne, Clifford.
EDUCATION: Reservation and public schools.
HONORS: Man of the year, Grays Harbor-Pacific County Area, *Aberdeen Daily World;* Indian Council Fire Achievement Award and honorary life membership (1969).

WOODROW W. PALMER (MIAMI-PEORIA) COLUMNIST

Woodrow Palmer is better known to his readers as "Injun Woody." His father was chief of the Miami tribe and his mother was second chief of the Peorias. His great-grandfather was Chief Richardville (Peshewah) who named the town of Miami, Oklahoma, and secured land from the government for the purpose of founding Bacone College.

A great-great-grandfather was also Richardville (Peppin-Sis-She-Wha), and the nephew of Little Turtle, the warrior, who defeated General St. Clair and General Harmar in battles for the Northwest Territory during Colonial times. Richardville is said to have been the wealthiest Indian in the country. His home still stands in Indiana.

When "Woody" was a child, the great humorist, Will Rogers, was a frequent visitor to his home. It may have been from Rogers that "Woody" picked up his sparkling style. He uses the barbs from the arrows of his ancestors and directs these with hilarious accuracy at everybody, just as Rogers did.

"Woody" calls his column "With Some Reservation." It runs five days a week in more than 30 newspapers of five states and is tailor-made for the conservative and the liberal, the rich man and the poor man, the industrialist - or just anybody. It is distined to have many more readers for it is considered one of the most refreshing columns in print.

BIRTHPLACE: Miami, Oklahoma.

MARRIED: Virginia Shoemaker.

EDUCATION: Seneca Indian School; Haskell Institute; Sherman Institute.

AUTHOR: *The Blouse and Skirt* (in publication).

WILFRED C. WASSON (COOS-CHEROKEE) PROFESSOR OF ETHNIC STUDIES AND ANTHROPOLOGY

Mr. Wasson is director of Indian Studies in the College of Ethnic Studies, Western Washington State College. He has been Coordinator of Special Services, Oregon State University; Consultant on Minorities to Counseling Center, University of Oregon; and Consultant to Northwest Regional Educational Laboratory.

BIRTHPLACE: Marshfield, Oregon, December 10, 1924.

MARRIED: Barbara. CHILDREN: (3).

EDUCATION: University of Oregon (B.A.); Graduate School, University of Oregon; Ph.D. candidate in education.

MILITARY SERVICE: U.S. Army Air Force, five years.

ORGANIZATIONS: Affiliated Tribes of Northwest Indians; American Association of University Professors; Oregon Personnel and Guidance Association; Commission on Humanism of Association for Supervision and Curriculum Development.

POPOVI DA (PUEBLO-SAN ILDEFONSO) ARTI-SAN *

Popovi Da is the son of the internationally famous potters, Julian and Maria Martinez. He has been governor of the Pueblo of San Ildefonso.

Like his father, he does his best work with symbolic designs and geometric figures. Since his father's death, he designed his mother's pottery and the pieces on which they collaborate are authographed Maria and Popovi Da.

Popovi Da has his own arts and crafts shop at his home pueblo. He also conducts pottery work shops for colleges, and lectures on Indian pottery.

BIRTHPLACE: Santa Fe, New Mexico, April 10, 1924.
MARRIED: Anita Montoya. CHILDREN: Janice, Joyce, Anthony.
EDUCATION: Private art school.
MILITARY SERVICE: U.S. Army, World War II, 2½ years. (Good Conduct Medal).
ORGANIZATIONS: School of American Research (director); Gallup Ceremonial (director); All-Indian Pueblo Council (past chairman).

* *See art section*

EBEN HOPSON (ESKIMO) EXECUTIVE

Mr. Hopson has been on the political scene for the past thirteen years. He served one term in the Territorial House of Representatives and was then elected a senator following Alaska's statehood in 1958. He lost his seat because of re-apportionment in 1965.

Mr. Hopson has lived all of his life, with the exception of the time away in military service, in Barrow. He has been a member of the City Council, since 1949; ten years of this period he served as president of the Council. He has also been a captain in the Alaska National Guard.

During World War II, Mr. Hopson was assigned to a tugboat which travelled the Aleutian Islands chain. He worked for the Naval Exploration and Arctic Contractors and now specializes in heavy equipment operation. He is an expert whaler.

Mr. Hopson is currently executive director of the Alaska Federation of Natives, a state-wide group which is carrying the fight for Native land claims. Just prior to this, he was executive director of the Arctic Slope Native Association.

BIRTHPLACE: Barrow, Alaska, November 7, 1912.
MARRIED: Rebecca Panigeo. CHILDREN (12).
EDUCATION: Barrow Indian School.
MILITARY SERVICE: U.S. Army, World War II, three years, three months. (Good Conduct Medal; Presidential Unit Citation).
ORGANIZATIONS: Veterans of Foreign Wars; Alpha Omega Club.

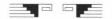

DALLAS CHIEF EAGLE (BORDEAUX) (DAKOTA--TETON) AUTHOR

Born in a tent on the Rosebud reservation, then orphaned and raised by the elders of his tribe, Dallas Chief Eagle is one of the most versatile of modern Indians. He writes - both prose and poetry well - he paints well, and is an excellent speaker. He sings well and is a popular radio and TV performer.

Dallas learned his first English words from a Jesuit missionary. He now speaks with an eloquent tongue, and always from the Indian point of view. His writings do not always agree with historians, but he is presenting what he has learned from his own people - and who should know better? He also speaks out for modernization of laws affecting Indians so as to remove artificial legal handicaps imposed on Indian people. In the past year, he has travelled more than 50,000 miles lecturing for the Indian cause. The proceeds from his writings and music are given to the support and education of Indian children.

In appreciation of his efforts for his people, the Teton Sioux conferred chieftainship upon Dallas Chief Eagle several years ago. The ceremony was one that had not been held for nearly a century.

BIRTHPLACE: Rosebud reservation, August 14, 1925.
MARRIED: Shirley Bennett. CHILDREN: Dallas, Rhonda, Theresa, Paul, Sheela, Takakwitha.
EDUCATION: Oklahoma A&M College.

MILITARY SERVICE: U.S. Marine Corps, World War II (Pacific Theatre).

AUTHOR: *Winter Count,* (this book has been made into a musical play); Golden Bell Press, 1967, *The Legend of the White Buffalo,* to be published in Japan.

ORGANIZATIONS: Colorado State Historical and Archeological Society; Pueblo Art Guild; International Platform Association; White Buffalo Council; American Indian Cultural Foundation; Pikes Peak Intertribal Club; United Churchmen's Organization of Pueblo.

SPECIAL ACTIVITIES: Superintendent of Indian Activities, Colorado State Fair.

ANDREW TSINAJINNIE (NAVAJO) ARTIST ✳

When "Andy" was five, he learned about pencils. With a pencil that he begged his mother to buy, he drew on paper bags and the labels from cans of food. Even so, his drawings had a charm that has continued throughout his years of painting.

When he was first sent to school, "Andy" ran away. He did complete his schooling, however, probably because there was an art department where he could find an outlet for his creativity. For a time after graduation, he worked as an illustrator. With the outbreak of World War II, he volunteered for service with the Marine Corps and spent the better part of three years in the South Pacific. For a time he was stationed in Tokyo and some of his postwar paintings reflected an Oriental influence.

The artist has painted seriously since 1940 and has his own studio. He is known for his "color periods" with a favored color of the moment dominant in the completed picture. He is also a "mood painter," turning to something new and different as the whim strikes him. He is especially fond of

161

painting horses, but his subject matter always centers around the daily life, or the ceremonials of his people. His delightful imagination gives originality to all that he does.

BIRTHPLACE: Rough Rock, Arizona, November 19, 1918.
MARRIED: Minnie McGirt. CHILDREN: Hulleah, Welake, Tsisie, Miquagekee, Bahe.
EDUCATION: Santa Fe Indian School.
HONORS: Palmes d'Academiques, French Government (1954); *Indian Painters; Southwest Indian Painting.*
MILITARY SERVICE: U.S. Army Air Force, World War II, five years - South Pacific and Asian Theatres.
EXHIBITIONS: More than 15 major exhibits; more than 30 public and private collections.
AWARDS: Several Grand Awards among others.

* *See art section*

VINA SMITH KIRK (DAKOTA) LIBRARIAN

Mrs. Kirk is a librarian for the Chiloquin, Oregon Schools.

She has been a teacher, counselor, newspaper reporter, and has also engaged in public relations.

She and her three sisters were orphaned at an early age so she had to work to complete her college education.

BIRTHPLACE: Poplar, Montana, 1908.
MARRIED: Friedman H. Kirk. CHILDREN: (2).
EDUCATION: Willamette University (B.A.).

CALVIN DUPREE (DAKOTA-TETON) MECHANICAL CRAFTSMAN AND SUPERVISOR

The first Dupree in South Dakota was an employee of the American Fur Company. He married Good Elk Woman and established a family on the Cheyenne River.

Calvin Dupree, after a typical reservation childhood, left home at 18 to join the Coast Guard, and to live through some very frightening experiences. While in service, he received training as a machinist and worked at this craft in Washington State.

He has spent the years following his times in service teaching mechanical crafts to Indian young people and teaching at Yakima Valley College as well. With a teaching degree he plans to return to reservation teaching and counseling and the organization of sports.

As of September 1, 1970, Calvin Dupree signed a contract as Coordinator of Special Programs and Assistant Vocational Education Director for Green River Community College of Auburn, Washington. He will continue working towards his M.Ed.

BIRTHPLACE: Timber Lake, South Dakota, November 1, 1922.
MARRIED: Frances Tollestrup; CHILDREN: Belva June.
EDUCATION: Cheyenne River Indian School; Columbia Basin Junior College; Wenatchee Valley Junior College; Yakima Valley Community College; Colorado State University (B.Ed.).

SCHOLARSHIPS: Colorado State University (two).
HONORS: Iota Lambda Sigma (honorary vocational education fraternity).
MILITARY SERVICE: U.S. Coast Guard, five years.
ORGANIZATIONS: South Dakota Historical Society (life member); American Vocational Association.

JOHN SACKETT (ATHABASCAN) STATE REPRESENTATIVE, ALASKA LEGISLATURE

Mr. Sackett, who has served in the Alaska Legislature for the past four years, is the youngest member ever to have been a legislator. He is the owner of a motel and general store in his native village, and has always been active in Alaska Native affairs.

He has been president of the Tanana Chiefs, an organization with representatives from 32 villages and vice-president of the Fairbanks Native Association.

BIRTHPLACE: Cutoff, Alaska, June 3, 1944.
EDUCATION: Ohio University; University of Alaska.
SCHOLARSHIPS: State of Alaska.
ORGANIZATIONS: Alpha Kappa Psi; Alaska Federation of Natives (treasurer); D.N.H. Development Corporation (board).
SPECIAL ACTIVITIES: Remote Housing Task Force; Advisory Council on Education; Alaska Task Force on Land Claims.

JAMES HOFFMAN (INDIAN-ESKIMO) PILOT

The first "air porter" service in the Kuskokwim country of Alaska was operated by 12-year-old Jimmy Hoffman at the village of Napamute. He would meet the bush pilot's plane and carry cargo. Since the landing strip was across the river from his village, Jimmy used a boat in summer and a dog sled in winter to reach the strip.

Orphaned when he was six years old, Jimmy worked in mining camps while going to school. Flying fascinated him and he managed to take flying lessons. He first soloed in 1941 and a year later he was handling ground service for bush planes.

Jimmy joined the Army in 1944 and was assigned to intelligence in the Alaska Scouts. In his two years in service, he continued to build up flying hours and bought his own Supercruiser Cab. Today, he has more than 18,000 hours in his flying log. By 1948, he was a pilot for Al Jones Airways, and the following year was hired by Wien to fly the bush out of Bethel. In 1963, he became chief check pilot, and in 1965 moved up to pilot of the F-27's

James Hoffman also served two years in the Alaska Territorial House of Representatives.

BIRTHPLACE: Napamute, Alaska.
MARRIED: Dorothy Marsh. CHILDREN: Marilyn Hoffman Jacobs; Robert, and seven others.

MARY NELSON (COL-VILLE-CREE-MOHAWK) EDUCATOR

Mrs. Nelson is director of the Indian education program at Eastern Washington State College. There are 56 Indian students on the campus with an attendance rate of over 90 percent - which speaks well for her program. Two years ago, the dropout rate of Indian students was more than half their number.

One of Mrs. Nelson's outstanding projects was the arrangement of a conference of Indian educators from the Northwest area.

She is an artist and sculptor of ability and has written excellent poetry in addition to her academic concerns.

BIRTHPLACE: Inchelium, Washington, May 17, 1933.
MARRIED: Raymond E. Nelson.
EDUCATION: Columbia Basin College (AAS); Washington State University (BFA); University of Idaho (BFA).
SCHOLARSHIPS: Colville Tribal.
EXHIBITIONS: Several major art centers.
ORGANIZATIONS: National Congress of American Indians; Affiliated Tribes of the Northwest; Native American Scholars-Northwest (a new organization of Indian college faculty members).

MESCAL MARTINEZ (ALGONQUIN-APACHE) SINGER

Mescal's maternal grandfather was a licensed Captain and First Mate on a number of whaling vessels. Her paternal grandfather was sent, with two other Apaches, into Mexico to induce Geronimo to surrender.

Miss Martinez started singing for audiences when she was in grade school. In her professional career she has studied under well-known opera singers. She has toured the country with a woman's choral club among other appearances. She is currently the featured woman singer in the Stand Rock Ceremonials held nightly during the summer at Wisconsin Dells, Wisconsin.

BIRTHPLACE: Southampton, L.I., New York.
EDUCATION' University of Oklahoma.

HENRY GATEWOOD (NAVAJO) SCHOOL DISTRICT SUPERINTENDENT

Mr. Gatewood is superintendent of the Chinle Public School District on the Navajo Reservation, geographically the largest school district in the United States. Included are nearly three thousand students in three elementary schools, junior high school, and high school. Housing for more than one hundred certificated personnel is provided on each of the five campuses. A fleet of forty buses transports the students.

Mr. Gatewood is the first Navajo Indian, and the first Indian of any Arizona tribe, to hold such a high position in the public school system of Arizona.

Typical of most Navajos of his generation, he lived in the traditional hogan, herded sheep, cut wood and grew up in the culture of his people. Orphaned at the age of nine, he was encouraged to get an education by the families that cared for him. Shortly after high school graduation, he left the reservation to enroll in college. This schooling was interrupted by enlistment in the army for service in the Korean Conflict.

Eventually completing his college work, Mr. Gatewood obtained his first position as a high school teacher and basketball coach in Tuba City. He became administrative assistant to the superintendent working as liaison person between the Navajo tribe and the Tuba City schools.

In 1961, Mr. Gatewood was appointed director of the newly constructed million dollar Navajo Community Center. He worked actively with the school, and with the churches and the community. He helped charter the local Lion's Club, Sportsman's Club, Youth Baseball Association and among other things brought the first television to the western portion of the reservation. He also served on the board of directors of Navajo Forest Products, which built a nine million dollar sawmill on the reservation; and on the board of the *Navajo Times,* the tribal newspaper. Mr. Gatewood enrolled in the Education Specialist Degree Program at Arisona State University. Upon completion of this course of study, he was appointed a consultant for the Arizona State Department of Public Instruction. In 1969, he returned home to his present position at Chinle.

Mr. Gatewood is a member of the Totsohnii or Big Water People clan and has several noted ancestors.

BIRTHPLACE: Fort Defiance, Arizona, March 17, 1929.
MARRIED: Mary Paul. CHILDREN: Shannon, Brooke.
EDUCATION: Northern Arizona University (B.S., M.A.).
SCHOLARSHIPS: Navajo Tribe (two scholarships).
HONORS: "Outstanding Navajo Educator," Award, Navajo Community College (1970).
MILITARY SERVICE: U.S. Army Paratroops, 2 years, Korean Conflict. (Divisional Outstanding Basic Training Recruit; several medals).
ORGANIZATIONS: Dine Bi Olta (charter member); Ganado Learning Center (board); Arizona Education Association; Arizona School Administrators; Association of Navajo Education Evaluators.

MARY ELLEN HILLAIRE (LUMMI) EDUCATION SPECIALIST

Mary Hillaire looks out upon the world through shining windows. She sees that "new Indian" as one who must move, not in a quest for power but for good will, in "the gentle harmony of humanity that makes life a worthwhile venture for all."

She sees the differences and similarities between Indians and non-Indians in such a way that she recognizes what must be done for and by her people in order "for them to live well in the common destiny."

Her first position was as a child welfare worker. She is currently education specialist for the new aquaculture project that has been started by her tribe for the raising of oysters, shellfish and other seafood as a means of economic revenue. This is a unique enterprise and one of the most exciting of the various tribal projects that have been initiated in recent times.

Before undertaking this assignment, Miss Hillaire was supervisor of manpower development and training involving special programs with the State Division of Vocational Education.

Although injured in an automobile accident earlier in her life, she overcame her disability, earned a college degree, and became a skilled professional woman using her skills to help others.

170

BIRTHPLACE: Lummi Reservation, Washington.

CHILDREN: Debra, Robert, Audrey.

EDUCATION: Western Washington State College (B.A., M.Ed.); University of British Columbia (B.S.W.).

SCHOLARSHIPS: John Hay Whitney Foundation Fellowship.

HONORS: Distinguished Alumna Award, Western Washington State College (1970) Rehabilitation Achievement Award, State of Washington (1970).

WILLIAM R. JEFFRIES (CHEROKEE-DAKOTA) SPECIAL ASSISTANT FOR INDIAN AFFAIRS TO GOVERNOR OF STATE OF WASHINGTON

In college, Mr. Jeffries majored in community organization. As his field placement for the school year, he was assigned to the staff of the Governor of Washington, his task to evaluate the Department of State programs which touched the lives of Indian people. The year's results produced an "outreach" proposal of working with Indian people, and not one of "for, to or at" them. It also led to his unprecedented appointment to the staff of the Governor as special assistant for Indian Affairs.

The first year's work has produced a reorganization of the Governor's Indian Advisory Committee into a social action committee run by Indian people representing 22 tribes of the State. This begins a more effective communication between the people and state government; more coordination between tribal, state and federal levels of government; more coordination with respect to Indian issues; and Indian participation on committees and commissions. An Indian Task Force in conjunction with the Indian Advisory Committee and the Urban Affairs Council has also evolved, and there will be increased hiring of Indians in the various State departments.

Mr. Jefferies provides technical assistance to Indian communities and organizations and will develop more effective state services.

It was not easy for him to secure an education. That he did, is an example of the classic saying, "where there is a will, there's a way." By doing odd jobs and pumping gas, he was able to obtain a double major in psychology and sociology over a ten-year period.

He served two years as a child welfare specialist in Los Angeles, counseling with children of all races and then was Child Welfare Specialist and Senior Social Worker in all phases of counseling for six years. He assisted in initiating a county Family Counseling Division and set up private practice in marriage and family counseling.

His next position was at the Colville Indian Agency as a social service representative for the Bureau of Indian Affairs. He left this position to return to school to work for his master's degree.

BIRTHPLACE: Venice, California, October 8, 1928.
MARRIED: Wanda Lee. CHILDREN: Connie, Patrick, Michael.
EDUCATION: University of California Graduate School of Social Work; University of Washington (M.S.W.).
SCHOLARSHIPS: California State Scholarship; Bureau of Indian Affairs Scholarship.
HONORS: Jaycee of the Year Award, Ventura, California.
SPECIAL ACTIVITIES: State Electoral Reform Council; Community Colleges Advisory Committee; American Revolution Bi-Centennial Commission; National Endowment for Humanities; Governors Inter-State Indian Council; National Congress of American Indians.

OVERTON M. CHEADLE (CHICKASAW) ATHLETIC COACH

Life began in a one-room sharecropper's shack for Overton Cheadle. Although his grandfather had been lieutenant of the Chickasaw Nation, the family came upon hard times. They were often without the bare necessities of life, and the children only went to school when there was a sandwich to share between them.

Although painfully shy, Overton had athletic ability that earned him several scholarships and a career as a coach. During World War II, he was a first class athletic specialist in the Navy. His leadership in the development of moral and physical qualities among his students has been noteworthy. He has had baseball and basketball teams in the finals of state tournament play. A number of his students have made All State First Team selections. One was All American at Iowa State College.

BIRTHPLACE: Milburn, Oklahoma, January 6, 1919.
CHILDREN: Robert, Thomas, Mary Alice, Elizabeth.
EDUCATION: Oklahoma Central State (B.A. - Dean's Honor Roll); Illinois Institute of Technology (M.S.).
HONORS: Nominated for Iowa Basketball Hall of Fame (1970).
MILITARY SERVICE: U.S. Navy, World War II, three years.
ORGANIZATIONS: Iowa High School Baseball Coaches (board).

CHARLES LOLOMA (HOPI) CRAFTSMAN

Although he has an international reputation as a painter, Charles Loloma has received greater recognition as a potter, silversmith and designer.

His creative talent is deeply rooted in ancient times. He takes part in all of the village life and ceremonial activities of his people, and his jewelry reflects this rich, cultural heritage. His sandcast silver work, gold work, mosaics in turquoise, coral and native woods, go beyond the silver tradition introduced by the Spaniards. Loloma jewelry is as much at home with the Hopi as it is with art collectors who seek it.

BIRTHPLACE: Hotevilla, Arizona, January 7, 1921.

MARRIED: Otellie Sequafenema.

EDUCATION: Oraibi High School; Phoenix Indian School; Alfred University, School for American Craftsmen; special studies.

HONORS: John A. Whitney Fellowship for research on Native Raw Material used in pottery.

MILITARY SERVICE: U.S. Army, World War II, 4½ years, U. S. and Aleutian Islands tours.

EXHIBITIONS: Three major exhibitions and national exhibitions sponsored by American Craftsmen Council.

COLLECTIONS: A number of public and private collections.

AWARDS: Several in state and national competitions.

COMMISSIONS: Murals´ - San Francisco World's Fair; Radio Station KOY; Oraibi High School; Kiami Lodge Scottsdale; Phoenix Indian School.

OTELLIE SEQUAFENEMA LOLOMA (HOPI) SCULPTOR

Mrs. Loloma is best known for her work in ceramic sculpture. Recently she has turned to painting with similar success. She has been a substitute teacher on her reservation and still offers her services when the need arises.

After World War II, Mrs. Loloma and her husband decided to return to school. A scholarship made it possible for her to enter college to study ceramics. When she returned to her home she set up a studio, and taught at the Shungopavy Day School for four years. Then, Mrs. Loloma and her husband, opened an arts and crafts shop in Scottsdale.

Since 1962, she has been teaching at the Institute of American Indian Arts in Santa Fe, working with Indian students from more than 70 tribes, all potential craftsmen in the arts. Mrs. Loloma strongly believes that sculpture in ceramics and bronze is a new expression for Indians and one in which they can excel.

BIRTHPLACE: Second Mesa, Arizona.
MARRIED: Charles Loloma.
EDUCATION: Oraibi High School; Alfred University, School of American Craftsmen.
EXHIBITS: A number of major exhibits.
COLLECTIONS: A number of public collections.
AWARDS: Three first awards.

HOMER L. MORAN (DAKOTA BRULE) COMMUNITY LIVING SPECIALIST

A combat hero and veteran of more than 20 years service to his country, Homer Moran is a retired Lieutenant-Colonel, U.S.A.F.

As a bomber in World War II, Mr. Moran received a number of military honors. He enlisted in the Army about three months before the attack on Pearl Harbor and was assigned to flight training with the Army Air Corps. When he won his wings, he was commissioned a second lieutenant.

His first combat mission was a bombing mission over France. A tour of duty in England followed and then he was sent to North Africa. Operating from the Libyan desert, he participated in bombing missions over Sicily and Italy.

While flying from Africa to England, Lt. Moran's plane was forced to make an emergency landing in Spanish Morocco. The crew was interned briefly but eventually was returned to England. Moran then flew a series of combat missions over Germany until re-assignment to North Africa. He and other pilots, in a daring sortie, swooped in low to bomb Ploesti.

Moran's last bombing mission was over Kiel, Germany, in 1943. In the months that followed he helped train pilots and aerial gunners and rose to the rank of squadron commander. Post-war assignments took him to seven states and Japan. In 1953 he was sent to Yokota air base, Japan, where he flew

176

KD-29's, air refueling tankers. While there he was named squadron executive officer.

Colonel Moran retired from military service in 1965. Joining the Bureau of Indian Affairs, he has been a community living specialist, vocational training specialist, and an employment assistance program officer in Los Angeles, at Aberdeen, South Dakota, and on the Navajo reservation. He is currently stationed in Anchorage, Alaska.

BIRTHPLACE: Wood, South Dakota, April 28, 1916.
MARRIED: Esther Fredberg.
EDUCATION: Northern State College (B.A., B.S.).
MILITARY SERVICE: Army Air Force, World War II. (Distinguished Flying Cross, one oak leaf cluster; Air Medal, three oak leaf clusters; Presidential Citation, one oak leaf cluster; six campaign battle stars).
ORGANIZATIONS: Elks.

BAHE BILLY (NAVAJO) AGRICULTURALIST

Bahe Billy is the first of his tribe to earn a Ph.D. His academic odyssey began nearly 20 years ago when an uncle took him to a farm where he lived and attended high school in exchange for farm work. His interest in soil science began at that point and he entered college prepared to pursue this subject.

When he began working toward his Ph.D., the foreign language requirements almost made him quit. "I just about threw up my hands several times because of the French language," he says, though he had no difficulty with German.

During his graduate research work, Billy evaluated the basic principles of integrating fertilization practices with climatic conditions, vegetation and soils to produce the maximum amount of range forage on an economic basis. He also studied the effects of water quality on plant production.

Dedicated to the betterment of his people he has great concern for reservation agricultural problems, and hopes to help his people make agrarian advances. He is greatly interested in the Navajo Irrigation Project underway which eventually will encompass 110,000 acres of land. A land reform program will be part of the project and crops and livestock will be raised.

MARRIED: Florence Boyd. CHILDREN: Julie, Ann, Christina, Brian.

EDUCATION: Utah State University (B.S.); University of Arizona (M.S., Ph.D.).

SCHOLARSHIPS: Standard Oil F.F.A.; 1955 - Standard Oil Company of California; Lamanite Leadership Award, 1970 L.D.S. church.

ORGANIZATIONS: American Society of Range Management; Soil Conservation Society of America.

BEATIEN YAZZ (JIMMY TODDY) (NAVAJO) ARTIST✱

Beatien Yazz has another name - "Little No Shirt." Like many other Navajo children he herded the family sheep and to ease the loneliness, drew pictures on craggy canyon walls with a sharp-edged stone. He was a very shy little boy, but he made friends with a couple who owned a trading post and they gave him scraps of paper and crayons so he could draw.

The little boy watched an artist who went about shirtless as he acquired a tan. To show his admiration he too went shirtless. The Navajos called the little boy "Little No Shirt" after his friend. And, as sometimes happens, a name given in friendly jest followed its owner to fame.

Because of his recognizable talent, artists tried to teach technique to "Little No Shirt," but this only confused him. He had his own way to go, and his work, crude as it then was, had the inward fire that belongs only to the gifted. He could never be poured into a mold of any kind.

For a time, his bewilderment over what could, or should, be done got in the way of his painting. Finally, an author came to the area and took an interest in the little boy. She was excited by his drawings, some of which had already found their way into private and museum collections. She wrote a book that told a good deal about him. He did the illustrations for her book.

This book aroused great interest in Beatien Yazz and his art. Requests for exhibits came from all parts of the country and buyers eagerly snapped up what ever he produced. From the start, he had a wide range of subject matter, but what he drew was nothing that he had been taught. He was painting for the pure joy of it, and he and his brush were friends who found pleasure in being together.

When his trader friends left, Beatien Yazz went away to school where there were art classes and he could have his fill of paper and pencils. He left because the routine instruction bothered him. He applied for a railroad job and "upped" his age to get a Social Security card - and this landed him in the Marines, although he was actually only fifteen.

Stationed in China, Beatien Yazz, or Jimmy, as he was then known, was greatly disturbed by all of the poverty he saw. It took him some time to get over the emotional impact of the War and in harmony again with his Navajo life.

Offered an art scholarship, he spent one year in study with a famous Japanese artist. The Japanese influence appears in some of his work during that period - exquisitely beautiful - with a touch of the Orient, yet, still the distictive style of Beatien Yazz. In protest against regimentation, during his art classes, he would add an extra fillip to the obligatory sketch of a nude by putting a rag around her big toe, and a feather in her hair.

Returning home, Jimmy married and had children and stopped painting altogether. Then a new book by the same author who originally started him on the road to fame, chronicled his story from adolescence to manhood. This helped him decide to take up his brush again, and at this time opened his own studio.

This artist, who is called the greatest living primitive painter, still experiments and demonstrates an amazing inventive skill, when he paints, and a sensitive response to the things that emotionally move him.

BIRTHPLACE: Wide Ruins, Arizona, March 5, 1928.

MARRIED: Elizabeth Roan (div.). CHILDREN: Irvin, Marvin, Calvin, Velma.

EDUCATION: Santa Fe Indian School; Sherman Institute.

MILITARY SERVICE: U.S. Marine Corps, World War II, two years, South Pacific (Navajo Code unit).

EXHIBITIONS: Many major exhibits; many public and private collections.

ILLUSTRATIONS: *Spin A Silver Dollar* and *Paint The Wind* (the two that are written about him); and *The Last Horse.*

✱ *See art section*

CHARLES E. GROUNDS (SEMINOLE) ATTORNEY

Charles Grounds, an attorney, has been concerned with Seminole affairs throughout his career.

He has been an assistant county attorney and counsel for the Tribe, and now represents the Seminoles in the Court of Claims. At one time during his career, he protested a scalping scene picture hanging in the conference hall of Congress and was successful in having it removed.

Especially interested in"Indian Sign Language,"Mr. Grounds is an expert in this "hand talk," and welcomed Hubert Humphrey to the Oklahoma Cowboy Hall of Fame in this language only.

BIRTHPLACE: Indian Territory.
MARRIED: Allene Cooper. CHILDREN: Charal; Charles.
EDUCATION: Haskell Institute; University of Kansas (A.B.); University of Tulsa, School of Law (AB., LLD).
ORGANIZATIONS: Elks; Shrine; Seminole City Bar Association (past president); National Congress of American Indians (charter member); Inter-Tribal Council, Five Civilized Tribes (charter member).

GEORGE OWL, JR. (CHEROKEE) AERONAUTIC ENGINEER

George Owl, for sixteen years a designer of planes for the Los Angeles Division of Advanced Concepts, has worked on the X-15, the B-70 and the TFX proposals. From his work, as air frame project engineer, came a patent on the compression life principle, a patent which he shares with two others.

Recently, he designed the "Owl Racer," a Formula One sports racing airplane. His design is somewhat different from anything previously developed. It utilizes an aerodynamic fundamental not commonly accepted by race plane designers because it involves the shape of the cowling and the frontal area. Although his technique isn't new, it has never before been applied to a Formula One racing plane.

This is the third racing plane that George Owl has designed. The others were not successful in competition. Designing racer planes has been a hobby since high school. His current plane is capable of speeds averaging between 230-240 miles per hour. George's plane, which took more than 3000 man-hours to construct, is said to be the most advanced in its class.

"Right now, we're continuing to explore the next generation of aircraft," Owl who has won national and international recognition as an aircraft designer, says. "I'm quite enthusiastic about the future of manned vehicles. There just doesn't seem to be any limit on speed or altitude. Man will be able to go out into space and come back again, landing just like a normal aircraft."

ROBERT STOPP (CHEROKEE) GENERAL BUSINESS MANAGER, DEPUTY PRINCIPAL CHIEF, CHEROKEE NATION

"Bob" Stopp has a highly responsible position as the executive administrator for the business affairs of the Cherokee Nation. He came to this position with a strong background of experience in teaching, and administration, and work with professional organizations. He has taught on both public high school and college faculties and has been president of a teacher's organization.

He is vitally interested in the history and culture of his people and helped to found the Eastern Missouri Indian Cultural and Ceremonial Association to educate the general public on Indian history.

BIRTHPLACE: Tahlequah, Oklahoma, October 10, 1938.
MARRIED: Margaret Peake. CHILDREN: Gary, Lisa.
EDUCATION: Northeastern State College (B.S., M.A.T.); Missouri University.

GOINGBACK CHILTOSKEY (CHEROKEE) WOOD CARVER, CRAFTS INSTRUCTOR *

Goingback Chiltoskey for many years worked for the U.S. Army Engineer Research and Development Laboratories at Fort Belvoir, Virginia. He was a model maker, fashioning miniature figures of men and equipment for the displays and dioramas depicting Engineer Corps activities. Much of his work was "top secret" and some of it was used to "iron out kinks" before expensive and actual building was undertaken.

Aside from this, Chiltoskey is one of the foremost woodcarvers in the country. He started to whittle before he learned to speak English. His beautiful carvings have won numerous awards and each one is a collector's piece. A carving that he made of St. Francis was exhibited at the Smithsonian Institution and was ordered in large dimension for a church in Washington, D.C.

Since his retirement, he spends his time in carving, in building a home, and in participating in community projects on the Cherokee Reservation. He is illustrating a book on Cherokee "cooklore" compiled by his wife and is also assisting his wife and brother in the compilation of a Cherokee dictionary.

Mr. Chiltoskey's name "Goingback" has an historical connotation. When the Cherokees were removed from their eastern homelands and sent to Indian Territory, some of the families made their way back. These were called the "goingbacks."

BIRTHPLACE: Cherokee, North Carolina, April 20, 1907.
MARRIED: Mary Ulmer.
EDUCATION: Haskell Institute; Santa Fe Indian School; Penland Handicraft School; Oklahoma A&M College; Purdue University; Chicago Art Institute.
ORGANIZATIONS: Cherokee Community Club (president); Qualla Arts and Crafts (vice-president).

* *See art section*

EVERETT R. RHOADES (KIOWA) PHYSICIAN

Dr. Rhoades is Chief of the Infectious Disease Center at the Veterans Administration Hospital in Oklahoma City. He is also Assistant Professor of Medicine and Microbiology at the Oklahoma Medical Center. He is the first Kiowa to win a doctorate degree and to complete medical school.

Dr. Rhoades interned at Gorgas Hospital in the Panama Canal Zone and returned to the Oklahoma Medical Center for Internal Medicine Specialty training. Following his residency, he served five years on active duty in the Air Force as Chief of the Infectious Disease Service, Wilford USAF Hospital. He is an authority in this particular field and has published more than 20 articles on the subject in various scientific journals.

As a member of the Kiowa Tribal Council and the Kiowa Tribal Land Management Committee, Dr. Rhoades has played a prominent role in the writing of the tribal constitution and in securing the passage by Congress of a bill authorizing disbursement of tribal judgment funds awarded by the Indian Claims Commission. He has also been active in several important land transactions for the tribe.

BIRTHPLACE: Lawton, Oklahoma, October 24, 1931.
Married; Bernadine Toyebo. CHILDREN: Lee, Melanie, Melinda, Dorothy, Lisa.
EDUCATION: Lafayette College; University of Oklahoma Schools of Medicine (M.D.).

185

SCHOLARSHIPS: Bureau of Indian Affairs; Zeta Psi American Indian Scholarship; John Hay Whitney Foundation Fellowship; Polio Foundation Fellowship.

HONORS: Phi Beta Kappa; Alpha Omega Alpha (honorary medical); Sigma Xi (honorary scientific); Student Research Achievement Award (1956); Outstanding Achievement Award, Veterans Administration Hospital (1960, 1961); Unit Citation Award, Wilford Hall USAF Hospital (1964); Markle Scholar in Academic Medicine (1967); Kiowa Tribal Black Legging Society (Veterans Honor Society).

MILITARY SERVICE: U.S. Air Force, 1957-1966, rank of Major. (Area Consultant in Infectious Disease and Internal Medicine for Surgeon General); (Air Force Certificate of Merit).

ORGANIZATIONS: Sigma Xi; American Federation of Clinical Research; American Medical Association; American Thoracic Society; American Board of Internal Medicine (diplomate); Air Force Society of Internists and Allied Specialties; American College of Physicians; Infectious Disease Society of America; National Congress of American Indians; Southwest Oklahoma Historical Society.

SPECIAL ACTIVITIES: Ad Hoc Committee on Long Range Planning, Indian Health Service; Oklahoma State Tuberculosis Planning Committee; Policy Advisory Committee, Community Action Program, Oklahoma City Indian Center.

SPECIAL INTERESTS: Consultant, University of Saigon Medical School, Vietnam; Kiowa history; archeology of Oklahoma and Texas.

BEATRICE MEDICINE (DAKOTA-STANDING ROCK) ANTHROPOLOGIST

Dr. Medicine is outstanding in her chosen field of anthropology. Tribal traditions were kept alive in her home while she attended public schools as a child. Her family actually kept alive her interest in her cultural background.

More and more she was drawn to anthropology, even though the subject was not one in which women were encouraged to enroll. Her graduate work was completed in anthropology. Since then, she has taught in a number of major universities, including the University of Washington, University of British Columbia, Michigan State University, and the University of South Dakota where she also directed an Indian research project. She is now Acting Director of Native American Studies and assistant professor of anthropology at San Francisco State College.

Dr. Medicine has written many professional papers and is currently working on two books. One of her books is a text to be used by South Dakota students. In 1968, she was one of six Americans who were invited to present papers at the International Congress of Americanists meetings held in Stuttgart, Germany. Her paper was accompanied by slides of Dakota ceremonies and recordings of music collected during her research.

BIRTHPLACE: Wakpala, South Dakota, August 1, 1924.
MARRIED: James Garner (div.). CHILDREN: Clarence.

EDUCATION: South Dakota State University (BSc.); Michigan State University (BA., Ph.D.).

SCHOLARSHIPS: Noyes Scholarship; Illinois Federation of Women's Clubs; American Council of Learned Societies Fellowship; John Hay Whitney Foundation Fellowship.

HONORS: Outstanding Alumnus, South Dakota State University (1956); Phi Upsilon Omicron (honorary); Alpha Kappa Delta (honorary).

ORGANIZATIONS: Society for Applied Anthrolology; American Anthropological Association; Canadian Sociology and Anthropology Association; National Congress of American Indians; Indian Association of Alberta; California Indian Education Association; American Indian Women's Service League (charter member); American Association of Indian Artists (associate member); Committee on Third World Association for Minorities; American Indians United consultant (text book committee).

SPECIAL INTERESTS: Major interests-the development of Indian leadership. Has worked to establish urban Indian centers. Although living in an academic atmosphere, she still has strong ties to her reservation home and participates in native religious and aesthetic affairs. She is raising her son as an Indian and he has undergone his naming ceremony in traditional fashion. He was given his grandfather's name of "Sitting Crow."

THE KLAUDT FAMILY (ARIKARA-MANDAN) GOSPEL SINGERS

The Klaudt Family, nationally known gospel singers, originated 41 years ago when Lillian Little Soldier married a German minister. The couple started a singing team, adding each of their children to the group, as soon as they were old enough to sing.

The family travels more than 75,000 miles a year in their own air conditioned bus. They perform at shopping centers, shows, fairs, company and church functions, concerts and other events. They are regulars on three national TV programs, and are in the process of producing their own 30-minute TV program on Indian culture, folklore and singing. They have also produced 10 long-play records.

The family has appeared in every state of the union and throughout Canada. All programs are given in full Indian costume.

Mrs. Klaudt is a descendant of One Feather and Little Soldier who were among the scouts employed by General George A. Custer in the battle against the Sioux at the Little Big Horn. Their names are inscribed in the granite memorial that stands on the battle site.

Raymond Klaudt, (a son) is a graduate of Northern State College, with A.A., B.S., and M.S., degrees. He is assistant principal in an Atlanta school.

Vernon, (a son) holds a B.A. from oglethorpe University, A B.D. from Emory University and a M.Ed., from the University of Georgia. He is a minister and a school principal in Atlanta.

J. WOODY COCHRAN (CHEROKEE) ARTIST

Associate Professor of Art at the University of Tulsa, the artist was once selected by the U.S. War Department to represent minority Americans at the *New York Herald Tribune* forum, "Pioneering for a Civilized World."

BIRTHPLACE: Tahlequah, Oklahoma.
MARRIED: Geraldine Berg. CHILDREN: Melanie Jo, Woody Kim.
EDUCATION: Oklahoma State University; University of Tulsa (B.A., M.A.).
MILITARY SERVICE: U.S. Air Force, World War II, four years, Southwest Pacific Theater. (Distinguished Flying Cross, Silver Star, Purple Heart, Air Medal, four Presidential Citations for combat action).
EXHIBITIONS: More than 17 major exhibits; four one-man shows; 18 public and private collections.
AWARDS: Ten awards.

190

JAMES DANIELSON (CHEROKEE) TRIBAL AFFAIRS OFFICER, PORTLAND AREA, INDIAN HEALTH SERVICE

James Danielson, as tribal affairs officer, is in a key position in the Indian Health Service. Before taking up a health career, he was a teacher and coach in Texas public schools, and a teacher with the Bureau of Indian Affairs.

BIRTHPLACE: Tahlequah, Oklahoma.
MARRIED: Laura Perry. CHILDREN: Robert, James, Thomas, Becky.
EDUCATION: Northeastern State College (B.A.); Utah State College.
MILITARY SERVICE: U.S. Navy, four years, Korean Conflict.
CORGANIZATIONS: Elks, Tatta Sigma, Fraternity.

THE GRANT SISTERS (Joy, Gloria, Ruth) (NAVAJO-OMA-HA) RODEO TRICK RIDERS

The Grant sisters are the only Indian rodeo trick riders in the country. Their interest in this profession began as children when they visited their grandfather's sheep ranch. The grandfather noticed that every time the little girls came, they managed to take his sheep herding horse, "Watson" behind a hill. After each visit, "Watson" was never the same. He would take off on a dead-run and stop short, and had to be re-trained back to his old style and duty.

It was discovered that the girls were galloping "Watson" at high speed while they hung upside down from the saddle, or did other stunts. They were imitating the trick riding they had seen in various rodeos.

A family council was called, and it was decided to have the youngsters trained by an expert horseman who was one of the world famous trick riders. This man said he had never seen three little girls with so much natural ability and talent for riding.

The girls practiced diligently with their father who had once been a professional rodeo star. An accident that cost him his right arm ended the father's career, but he could still teach rodeo skills. Riding since they were tiny tots, the girls were a sensation in their first rodeo appearance. They have traveled the country over, have won numerous awards, and have been invited to appear at the 1970 Tokyo World's Fair.

Gloria and Joy are working their way through college. Ruth was named "Miss Congeniality, USA" in the Miss Teen-Age America Contest in 1968. Together, the three girls have started a business of making splash guards for cars and trucks.

RAYMOND G. BAINES (TLINGLIT-TSIMPSHEAN) RELIGIOUS ADMINIS-TRATOR

Reverend Baines has much to his credit in the field of administration. He is currently Associate Director of Cook Christian Training School for Indians, in charge of campus and student activities.

While serving as student pastor for the Berkeley Westminster Presbyterian Church his congregation was comprised of Orientals, Indonesians, American Indians, Spanish Americans, Negroes and Caucasians. Through this service, he came to understand not only the problems connected with minority groups and poverty, but also those which immigrants to this country face.

From here, he went as pastor to a church in his home town in Alaska. He was one of two pastors in the community. He was also civilian Chaplain to an F.A.A. facility and a U.S. Coast Guard Air-Sea Rescue Squadron. He was vice-president of the P.T.A., a member of the local school board, and executive-treasurer of the Tlingit-Haida Land Claim Organization representing some 12,000 Alaskan Indians.

This background of experience was to serve well when Mr. Baines was named to head the Department of Indian Work for the Minnesota Council of Churches. The department is an ecumenical effort of 16 Protestant denominations in the State and especially in the Twin Cities. As director of this department, he was deeply involved in the areas of housing, employment, education and training, health needs, law enforcement, family problems, welfare and spiritual needs.

Also involved in his work were many other activities. He was a board member of the Upper Midwest American Indian Center; one of the organizers of the first Indian Advisory Committee, Minneapolis Public School system; a charter member and officer of the Minneapolis Upward Bound Program for Indian children; Chairman of the American Indian Employment and Guidance Center of Minneapolis; a charter member of the Indian Task Force of the Mayor of Minneapolis; an organizer of the American Indian Federation of the Twin Cities; and, an initiator of the St. Paul American Indian Center.

He was also a member of the Minneapolis Public Health Department Advisory Board; a member of the Minneapolis Welfare Association and of the Minneapolis Urban Coalition and on the board of the Citizens Community Centers of Hennepin County. He worked with the Indian Housing Council of the Twin Cities; was a resource person for the Minneapolis Police Department Recruit Training Program; and served, by governor's appointment, on the Governor's Human Rights Council. Again, by governor's appointment, he served on the board of the State Human Rights Commission.

BIRTHPLACE: Ketchikan, Alaska, September 26, 1926.
MARRIED: Carolyn M. Fenton. CHILDREN: David, Deborah, Rebecca, Jonathan.
EDUCATION: Phillips University (A.B.); Pacific School of Religion (B.D.)
SCHOLARSHIPS: Methodist Church for graduate work.
MILITARY SERVICE: U.S. Army, Infantry 1944-1946.
ORGANIZATIONS: United Methodist Church (Chairman, Advisory Committee on Indian Work) Chairman, Indian Task Force; Program Council, American Indians-United (a founder); Phoenix Indian Center (board).

ARTHUR RAYMOND
(DAKOTA-OGLALA)
JOURNALIST

Arthur Raymond was orphaned when he was fourteen. He has been on his own since then, and held his first steady job when he was eleven. In the ensuing years he has been a laborer, truck driver, archery instructor, life guard, dairy worker, assistant physiotherapist, cook, hospital orderly, janitor, dishwasher and salesman. He graduated from grade school and high school at the head of his class. In high school, he held a number of class offices and was active in many school affairs.

Arthur enlisted in the Army in World War II. He worked his way through the ranks, and when he was commissioned a second Lieutenant, he was the youngest person to hold this rank. Before transferring to the infantry, he served in the medical corps and was graduated from Surgical Technician School at the top of his class. He served in the infantry as a first lieutenant and as commander of an infantry company.

Returned to civilian life, Mr. Raymond was an assistant boy's adviser at Rosebud Indian school for a brief time, and then worked as a physiotherapy assistant at a polio center. He then entered college and worked his way through in some of the various jobs listed above. Editor of the student newspaper, his editorials won him a top award. He revamped the paper, converting it from a school-subsidized one to a self-supporting journal. Through his editorials, a scholarship program for Sioux Indians was started.

196

With graduation, Mr. Raymond joined the staff of the *Mitchell Daily Republic* and a few months later was named city editor. A news-feature article that he wrote while there won the national first prize from the Associated Press and was selected by the Pulitzer Awards Committee for award consideration.

Moving to North Dakota as managing editor of the *Williston Herald* he continued to participate in many community activities, as he had done in South Dakota. The positions that he has held in community service are too numerous to mention.

Currently Sunday Editor with the *Grand Forks Herald,* Mr. Raymond is proud of his Indian heritage, but says that heritage will not put food in the stomach or clothing on the back.

"I am convinced that I can do more to help my people by making my mark in the free competitive society of America against all comers," he says. "The Sioux are in dire need of men and women who can make this kind of mark."

BIRTHPLACE: Winner, South Dakota.

MARRIED: Rose Marie Schone. CHILDREN: Arthur, Jr., Eric, Mary, Mark, Rebekah.

EDUCATION: Rosebud Indian School; Dakota Wesleyan University (B.A.).

HONORS: Named "outstanding economics student of year, *Wall Street Journal;* Sigma Delta Chi top award (1950); Associated Press National First Prize (1958); 4-H Community Service Award (1958); many others.

MILITARY SERVICE: U.S. Army, World War II, 1942-46, infantry, Europe.

ROBERT G. RAYMOND (DAKOTA-OBLALA) SANITARY ENGINEER, PUBLIC HEALTH SERVICE

Robert Raymond is the first Indian to be commissioned a sanitary engineer in the Public Health Service. His first position was on the Red Lake Reservation in Minnesota. Presently he is stationed at the Indian Health Service Area Office in Billings, Montana. His rank is equivalent to that of major in the army.

BIRTHPLACE: Milboro, South Dakota, February 6, 1931.
MARRIED: Elrita Lysne. CHILDREN: Deborah, Teresa, Gail, Michael.
EDUCATION: Dakota Wesleyan College; South Dakota State University (B.S.); University of Minnesota (MPH).
ORGANIZATIONS: National Society of Professional Engineers; Oklahoma Society of Professional Engineers; Commissioned Officers Association of the U.S. Public Health Service; American Public Health Association; American Society of Civil Engineers.
SPECIAL ACTIVITIES: Vestryman, lay reader, Episcopal Church, delegate of Church state conventions.

ANNA MOORE SHAW (PIMA) TEACHER, AUTHOR

Mrs. Shaw is the writer of a book on Pima legends. She began to collect these when she realized they might someday be lost forever. She also teaches the Pima language to children in kindergarten classes on her reservation.

She was born in the shadow of the Estrella Mountains in a lowly place among the bushes. Among her interesting memories is the time she helped nurse the renowned Dr. Carlos Montezuma. He was an Apache who became a prominent surgeon in Chicago and returned to Arizona when his health failed.

Mrs. Shaw is active in tribal and non-tribal affairs and for several years has edited the Salt River Pima monthly newsletter.

BIRTHPLACE: Pima Reservation.
MARRIED: Ross Shaw. CHILDREN: Roderick, Adeline.
EDUCATION: Reservation schools, high school.
AUTHOR: *Pima Indian Legends,* University of Arizona Press (1968).
ORGANIZATIONS: P.T.A.; Church Women United; State Synodical Presbyterian Church; Cook Christian Training School (board).
SPECIAL ACTIVITIES: Commission of Self-Help Housing Authority.

FRANCIS BLACKBEAR BOSIN (KIOWA-COMANCHE) ARTIST *

Entirely self-taught. Blackbear paints in a unique style and with imaginative flair while retaining the spirit and verve of the traditional.

The eldest of four children, he helped to maintain the family, painting only in spare moments. His family obligations prevented the acceptance of two university scholarships. However, in spite of difficulty, the artist has achieved great success and stands on a high pinnacle. His paintings are always sought for art exhibitions, and he is the only Indian artist to be represented in the 1965 White House Festival of Arts.

Blackbear's ability was first recognized when he was in military service. At one time he was an illustrator for Boeing Aircraft Company and art director for the Training Aids Section, McConnel AFB, Nuclear Weapons. He, is presently owner of the Great Plains Studio and Gallery in Wichita.

BIRTHPLACE: Anadarko, Oklahoma, June 5, 1921.
MARRIED: Nola Simmonds. CHILDREN: Rowene, Patricia, Francis, Jr., Niles (by previous marriage).
EDUCATION: Public high school and mission school.
MILITARY SERVICE: U.S. Marines Corps, World War II, two years, Pacific Theatre.
HONORS: Civil Servant Award, U.S. Chamber of Commerce (1959); Certificate of Appreciation, Indian Arts and Crafts Board (1966); *Who's Who in American Art; Who's Who in Greater*

Wichita; American Indian Painters. Fellow, International Arts and Letters, Switzerland.

EXHIBITIONS: More than 60 museums, galleries and art centers; six one-man shows. Represented in many public and private collections.

WORKS PUBLISHED IN: *American Medical Journal; National Geographic* (March, 1955); *Life, International* (March 16, 1959); *Book of the American Indian* (1956-1960); *Saturday Review; American West* (March, 1968); *Oklahoma Today* (1958, 1965); *American Indian Paintings from Collection of Philbrook Art Center* (1964); *Sunday Bonanza, San Francisco Chronicle* (August 22, 1965); and others.

AWARDS: Many, including five Purchase Awards and two Grand Awards.

ORGANIZATIONS: Wichita Artist Guild (director); Mid-America All Indian Center, Wichita (advisory board).

SPECIAL ACTIVITIES AND INTERESTS: Collecting Indian artifacts from southern plains area; writing Indian poetry.

✳ See art section

LEAH HICKS MANNING (SHOSHONE-PAIUTE-CHEROKEE) SOCIAL WORKER

Her life began in a Nevada Indian reservation village where the land was divided between the Washoes and Shoshone-Paiutes, Mrs. Hicks says. When a Paiute aunt of hers married a Washoe, both tribes denied the couple residence on their side of the reserve - so the family lived in the middle of the reservation.

As a girl, Leah was taught to respect and function in both tribal languages and culture. She was the first Indian student to be enrolled in a public school kindergarten and to continue on to high school where she earned her share of honors and offices. Her family pioneered in changing the trend of keeping children at home to that of sending them away to government boarding schools. Public school expectations at that time were difficult to meet either financially or in reference to grade requirements.

After completing her college studies, Mrs. Manning taught in the Nevada public schools. She then attended graduate school for two years. After her marriage, she, raised her family and worked for a social service agency while her husband went through college. When her children were grown, she completed the work necessary for her master's degree.

Returning to Nevada, where her husband owns a cattle ranch, Mrs. Manning has continued to serve as a social worker. She has also been acting assistant to the superintendent of the

Nevada Indian Agency and continues to carry that responsibility when her personal services are required.

Mrs. Hicks has two noted ancestors - one is Elijah Hicks, who was a Cherokee councilman at the time of the Cherokee Removal; the other is Chief Winnamucca, an early leader among the Paiute and well-known in Nevada history.

BIRTHPLACE: Reno, Nevada.
MARRIED: Arthur T. Manning. CHILDREN: Winona Manning Holmes, Tina, Claire, Teela.
EDUCATION: Bacone Junior College; Keuka College for Women; Graduate School for Social Work Administration, University of Chicago; University of Utah.
SCHOLARSHIPS: DAR; American Baptist; Illinois Federation of Women's Clubs.
HONORS: Blanche Snowcroft Willey Award, University of Utah, for outstanding social work student of year; Alumnae Professional Achievement Award, Keuka College (1968).
ORGANIZATIONS: National Congress of American Indians; a number of state, community and county welfare organizations.
SPECIAL INTERESTS: National Presbyterian women's activities; Indian arts and crafts and the recording of Indian music.

SOLOMON McCOMBS (CREEK) ARTIST *

Solomon McCombs is descended from forebears who travelled the tragic "Trail of Tears" during the time of the Indian removal from Georgia to Oklahoma. A great-uncle was one of the founders of Bacone College and the Memorial art gallery there is named for him. On his mother's side, Solomon is descended from Chief William McIntosh.

An injury in his youth confined Solomon to bed for some time. During this period, he became interested in art. He was one of the first Indian students to enroll in the art department at Bacone College when it was officially opened.

Painting the history of his own Creek people is a major interest, but the artist does not restrict himself to this subject in his range of art. In his portrayals of Indian life and custom, he tries to keep alive the beautiful old techniques of Indian painting. His interpretations are entirely authentic.

Mr. McCombs is employed by the State Department as an audio visual officer and has served in the capacities of illustrator, architectural, cartography, model making, and as art ambassador. In 1945, he was sent by the Department's International Educational Exchange Service to Lebanon, Syria, Jordan, Uganda, Kenya, the Belgian Congo, French Equatorial Africa, Libya, India and Burma. He exhibited his paintings and explained American Indian contributions to our country's national development and culture as the first Indian good will art ambassador. After his return from this tour, in which he met informally with many high ranking officials, he was interviewed for the Voice of America. This was later beamed to countries around the world, and also to Africa for the French speaking people.

Solomon McComb's works can be found in museums and collections throughout the country. In addition to his creative art, he has been a technical artist with Douglas Aircraft, U.S. Engineers Corps; Clovis Air Force Base; and the U.S. Bureau of Reclamation.

BIRTHPLACE: Eufaula, Oklahoma, May 17, 1913.

MARRIED: Margaret Sauer.

EDUCATION: Bacone College; Tulsa University.

HONORS: Waite Phillips Trophy for outstanding contribution to art through the years, Philbrook Museum (1965); Shield Award for outstanding contributions to the advancement and encouragement of Indian arts and crafts (1968); *Who's Who in the South and Southwest; Register of United States Living Artists; Dictionary of International Biography; American Indian Painters.*

EXHIBITIONS: Many major exhibitions; more than 30 public and private collections.

AWARDS: Two Grand Awards among many others.

PUBLISHED WORKS: Jacobson and D'Ucel (1950); Jacobson (1964); *Sunday Oklahoman, Orbit Magazine* (May 26, 1963); *Smoke Signals,* Indian Arts and Crafts Board (Autumn, 1965).

ORGANIZATIONS: Artists Equity Association of New York, Inc., Interantional Platform Association.

* *See art section*

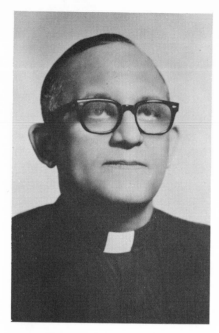

JOSEPH BROWN, S.J.
(BLACKFEET) PRIEST

Father Brown was educated by the Society of Jesus. He was ordained in 1948 and solemnly professed at the historic old mission of Cataldo, Idaho.

Twenty-five years in Indian missions have proved to him that old Indian values persist with dynamic vigor, he says. In spite of attempts to dissipate this great heritage or to downgrade and destroy it he believes it survives and still flourishes.

Father Brown believes the Indian past should be built upon because it is very real in profound spiritual reverence for the Holy Spirit, concern for neighbors, personal growth, fulfillment, beauty and dignity.

He has dedicated himself to the promotion of studies for and by Indians.

BIRTHPLACE: Browning, Montana, September 8, 1916.
EDUCATION: West Baden College (A.B.); Loyola University (M.A. History); Alma College (M.A. Theology).
ORGANIZATIONS: American Indian Historical Society; National Congress of American Indians.
SPECIAL ACTIVITIES: Pacific Northwest Indian Center (Indian studies and education).

BRONSON EDWARDS (OTTAWA) ARTIST *

Bronson Edwards did not become seriously interested in art until 1947. His subjects are mostly Indian in theme and he does a great deal of research in connection with his art.

The artist has sold more than 300 paintings - two of these were purchased by the late Senator Robert Kennedy. He has exhibited in more than twelve states.

BIRTHPLACE: Miami, Oklahoma, May 22, 1910.
MARRIED: Daisy Bonner. CHILDREN: Larry, Karen, Duane.
EDUCATION: Art Instruction, Inc.
EXHIBITIONS: More than 17 major exhibitions; two one-man shows; 15 public and private collections.
AWARDS: More than 39.
ORGANIZATIONS: Arts and Crafts Club, Inc.
SPECIAL INTERESTS: Secretary-treasurer, Ottawa Tribe for past 18 years.

* *See art section*

EDWARD P. DOZIER (PUEBLO-SANTA CLARA) PROFESSOR OF ANTHROPOLOGY

Dr. Dozier was raised entirely within the Pueblo tradition and culture. His English was limited and his contact with the outside world was scanty. He did not begin to appreciate the value of schooling until he enrolled in off-reservation schools.

His interest in anthropology was stimulated while in military service and he decided to pursue this profession with aid from the GI Bill of Rights.

Dozier, who still speaks his childhood language, has a home at his native pueblo and has earned an international reputation in the field of anthropology. He has taught at the University of Oregon, Northwestern University, and the University of Arizona where he was professor of anthropology and linguistics. He recently completed a study of American Indians in urban centers at the Center for Advanced Studies in the Behaviorial Sciences at Stanford. Late in 1969, he was named a professor of American Indian Studies and anthropology at the University of Minnesota, and chairman of the newly created Indian Studies department.

BIRTHPLACE: Santa Clara Pueblo, New Mexico, April 23, 1916.
MARRIED: Marianne Fink. CHILDREN: Wanda Dozier Kabotie, Miguel, Adya.
EDUCATION: University of New Mexico (B.A., M.A.); University

of California, Los Angeles (Ph.D.).

MILITARY SERVICE: U.S. Air Force (staff sergeant) World War II -4½ years.

SCHOLARSHIPS: Social Science Research Council; John Hay Whitney Fellowship; Wenner-Gren Foundation.

ORGANIZATIONS: Linguistic Society of America; American Folklore Society; American Anthropological Association; American Association for Advanced Science (Fellow).

KENNETH G. ROSS (DAKOTA-SANTEE) DIRECTOR OF INDIAN EDUCATION, STATE OF SOUTH DAKOTA

Kenneth Ross comes from a family of four boys, all of whom have a substantial background in education. This appreciation for learning was instilled in them by their mother, a classroom teacher.

Through most of his grade school years, Kenneth lived in the city. Then the family returned to Indian country and he attended government Indian schools. Before coming to his present responsible position, he was a teacher, supervisory teacher, and guidance counselor in the Gallup, New Mexico area.

Kenneth is a descendant of Chief Little Crow.

BIRTHPLACE: Pipestone, Minnesota, November 25, 1941.
MARRIED: Lucille Martin. CHILDREN: Kimberly, Kelly.
EDUCATION: Black Hills State College (BS); Northern Arizona University (MA).
SCHOLARSHIPS: United Scholarship Service; Bureau of Indian Affairs; South Dakota Indian Scholarship.

FRANCIS McKINLEY (UTE-NAVAJO) EDUCATIONAL DIRECTOR

From the time he was twelve years old, Francis McKinley had the responsibility for the care of two younger sisters and an invalid father.

He attended public schools, most of the time the only Indian student. In high school, he became interested in journalism and was editor of the school paper. In later years, when he returned to the reservation, he produced an excellent newspaper for his tribe.

Francis says his first job was with the Bureau of Indian Affairs when he was fourteen. He was hired to help with the reconstruction of a community building. Through necessity, he has worked hard all of his life.

Mr. McKinley has worked for the Ute Tribe in several capacities. He helped develop a reservation program for presentation to Congress so that the tribe could collect a $17.5 million award from the Court of Indian Claims. He included in this plan, a program for the future that presented broad programs in education, recreation, housing, resource development and other social progress. It was his task to implement the proposed programs.

In 1954, the Utes were divided on seeking termination of the services of the federal government. Full blood Indians decided to remain under government jurisdiction. Francis was given the responsibility for planning and organizing a long range development plan for them. At one time in his work with his tribe, Mr. McKinley was concerned with the development of housing projects and community recreation centers: and served as the director of education and public relations. He also served a number of years on the Tribal Council.

In order to academically prepare for employment in education, Francis continued his schooling with graduate studies and night school. He earned his way through all of his college training with part time work. While counseling students at the University of Utah, he drove 150 miles to the University, took courses until 10:00 p.m., and then returned the 150 miles, arriving home during the "wee hours of the morning."

Francis is now employed with the Far West Laboratory for Educational Research as Director of the Indian Studies Project.

BIRTHPLACE: Randlett, Utah, September 20, 1920.
MARRIED: Frances Cesspooch.
EDUCATION: Riverside Junior College; George Washington University (AB); University of Utah (MA).
HONORS: Indian Council Fire Achievement Award and honorary life membership (1964).
MILITARY SERVICE: U.S. Army 1942-46 - England, France, Germany.
SPECIAL INTERESTS: Working with Indian young people to assist them along educational lines.

ROBERT L. BENNETT (ONEIDA) DIRECTOR, AMERICAN INDIAN LAW CENTER, UNIVERSITY OF NEW MEXICO LAW SCHOOL

Mr. Bennett, who has spent his entire life until recently, in government service, is the only individual to come up through the ranks of Bureau Of Indian Affairs to serve in the position of Commissioner. He served in that capacity for three years. Mr. Bennett was the second Indian in 100 years to be so appointed.

For 33 years prior to his appointment by President Lyndon B. Johnson, Mr. Bennett was engaged in work with Indians throughout the country, including Alaska. He began his career in the Bureau of Indian Affairs immediately after his graduation while continuing studies for his law degree.

With the Bureau of Indian Affairs, Mr. Bennett was a specialist in tribal affairs, administrative assistant, job placement officer, an agency superintendent, and an area director. He also served in other capacities during his tenure with the Bureau.

Following his military service, he directed a training program for World War II Indian veterans for the Veterans Administration, which enabled several hundred Indians to obtain G.I. benefits. Returning to the Bureau of Indian Affairs, as placement officer, he arranged the first agreement with a state employment agency for special services to South Dakota

Indians. He also assisted in the development of the Southern Ute Tribal and Family Plan Program and the Partition Act for the Utes.

As Area Director for the BIA in Alaska, Bob Bennett worked to develop better education, utilize native resources, and provide better housing for the Native and Indian people. He was called to the Commissioner's office from Alaska and then stepped out of the position in 1969.

Now is the time to start writing a new chapter in the annals of the Indian people, Mr. Bennett believes. "There aren't enough of us who are climbing the highest mountain . . . who walk with dignity through troubles . . . who are striving to build a solid future in which Indians will not merely play a part in surviving the new civilization, but will make a better one," he says.

BIRTHPLACE: Oneida, Wisconsin, November 16, 1912.
MARRIED: Cleota Minor.   CHILDREN: John, William, Leo, Joanne, David, Robert.   (The first three have University degrees.)
EDUCATION: Haskell Institute; Southeastern University School of Law (LLB).
HONORS: Indian Council Fire Achievement Award and honorary life membership (1962); America's Outstanding Indian Citizen, American Indian Exposition (1966); Honorary Membership, Southern Ute Tribe (1969); Adoption, Whistling Water Clan, Crow Tribe (1967); Lifetime Member, Haskell Alumni Association and Outstanding Alumnus (1968); Honoring Name, Seminole Tribe (1969); Honorary Life Membership, Aberdeen Area Employees Association (1970); Annual Honorary Award, American Indian Society, Washington, D.C. (1969); Adoption, Cheyenne and Arapaho Tribes (1968); Adopted, Sacred Indian Gourd Society.
MILITARY SERVICE: U.S. Marines (1943-1945).
ORGANIZATIONS: Arrow, Inc.; American Legion; American Society for Public Administration; American Academy of Political and Social Science; American Association of Applied Anthropology; American Indian Development, Inc. (president); Gallup Ceremonial Association (chairman of board); Kit Carson Council,

Boy Scouts of America (member Executive Board); National Congress of American Indians; National Advisory Council on Indian Youth.

SPECIAL ACTIVITY: Consultant, William H. Donner Foundation.

TAYLOR McKENZIE (NAVAJO) PHYSICIAN

Dr. McKenzie, the grandson of a medicine man, is the first Navajo to become a physician. After completing his medical training, he joined the U.S. Public Health Service with the request that he be assigned to practice on the Navajo Reservation.

"Navajos have an acute health problem. Because of the language barrier and hostile attitudes, doctors· have not had an easy time among my people. I want to help," he said.

His first assignment was in the Kayenta Health Center. He was then appointed Chief of Surgery for the Indian Hospital at Shiprock, and is now Director of the Indian Health Service Unit there.

Dr. McKenzie strongly believes that the Navajos should take over reservation schools without further delay, and assume the responsibility for the education of their children.

BIRTHPLACE: Shiprock, New Mexico.
MARRIED: Betty Jean Smith. CHILDREN: Michael, Marvin, Judith, Gilbert, Patricia, Claire, Kathleen, Edward.
EDUCATION: Navajo Mission School; Wheaton College (B.S.); Baylor University College of Medicine (M.D.); University of Michigan Medical School.
SCHOLARSHIPS: Navajo Methodist Mission.

OSCAR WELCH (CHERO-KEE) HOSPITAL EXECUTIVE

Oscar Welch is Deputy Service Unit Director for the Hastings Hospital in Tahlequah. He has been an employee of the Indian Health Service for the past five years and before that has been a health educator, athletic director, teacher and principal.

When he was health educator on the Cherokee Reservation in North Carolina, he wrote a series of weekly health education articles for the reservation newspaper.

Mr. Welch is the first Indian to hold his present position.

BIRTHPLACE: Cherokee, North Carolina, May 24, 1921.
MARRIED: Elizabeth Barnett. CHILDREN: Anita Elizabeth.
EDUCATION: Cherokee High School; Northeastern State College (B.S.); Western Carolina University (M.A.).
SCHOLARSHIPS: Public Health Service Traineeship.
MILITARY SERVICE: U.S. Army Air Force, World War II, four years, ten months.
ORGANIZATIONS: Kiwanis (past president); American Legion (past commander); Lions; Masons; American Public Health Association.

JAMES SOMDAY (COLVILLE) TEACHER

James Somday is a "global teacher." He has taught high school in Alaska, and spent three years with the Peace Corps training teachers in Peru. He also taught in a Peruvian copper mining community.

Mr. Somday has been an athletic coach and guidance counselor.

He completed his education by part-time work; with the help of GI money; and with a tribal scholarship.

BIRTHPLACE: Koonteville, Washington, April 25, 1934.
MARRIED: Francisca Caceres.
EDUCATION: Gonzaga University; University of Colorado; Eastern Washington State College; University of Washington.
SCHOLARSHIPS: Colville Tribal Scholarship.
MILITARY SERVICE: U.S. Coast Guard, 4 years.

ROBERT E. POWLESS (ONEIDA) YOUTH WORKER

Robert Powless is Director of Programs for Recognizing Individual Determination Through Education at Wisconsin State University (Stevens Point). This organization is better known as PRIDE.

The main problem hindering the culturally diverse student is a conceptual one, Mr. Powless says. "If an Indian youth's concepts of school, of being an Indian in a white society, and of himself can be guided from the negative to the positive, he will then be able to utilize his individual academic potential in the educational programs made available to him."

This is the philosophy by which Mr. Powless works. It has been the keynote of all his relationships with Indian young people as high school teacher and coach, as recreation leader, adviser to university students and counselor and skills instructor. He has also been director of the Upward Bound Program at the University where he is now located.

BIRTHPLACE: Oneida, Wisconsin, March 6, 1933.
MARRIED: Linda Graham. CHILDREN: Blair.
EDUCATION: University of Wisconsin (B.S., M.S.).
MILITARY SERVICE: U.S. Army 1956-58, Medical Aidman.

NED HATATHLI (NAVA-JO) COLLEGE PRESI-DENT

Ned Hatathli was born in a hogan. He learned very early to care for the few sheep and horses owned by his parents which were their only livelihood.

The one close relative who had any school experience was an uncle who was an Indian Service policeman. He constantly tried to "sell" the Navajos on the value of an education and finally pursuaded Ned's parents to permit the boy to attend government boarding school.

School was bewildering, but Ned finally settled down to what would be a lifetime process - education. The importance did not become apparent to him, however, until he was twelve. At this time he was taken on a student trip to the "outside" world and what he saw made a tremendous impression on him.

Ned graduated from high school as valedictorian of his class. Nine months later, at the age of 19, he enlisted in the Navy for service in World War II. He studied radio communication and was a radio operator aboard a tanker.

Following his honorable discharge, Ned immediately returned to school. For a year after graduation he was a property clerk for the Bureau of Indian Affairs. After marriage and the birth of his first child, he decided to continue his education and paid his expenses by selling paintings and moccasins that he had made. He graduated from college with distinction.

His first professional position was that of manager of the Navajo Arts and Crafts Guild, sponsored by the tribe. He was the first Navajo manager of that organization which he helped build into one of the tribe's most important resources. A master of design, he modernized traditional silver work to achieve higher sales value. No matter how modern the new pieces were, something of the old was always retained.

Navajo weaving, as a craft, was then at its lowest level. Ned brought new life to the weaving industry and restored the traditional designs and top quality work of this Navajo art. Not only did he revitalize Navajo arts and crafts, but he developed and directed a sound and profitable program of marketing.

It was not long before he was elected to the Navajo Tribal Council and to the Advisory Council of this group. He was made chairman of the Resources Committee and charter board member of the Navajo Forest Products Industry.

He next became Director of Resources for the Navajo Tribe, the first person to head this new tribal organization. He proceeded to initiate the most extensive natural resource development that the reservation has known. Oil and gas production boomed, coal mining was pushed, and a huge coal-fired power plant was built by private utility firms to provide electricity for a vast area of the Southwest. Uranium was mined and processing plants for this were erected.

As the Tribe's land purchaser, Ned was instrumental in acquiring a number of ranches, made many profitable land consolidations and exchanges.

In this period of growth and promise Ned Hatathli played a definite and important role.

He was named Education Specialist with the Navajo Indian

Irrigation Project in 1967. One of his responsibilities was to develop agri-education program with schools. With the opening of the Navajo Community College, founded by the Tribe and the only Indian founded and operated college in the country, Mr. Hatathli was chosen Executive Vice President. He helped to organize this new institution of higher learning and in 1969 became the first Indian president of this, the first Indian college.

BIRTHPLACE: Coalmine Mesa, Arizona, October 11, 1923.

MARRIED: Florence Smiley. CHILDREN: Gloria, Janice, Glenna, Edison.

EDUCATION: Tuba City Indian School; Haskell Institute; Northern Arizona University (B.A.); graduate studies, University of Colorado.

HONORS: Kappa Delta Phi (honorary for Freshman); Phi Eta Sigma; Blue Key; Phi Kappa Phi -with distinction.

MILITARY SERVICE: U.S. Navy, World War II - two years, South Pacific.

PROFESSIONAL PAPERS PUBLISHED: Several.

ORGANIZATIONS: Boy Scouts of America (vice president, Kit Carson Council).

SPECIAL INTERESTS: The development of human resources.

RICHARD FRENCH (YA-KIMA) FORESTER

Richard French is thought to be the only Indian with a degree in forest management. Coming from the heavily forested Yakima reservation, it is natural that his interests would lie in this direction. He is presently in charge of the cutting back of tribally-owned timber in the Fort Apache Reservation forest.

BIRTHPLACE: Toppenish, Washington, June 22, 1939.
MARRIED: Viola Sohappy. CHILDREN: Tess Naomi.
EDUCATION: Yakima Valley College (A.A.); Washington State University (B.S.) (University honor roll twice).
SCHOLARSHIPS: Yakima Tribal Scholarship.
MILITARY SERVICE: U.S. Army, 1963-1965. (staff sergeant).
PROFESSIONAL PAPERS PUBLISHED: *Logging Effects Upon Fishery Resources in the West.*
ORGANIZATIONS: Society of American Foresters; American Forest Association; Yakima Nation All-Indian Invitation Basketball Association (past vice-president, treasurer). Washington State University Cougar Club.

OVERTON JAMES (CHICKASAW) EDUCATIONAL ADMINISTRATOR

Overton James has been a teacher, an athletic coach and a principal in the public schools of his native Oklahoma for ten years.

In 1965, he was appointed Assistant Administrator of Indian Education for the State. In that same year, he became Governor of the Chickasaw Nation, its' 27th governor and the youngest ever to fill the office.

BIRTHPLACE: Bromide, Oklahoma, July 21, 1925.

MARRIED: Evelyn Richardson. CHILDREN: Wynona James Childress.

EDUCATION: Southeastern State College (B.A., M.A.).

MILITARY SERVICE: U.S. Navy 2½ years, World War II, South Pacific.

ORGANIZATIONS: Inter-tribal Council Five Civilized Tribes (past president); Choctaw-Chickasaw Confederation (president); Oklahoma Indian Affairs Commission (past chairman); National Indian Athletic Hall of Fame (trustee); National Congress of American Indians (chairman, education committee); Women's Gridiron Club of Oklahoma (director); Masons (32nd degree); Shrine.

SPECIAL ACTIVITIES: Oklahoma Indian Affairs Commission (past chairman); Five Civilized Tribes Museum (director); Second National Indian Workshop on Indian Affairs (general chairman); Governor's Full Employment Advisory Committee; Southeastern State College Advisory Board on Training of Teachers to Teach Teachers; Consultative Center for School Desegregation, Oklahoma University); National Indian Education Advisory Committee (chairman).

MONTANA HOPKINS RICKARD (CHEROKEE) COLLEGE PROFESSOR, HUMANITIES

On the maternal side of her family, Dr. Rickard can trace her line back to Queen Christina of Sweden. There have been two Cherokee marriages among her grandparents - one in North Carolina before the Cherokee Removal, and one in Arkansas.

Presently on the faculty of the Oregon College of Education, she has taught in several other colleges and in secondary schools in Oklahoma, Texas and Oregon.

BIRTHPLACE: Butte, Montana, January 22, 1913.
MARRIED: George G. Rickard (div). CHILDREN: George, II; Earl.
EDUCATION: University of Oklahoma (B.A., M.Ed); University of Oregon (D.Ed).
SCHOLARSHIPS: Methodist Episcopal Church.
HONORS: Achievement Award, National Council of Teaching of English (1964-67); *Two Thousand Women of Achievement; Who's Who of American Women.*
ORGANIZATIONS: Oregon Teacher Association (past chairman); Oregon Council of English (past chairman); Oregon Education Association (past chairman); National Council of Teachers of English; American Association of University Professors; Modern Language Association; American Indian Education Association (secretary and a founder).

ARCHIE W. DEMMERT (TLINGIT) EDUCATOR, ADMINISTRATOR, TEACHER

Standing high in his chosen career, Mr. Demmert's battle for an education was tough and uphill. As a World War II veteran, he entered teachers college at the age of 41. After he had completed his junior year, his wife died and he was left with the care of two small daughters.

Three years later he received his degree and with several summers of study completed the work for his master's.

Mr. Demmert began his teaching career as a substitute in 1930. Since then, he has taught all over Alaska. It has been said of him that no "Alaskan has added more to the quality and length of schooling among natives than this "gentle, iron man." In his more than forty-year career he has urged, aided, pursuaded, even "deviled" many hundreds of Alaskan natives to continue their education. Many who finished college or hold degrees are in some way indebted to him.

A sixth-grade teacher in Sitka, Alaska, Mr. Demmert was named to the National Teacher of the Year honor roll in 1969 - the first American Indian honored in the program since 1952. Both of his daughters are preparing for teaching careers.

BIRTHPLACE: A boat north of Prince of Wales Islands, May 17, 1909.
MARRIED: Ella Mae Gidding. CHILDREN: Ruth, Frances.

EDUCATION: Chemawa Indian School; University of Wisconsin (B.S.); University of Alaska (M.Ed.).

HONORS: Service certificate (1965); Teacher of Year, Sitka (1969); honorary doctorate, University of Alaska (1970).

MILITARY SERVICE: U.S. Army, 1944-1946. (Sharpshooter, Honorable, Asiatic Pacific; Campaign Medal; Good Conduct Medal).

ORGANIZATIONS: Alaska Native Brotherhood; Tlingit and Haida Association; Sitka Teachers Association (president); Alaska Education Association; National Education Association; Association of Classroom Teachers.

SPECIAL ACTIVITIES: Greater Sitka Borough School District (advisory board); member, by governor's appointment, Commission on Cross-Cultural Education; member, State of Alaska Textbook Commission.

MICHAEL R. CRAWFORD (PENOBSCOT) EDUCATOR

Michael Crawford is Deputy Commissioner, State Department of Indian Affairs, a highly responsible position for one who "is just starting out." The State of Maine is the only one to have such a department. It was organized only a few years ago.

Previous to this appointment, Michael was a junior high school teacher in mathematics and science for the Bangor School System. During this time he was Economic Consultant to the Penobscot Indian Corporation.

BIRTHPLACE: Penobscot Indian Reservation, Indian Island, Old Town, Maine, December 5, 1943.

MARRIED: Barbara Harper. CHILDREN: Emily, Jason.

EDUCATION: Washington State College; University of Maine.

DANIEL SAHMAUNT (KIOWA) SCHOOL ADMINISTRATOR

Mr. Sahmaunt is superintendent of the Chilocco Indian School, one of the large Federal boarding schools. He has been a teacher and principal in public schools and at Riverside and Shiprock Indian schools.

His great concern is helping young Indian people develop and maintain a sound self-image and pride in themselves. "I meet hundreds of young Indians who need someone to believe in them and to whom they may confide their hopes and dreams," he says, "I have dedicated my life toward helping them reach an adulthood that they will be proud to live."

Mr. Sahmaunt's great-grandparents were Chief Stumbling Bear and Chief Kicking Bird, who were noted leaders in Southern Plains history.

BIRTHPLACE: Meeks, Oklahoma, December 10, 1924.
MARRIED: Fern Burch. CHILDREN: Dana, Kathryn, Kim, Mark, Jay, Andrea.
EDUCATION: East Central State College (B.A.); University of Oklahoma (M.Ed.).
ORGANIZATIONS: Kiwanis (vice-president).

BARNEY OLD COYOTE (CROW) GOVERNMENT ADMINISTRATOR

Barney Old Coyote, the grandson of Mountain Sheep, a noted Crow warrior, grew up on the reservation.

His grandfather, Old Coyote, was a Scout with General Crook, and his great--grandfather, Big Forehead, was the Crow hero of the Battle of Rainy Butte.

One day, on his way to high school, the news came that Pearl Harbor had been attacked. Serving his country was important to Barney. He rushed home, borrowed some money and headed for the nearest Navy recruiting office in Billings. Although he had enlisted, an older brother prevailed upon him to join the air force with him. After basic training, the two were sent on a flight to Africa. Barney's plane was caught in a hurricane and made a crash landing in Puerto Rico. Since his records were lost when the plane went down, he was "a man without a country" until new papers arrived.

When the records came, he re-enlisted and, upon a plea to the government from his mother, was reunited with his brother in Tunisia. Before their honorable discharge, the two brothers completed 50 missions and received 150 points. They were both decorated several times. Barney was decorated for "extraordinary heroism."

After Barney returned home, he passed a test for his high school diploma; entered college and earned his degree. He has held a number of positions, mostly with the Bureau of Indian

227

Affairs on western reservations until he was selected as Special Assistant to Secretary of Interior Udall, as Job Corps Coordinator. His work was to help young men and women train for useful and productive lives.

Mr. Old Coyote has recently been an administrator with the Bureau of Indian Affairs Area Field Office in Sacramento. He is now Professor of Indian Studies and Director of the Institute for American Indian Studies, at Montana State University.

Barney takes part in all of the official ceremonies of his tribe. His exploits as a military pilot earned him the right to carry the pipe, an honor given to leaders of Crow war parties. He also wears the chief's jacket decorated with skins of the white weasel. His enlistment entitled him to carry one pipe and the fact that he volunteered for European duty, earned him the right to carry two pipes. For each mission that he flew, he is entitled to wear a white weasel skin on his jacket and another on his leggings.

When he first put on the complete costume, many ceremonies were necessary. Honor songs were sung. He took part in the War Bonnet Dance, regaling his war deeds that deserved the respect of the people. A "giveaway" feast followed the ceremonies.

Although he is a prototype of the modern Indian leader, Mr. Old Coyote has been very successful in his government career, but the traditions of his people are equally important to him. Not only does he have a genuine interest in the welfare of Indians, but for youth of all races.

BIRTHPLACE: St. Xavier, Montana, April 10, 1923.
MARRIED: Clara Teboe. CHILDREN: Kenneth, Patricia, Gary, Bernard, Rachel, Jacqueline, Edwina.
EDUCATION: Haskell Institute; Morningside College (B.S.).
HONORS: Honorary Doctorate, Humane Letters, Montana State University (1969); Distinguished Service Award, Department of

Interior (1969).

MILITARY SERVICE: U.S. Air Force, 1941-45 (Air Medal, 14 Oak Clusters).

ORGANIZATIONS: Boy Scouts; Lions; Knights of Columbus; P.T.A.; National Congress of American Indians; American Legion (past commander).

EMMA G. WIDMARK (TLINGIT) HOME ECONOMIST

Miss Widmark spent her high school years at Sheldon Jackson school, one of the first schools for Indians in Alaska.

Her first position as a home economist was on the Mescalero Apache Reservation in New Mexico. Later, she returned to Alaska and taught at her old high school.

She is presently home economist for the Yukon and Upper and Lower Kuskokwim Rivers as a staff member of the University of Alaska Extension Service. This district is larger than the state of Texas and has 80 villages within its borders. The people are primarily Athabascan Indians and Eskimos - and Miss Widmark says she is grateful for the opportunity to work with them.

BIRTHPLACE: Ketchikan, Alaska.

EDUCATION: Oregon State University (B.S.).

ORGANIZATIONS: Fairbanks Native Association; Alaska Native Sisterhood (treasurer); American Home Economics Association; National Extension Home Economics Association.

DOROTHY L. ANDERSON (FLATHEAD) AIR TRAFFIC CONTROL SPECIALIST (COMMUNICATIONS)

A granddaughter of Chief Michele, Dorothy Anderson is one of the few Indian women in the field of aviation. She is employed by the Federal Aviation Administration.

BIRTHPLACE: St. Ignatius, Montana.

EDUCATION: Ursuline Mission School; public high school; Seattle University (B.A.).

HONORS: Sustained Superior Performance, FAA (1965); UN Fellowship Award, National Federation of Business and Professional Women (1968).

MILITARY SERVICE: Women's Air Force, World War II, 1949-1953.

ORGANIZATIONS: Seattle University Alumni; American Institute of Parliamentarians; UNA-USA; Camellia City Business & Professional Women's Club (past president); Davis Business & Professional Women's Club (president); Sacramento Valley Chapter 99's (women pilots); Altrusa; Sacramento Safety Council (vice-president, women's division).

SPECIAL ACTIVITIES: Equal Employment Opportunity Counselor for FAA; Chancellor's Advisory Committee on Extended Opportunities and Service, California Community Colleges; Organization of a World Refugee Chapter, Sacramento.

ACEY OBERLY, JR. (OSAGE-COMANCHE) EDUCATION SPECIALIST

Since his graduation from college, Acey Oberly has worked with or among Indian youngsters. His first teaching position was on the Coeur d' Alene Reservation. Next, he managed the Recreation Center on the Nez Perce Reservation.

Presently, Mr. Oberly is coordinator for the Adult Indian High School Program, sponsored by the Yakima Tribe. He is also coordinator of the Yakima Tribal Education Camp, a summer remedial education program for students on the Yakima Reservation.

Mr. Oberly's grandfather was principal chief of the Osages.

BIRTHPLACE: Lawton, Oklahoma, September 9, 1940.
MARRIED: Thelma Thomas. CHILDREN: Jorja, Yvonne.
EDUCATION: Bacone Junior College; Northeastern State College (B.S.).
ORGANIZATIONS: Yakima Agency Employees Club (board).

JOHN H. ARTICHOKER, Jr. (DAKOTA-OGLALA-WINNEBAGO) SUPERINTENDENT, COLORADO INDIAN AGENCY

John Artichoker is the son of a well-known educator who, as head of Hare Mission School, has assisted many Indian boys obtain an education and make a good adjustment to American society.

"Young John" says that he attended college only because of the help of "my wonderful family. They assisted me in financing my education at great sacrifice. At the time I was first in college, my parents were earning $180 a months with several other children to support. Almost one-fourth of their income was given me to go to school."

John financed his schooling, also, through loans and scholarships, and by working as a field hand and a construction laborer. In college, he was the first Indian to become a member of a campus fraternity. His first position after college was as director of Indian education for the state of South Dakota. When he took the position, he had one suit of clothes and only $175 in borrowed money.

Later positions were as tribal affairs officer for the Bureau of Indian Affairs and the Public Health Service. He was the first Indian superintendent of the Northern Cheyenne Agency and as a pioneer step helped the Tribal Council set up a number of new projects– without including a number of hampering restrictions. He also brought a small industry to the reservation. Because of his accomplishments at the Northern

Cheyenne Agency, he was named one of ten outstanding young men of the country by the U.S. Junior Chamber of Commerce.

At Colorado River John has assisted the people undertake an extensive development program and is helping the community in other constructive ways. He staunchly advocates the bringing forward of a large number of well-educated and well-trained Indian people for the protection of Indian interests and for assistance in working out social handicaps.

BIRTHPLACE: Pine Ridge, South Dakota, January 17, 1930.
MARRIED: June Boettiger. CHILDREN: John H., III, David.
EDUCATION: University of South Dakota (B.S., Ed., M.A.).
SCHOLARSHIPS: Illinois Federation of Women's Clubs; State of South Dakota; John Hay Whitney Foundation Fellowship.
HONORS: Indian Council Fire Achievement Award and honorary life membership (1965); Ten Outstanding Young Men Award, U.S. Jaycees (1964); Member, National Advisory Committee on Children and Youth for White House Conference (1960-1961); Member, 16-man National Advisory Committee on Human Resource Development, United State Jaycees (1969).
ORGANIZATIONS: Governor's Interstate Indian Council (past president, two terms); Lambda Chi Alpha; Masons.
PUBLICATIONS: *Indians of South Dakota* (1954); *The Sioux Indian Goes to College* (1959).

ALLAN A. FREDERICK (DAKOTA-YANKTON) PLANT MANAGEMENT SPECIALIST

Hard work and persistence in the face of adversity brought success and reward to Allen Frederick. During his life, he has had to overcome a host of hardships.

Frederick, who once worked as a fish peddler and railroad section hand, rose to executive status through sheer determination.

While in a federal boarding school, Mr. Frederick developed an interest in mechanics. High school years were tough and when the depression hit, he entered the Civilian Conservation Corps.

Miscellaneous jobs followed which gave him additional mechanical experience and ultimately led to a position as a mechanic and an instructor. During these formative years, he bought all the books he could afford on the subject of his interest and completed several correspondence courses.

Except for a brief period, Mr. Frederick has been in the employ of the Bureau of Indian Affairs. He received a number of promotions and then was named to the plant management position for the BIA in North and South Dakota with nearly 250 men and women employees in the department. Because he lacked formal training, the position imposed extreme mental stress on him, so he took additional correspondence courses to gain additional educational experience.

Knowing the many problems he experienced over a period of many years because of his lack of formal education, Mr. Frederick advises Indian young people to make every effort to get an education. In order to pass his examination as an electrical engineer, a gruelling regimen of correspondence study was necessary. This pace would have discouraged a lesser man. Later in his life, however, these strenuous activities took their toll on his physical well-being.

BIRTHPLACE: Wagner, South Dakota, July 22, 1910.
MARRIED: Olive DuBray.
EDUCATION: Flandreau Indian School; correspondence courses.
HONORS: Several recognition awards; Superior Performance Award, Bureau of INdian Affairs (1966); Special Commendable Service Medal, Bureau of Indian Affairs (1966); Certificate for war service work on lighting and guarding of Owyhee, Nevada dam (with Indian crews).
ORGANIZATIONS: Blue Lodge Masons; Scottish Rite Masons; Shrine; Eastern Star (Past Patron); Elks.

IRVIN COIN (HOPI) ETHNOMUSICOLOGIST

Irvin Coin has been a vocal and instrumental teacher at a high school in Tempe, Arizona. Starting with the fall of 1970, he will be on the faculty of Pima College in Tucson.

An ethnomusicologist is concerned with the history of music associated with culture. Dr. Coin, one of two Hopis to receive a Ph.D., the first in the tribe to earn a doctorate. He plans to record the music of all Arizona tribes.

The son of the long time director of the Santa Fe Indian Band, Dr. Coin credits his father with encouraging him to work hard and make a place for himself in the world.

EDUCATION: Arizona State University (BA, MA, Ph.D.).
SCHOLARSHIPS: Phoenix Newspapers, Inc. among others.

LUCILLE AHNAWAKE HASTINGS (CHEROKEE) SOCIAL WORKER (RETIRED)

Miss Hastings is the daughter of the late Congressman W. W. Hastings.

After pioneer experience in the Oklahoma State Department of Public Welfare programs in public assistance and rural child welfare services, she entered the Bureau of Indian Affairs as Field Service Assistant to the Supervisor of Social Work. She advanced through several positions to that of Assistant Chief, Branch of Welfare, Division of Community Services from which she retired in 1968.

She pioneered in introducing and developing social work programs on isolated Indian reservations and undertook extensive assignments in these areas to demonstrate modern methods and procedures. For her services on the Navajo reservation in "Operation Snow Bound" she was one to receive a Unit Citation for Meritorious Service in the Fifth Convocation of Honor Awards from the Department of the Interior.

She played a major role in changing methods of assistance so that families could purchase their own supplies and gain experience in handling funds. She also introduced state public assistance budgetary standards in the BIA general assistance program. She introduced other innovations for improvement, prepared social work instructional materials for field use and played the major role in developing the BIA's first manual section on general assistance and social services. She also developed an in-training program for staff workers.

Miss Hastings was designated by the BIA to work with the Civil Service Commission in establishing a rating system for the examination of social workers and served as chairman of the Board of Examiners. Because of her outstanding work in this connection, she was requested to serve as one of a committee to establish the present system of examinations and rating schedules of the Civil Service Examination for Social Workers.

It was mainly through her efforts that the BIA "Long Term Training Program for Social Workers" was developed. This has greatly improved social work service to Indian people.

Miss Hastings also had a significant role in the first housing improvement program conducted by the BIA and she developed the first standards for the selection of families for these first houses.

BIRTHPLACE: Tahlequah, Oklahoma.
EDUCATION: National Cathedral School for Girls; Vassar College (outstanding student); Tulane University, School of Social Work (B.SW); University of Chicago, School of Social Service Administration (M.SW).
HONORS: Special Citation, Outstanding Alumna, National Cathedral School for Girls; Distinguished Service Award, Department of the Interior, 1970.
ORGANIZATIONS: Academy of Certified Social Workers; U.S. Committee, International Conference of Social Work (has attended, at her own expense, conferences in Tokyo, Rio de Janiero, and Athens).

WILLIAM H. BEAN (CHEROKEE) GUIDANCE COUNSELOR AND ATHLETIC COACH

William Bean has coached in a number of fields. His teams have won five football conference championships.

BIRTHPLACE: Spearman, Texas, June 13, 1929.
MARRIED: Frances Cheadle. CHILDREN: William, HOward, Telitha.
EDUCATION: Chilocco Indian School; Northeastern State College (B.A.); Northeast Missouri State College (M.A.).
ORGANIZATIONS: Phi Delta Kappa; Masons; Iowa Personnel and Guidance (past board member); Southeast Iowa Association (past president); Waco Education Association (past president).

PATRICK DESJARLAIT (CHIPPEWA) ARTIST *

Patrick Desjarlait is rapidly building a national reputation with his paintings of life on the Red Lake Reservation in Minnesota.

Desjarlait says that he always wanted to paint, but his father was not at all sympathetic. Encouraged by a teacher, he soon found his niche and never left it.

As a commercial artist, he does much visual and advertising art. He helped to originate the original drawings for Hamm's beer, and he specializes in film animation for TV, training and industrial films.

Before World War II, the artist organized an art department in an Arizona War Relocation Center. On his return to Minnesota, he began to document the life of his people. He works in tempera using fine-point light brush strokes on flat tones to create a thin-line technique of unusual high lights.

BIRTHPLACE: Red Lake, Minnesota, March 1, 1921.
MARRIED: Ramona Needham. CHILDREN: Robert, Patrick, Charmaine, Delmar, Ronald.
EDUCATION: Pipestone Indian School; Phoenix Junior College; visual training, U.S. Navy, World War II.
SCHOLARSHIP: U.S. Department of Interior.
MILITARY SERVICE: U.S. Navy-four years.
HONORS: *Who's Who in American Art Vol. 4; American Indian Painters;* nine art awards including one grand award.
EXHIBITIONS: Eleven; two one-man shows.

* *See art section*   239

MARY OWL MELQUIST (CHEROKEE) CHOIR DIRECTOR

Mrs. Melquist is the daughter of Frell Owl who also appears in this book. The Owls are a distinguished family who have contributed importantly to Indian and non-Indian society. The Owls have all made their own way and have been very successful in various endeavors.

Mrs. Melquist has been a home economics teacher but now directs a church choir of 50 members. The group performs major works. As a harpsichordist, she often plays with chamber music groups and has organized and supervised such programs. She has also organized and directed musical productions in the churches of her community.

BIRTHPLACE: Hayward, Wisconsin, March 17, 1936.
MARRIED: Dean Melquist. CHILDREN: Ben, Tiana.
EDUCATION: Abbot Academy; Mt. Holyoke College (B.S.); University of Idaho.
HONORS: One of ten top seniors, University of Idaho; Phi Upsilon Omicron (honorary).
ORGANIZATIONS: Longmont Symphony Society (vice-president); Music Club (president).

VIRGIL L. GUNN (COLVILLE) HOME-SCHOOL COUNSELOR

Help for Indian students in the public schools of Omak, Washington, is being given by Virgil Gunn who is Indian Adviser in that area. He joined the Omak school staff under a program sponsored with Johnson-O'Malley funds.

Omak straddles the boundary of the Colville reservation. There are 200 Indian children in the schools from on or near the reservation.

Mr. Gunn's duties as Indian Adviser are varied. His duties consist mainly of helping Indian children and their families, making certain that the children remain in school, maintain good attendance, and receive understanding assistance with problems. He hopes to increase the number of granduates and to improve opportunities for Indian children.

Much of his work is involved with parents and with the development of parent participation in advisory groups and other activities. It is his belief that before Indian students will remain in school they must find Social acceptance, and have help and support at home.

BIRTHPLACE: Nespelem, Washington, March 22, 1942.
MARRIED: Maxine Dachal.
EDUCATION: Wenatchee Valley Junior College.
SCHOLARSHIPS: Tribal.
MILITARY SERVICE: U.S. Army, 1964-1966.

LOUIS W. BALLARD (QUAPAW-CHEROKEE) COMPOSER, MUSIC CURRICULUM SPECIALIST FOR ALL BUREAU OF INDIAN AFFAIRS SCHOOLS; DEPARTMENT HEAD, MUSICAL ARTS; INSTITUTE OF AMERICAN INDIAN STUDIES; LECTURER; TEACHER

Louis Ballard, one of the foremost composers of today, is a descendant of Joel B. Mayes, a principal chief of the Cherokees, and Louis Tallchief, a Quapaw chief.

He has many things to his credit musically - the music for three ballets based on Indian themes; two compositions for band, winds and percussion music; three compositions for chamber music; two compositions for chorus groups; three compositions for orchestra and five solo instrumental pieces.

His work as curriculum specialist includes the compilation of Indian music materials for key educational centers, the development of ideas through music in teaching English as a second language for Indians; and the conduct of music workshops and in-teacher training programs in reservation areas. Indian instruments will also play a key role in familiarizing with the ethnic resources of Indian music in the classroom. He is the first composer to develop a philosophy of ethnic music education in the field of Indian music.

Education was obtained the hard way - by working as a dishwasher, ambulance driver, drug store clerk, waiter, undertaker, bar-room piano player, vocal accompanist and janitor.

Projecting himself into another area, he is the founder and president of *First American Indian Films, Inc.,* the first all-Indian film company in this country. Louis is vitally interested in having Indians get involved in business enterprises and he seeks the support of all tribes in his film productions.

BIRTHPLACE: Miami, Oklahoma.
MARRIED: Ruth Dore (concert pianist, specialist of classical

Spanish repertoire). CHILDREN: Louis, Charles, Anne.

EDUCATION: University of Tulsa (B.A., B.A. Mus. Ed., Master of Music, Composition); Studied with a number of noted European teachers.

HONORS: Parriott Graduate Fellowship (1962); first Marion Nevins MacDowell Award for chamber music at MacDowell Festival of American Music (1969); Ford Foundation grant for one-year work-study (1970); A.S.C.A.P. awards annually (1966-1969).

COMMISSIONS: Many, including Santa Fe Symphony Orchestra; Harkness Ballet Company; William Jewell College; National Endowment for the Arts; State of Oklahoma 60th anniversary of Statehood; Youth Concerts of New Mexico.

AUTHOR: A number of professional articles.

SPECIAL ACTIVITY: State Department tour of Switzerland (1964).

GARY F. BASS (COLVILLE) ATTORNEY

Gary Bass is an ardent worker for Indian civil rights projects. He is director of a project sponsored by the National Institute for the Endowment of the Humanities which prepared and distributed pamphlets to Indian people explaining their legal rights and which conducts legal clinics on reservations. He is legal counsel for United Indians of All Tribes, a coalition of Indian people laying claim to Fort Lawton in Seattle. He assisted in the legal services proposal for Small Tribes of Western Washington, Inc.

BIRTHPLACE: Colville, Washington, April 8, 1936.
MARRIED: Rita Elliott. CHILDREN: Gary, Lance, Julia.
EDUCATION: Gonzaga University (BA); University of Washington (LLB).
SCHOLARSHIP: Colville Tribal.
MILITARY SERVICE: U.S. Army, 1960-62.

LORENZO MARTIN (NAVAJO) FRANCISCAN BROTHER

When people ask why he became a Religious Franciscan Brother, Lorenzo Martin answers in this way:

"A 'Religious' is one who gives himself to God in order to dedicate his whole life to being a 'pro' at love - the love of Christ that must live in the world.

"Today, in Navajoland, you have 'Religious' who have left their homes, families and friends to be witnesses to the fact that the life of Charity 'in action' is necessary. That is why I joined and why I follow the life of religious service. All of the Franciscan Brothers profess and love the same kind of life. My very name 'Brother' tells you I'm wide open, I *am* your Brother. It's not an easy life, but it's worth it."

Brother Martin works with young people - he teaches religion and spreads the message of the Gospel through radio programs, group discussions and newspaper articles.

His grandfather was a medicine man, a religious leader of the tribe.

Editor's note: Brother Lorenzo Martin, O.F.M., professed his solemn vows in the Order of Friars Minor on September 5, 1970.

BIRTHPLACE: Chinle, Arizona, April 20, 1945.
EDUCATION: St. Catherine Indian High School; Northern Arizona University; Duns Scotus College.

245

JAKE C. CHEE (NAVAJO) STATE REPRESENTATIVE

In private life a stock raiser, Mr. Chee is one of several Navajos in the New Mexico Legislature.

Trouble with his eyesight prevented his continuing schooling, but his life has been one of service for his people.

He has been chairman of the Navajo Land Development Board for the past 17 years and a deputy sheriff for three years.

BIRTHPLACE: Sand Spring, New Mexico, July 20, 1912.
MARRIED: Alice. CHILDREN: (6).
EDUCATION: Reservation schools.
MILITARY SERVICE: U.S. Army, World War II, three years Asiatic Pacific Medal, European Theatre Medal, Good Conduct Medal, North Africa Medal.
ORGANIZATIONS: Lions.

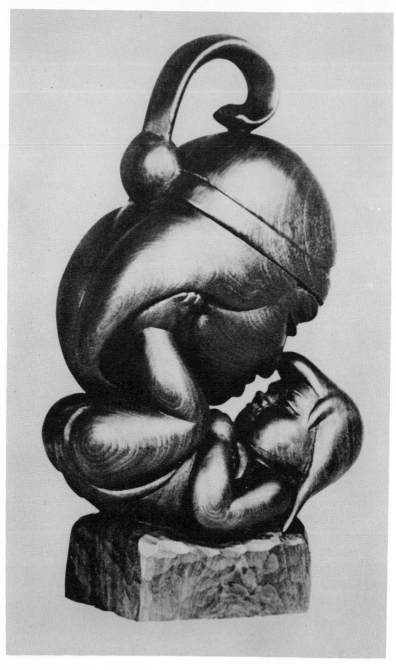

"Turkey Feather Halo" Willard Stone

Woody Crumbo

"*Spotted Wolf's Last Request*"

249

"Death Went Riding"   Blackbear Bosin

"Pawnee Winter Hunt"   Bronson Edwards

"Seed Gathering"   Pablita Velarde

251

Pottery by Maria Martinez and Popovi Da

Allan Houser

"Fresh Trails Apache War Party"

Photo: Philbrook Art Center

Brummett Echohawk

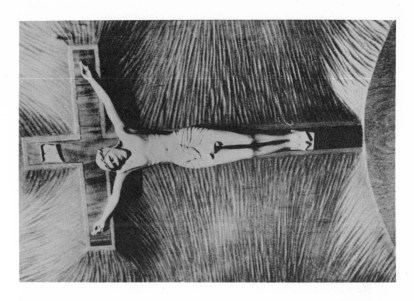

"Way Of The Cross"   Goingback Chiltoskey

"Black Squirrels Eating The Sun"   C. Terry Saul

"Francis The Prophet"   Joan Hill

256

Photo: Philbrook Art Center   *"The Medicine Man And His Helpers"*   Solomon McCombs

"Old Medicine Man"   Yeffe Kimball

Patrick Desjarlait

"Wild Rice Gathering"

"Peace On Earth"   Waano - Gano

"Navajo Mother In Supplication"   R.C. Gorman

260

"Buffalo Dancer"   Oscar Howe

Photo: Philbrook Art Center   *"Wild Horses"*   Andrew Tsinajinnie

Photo: Philbrook Art Center

"Seminole Women Grinding Corn"   Fred Beaver

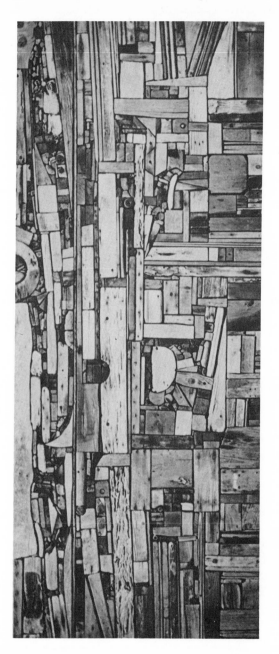

George Morrison

"New England Landscape III"

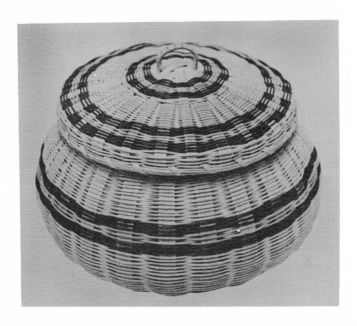

Honeysuckle Baskets   Lucy George

"Washing Hair"   Harrison Begay

Photo: Philbrook Art Center

AXEL C. JOHNSON (ESKIMO) CANNERY OPERATOR

Axel Johnson was a member of the Alaska Legislature for six years. He played a major role in securing one of the largest land claims in the State for his people.

At one time, Johnson flew his own plane into remote villages in which there was no doctor. He would administer penicillin shots while talking by radio with doctors, making certain that proper treatment was being given. He was able to keep charts, give drugs, and see to the needs of tubercular patients in his area. After he had taught himself the duties of a mid-wife, he passed his knowledge and skill on to his wife. When plane travel was impossible, Johnson used a dog sled. It is said that he considered his dogs more reliable than a motor.

Mr. Johnson is a man of many skills. He not only operates a cannery, he is a licensed boat operator and a diesel engineer. Even though he founded a fish marketing cooperative, he finds time to serve as its refrigeration engineer.

BIRTHPLACE: St. Michaels, Alaska, September 7, 1911.
MARRIED: Pearly Johnson. CHILDREN: Jacob, Mary, Cecilia.
EDUCATION: Territorial School.
MILITARY SERVICE: Alaska Territorial Guard, World War II, six years (Captain).
SPECIAL ACTIVITIES: President, Emmonak Village Council.

EDMUND J. LADD (PUEBLO-ZUNI) ARCHE-OLOGIST

Mr. Ladd has been an archeologist with the National Park Service since 1956. He is presently stationed in Hawaii.

Ladd is the first Zuni to have a college degree. His grandmother was one of the first school teachers to come to Zuni. His grandfather was for many years tribal governor.

BIRTHPLACE: Fort Yuma, California, January 4, 1926.
MARRIED: Marceline Kimbrell. CHILDREN: Halone, Edmund.
EDUCATION: Albuquerque Indian School; University of New Mexico (BA; MA.)
SCHOLARSHIPS: John Hay Whitney Fellowship.
MILITARY SERVICE: U.S. Army, 1944-1948).
PROFESSIONAL PAPERS: six on Hawaiian archeology.
ORGANIZATIONS: Kona Coast Civitan (past president).
SPECIAL INTERESTS: Pacific and Southwestern archeology, community planning; archery hunting; scuba diving.

G. WILLIAM CRAIG (MO-HAWK) ANTHROPOLOGIST, HISTORIAN, UNIVERSITY LECTURER

Mr. Craig is one of the first to lobby for academic recognition of the American Indian. As president of the American Indian Student Association at the University of Minnesota, he requested consideration of a structured Indian program. As a result, a unique department of American Indian Studies has been established at the University.

BIRTHPLACE: Montreal, Quebec, Canada, March 11, 1920.

MARRIED: Arlene. CHILDREN: Gregory, Geoffrey, Judity, John.

EDUCATION: University of Minnesota; Columbia University; University of Notre Dame.

MILITARY SERVICE: Royal Highland Regiment of Canada; U.S. Marine Corps.

ORGANIZATIONS: American Indians United; American Legion; National Congress of American Indians; Eastern Seaboard Federation of Indian Tribes; Indian Federation of Minnesota (chairman, legislative committee); American Indian Student Association (past president); Fort Saint Historical Society and historical societies of Indiana, Ohio, Minnesota, Wisconsin.

SPECIAL ACTIVITIES: Program Director, Education for Indians in Minnesota Correctional Institutions; consultant or advisor to many groups and committees.

C. TERRY SAUL (CHOCTAW-CHICKASAW) ARTIST *

Mr. Saul's given name is "Chief" and he was so known during his entire school and army career.

Currently director of the art department at Bacone College, Mr. Saul says that an artist cannot afford to become stagnant. "You have to keep growing and improving-each painting must be better than the one before."

The artist exemplifies this philosophy. Throughout his professional life, he has been a consistent award winner. He is one of the original exhibitors in the Indian annual art show at Philbrook Art Center. About 1961, he began to perfect an oil-on-gesso technique using dentist tools to etch away the oil over-painting to form the picture. He received his largest fee for the painting of an Indian "madonna and child" in this technique.

BIRTHPLACE: Sardis, Oklahoma, April 2, 1921.

MARRIED: Anna Peterson. CHILDREN: William, John.

EDUCATION: Jones Academy; Bacone Junior College; Oklahoma University (BFA., MFA).

MILITARY SERVICE: U.S. Army, World War II, five years (European and African Theatres. (1st Sergeant).

EXHIBITIONS: More than 20 major exhibitions; more than 14 public and private collections, in this Country and Museums of Denmark, Austria, The Netherlands, Germany, and several Foreign Embassies; several one-man shows.

AWARDS: Many including Special Indian Artists Award, Philbrook Art Center (1970).

* See art section

THOMAS H. YOUNKER (COOS-COQUILLE) HIGH SCHOOL COACH

Tom Younker was "born" to his profession. In high school, he made Honorable Mention All-State in football and basketball and All-State First Team in baseball. He was asked to play professional baseball but decided to get his college education, instead.

During his college years, he played in the NAIA Camellia Bowl (1961) and by the end of his senior year, he had gained All-Conference honors-3 years in football and 4 years in baseball. Immediately after graduation, he signed a professional baseball contract.

Deeply interested in young people, he turned to high school coaching at the varsity levels in football and baseball and at the sophomore level in basketball. Coaching is not only his vocation, but his special interest. He spends much of his extra time working with teenagers.

BIRTHPLACE: North Bend, Oregon.
MARRIED: Diana Allado. CHILDREN: Jason.
EDUCATION: Linfield College (B.S., M.Ed.); University of Hawaii.
SCHOLARSHIPS: Athletic; United Scholarship Service.
ORGANIZATIONS: Oregon Education Association; Linfield Alumni Association.
SPECIAL ACTIVITIES: Governor's Commission on Youth (vice chairman).

EDNA HOGNER MASSEY (CHEROKEE) ARTS AND CRAFTS SPECIALIST, ART TEACHER, INTERIOR AND TEXTILE DESIGNER

Mrs. Massey is an interior designer and an arts and crafts specialist for the Bureau of Indian Affairs. She has had her own design studio for more than 25 years.

Her works are exhibited in various art galleries and museums in this country and abroad. She is highly rated in her field.

BIRTHPLACE: Stilwell, Oklahoma.
MARRIED: Fred H. Massey. CHILDREN: William, and Fred, Jr.
EDUCATION: Haskell Institute; studies under noted art teachers.
AWARDS: First prize, textile design, Fourth Biennial Creative Crafts Exhibition and second prize, fifth Creative Crafts Exhibition.
ORGANIZATIONS: Center for Arts of Indian America (secretary); Cherry Tree Textile Designers, Inc.; American Craftsmen Council (craftsman member); Smithsonian Creative Crafts Council; local art and cultural organizations.

FRED H. MASSEY (CHOCTAW) GOVERN- MENT ADMINISTRATOR

Fred Massey is the first Indian to have been appointed to the post of Assistant Commissioner of Indian Affairs in the history of the Bureau of Indian Affairs.

He has been in government service since his graduation from college, rising steadily through positions of increasing responsibility. Retirement comes for Fred H. Massey in 1970 after 34 years of service.

Mr. Massey is a descendant of Greenwood LeFlore who was educated in France and who had a beautiful mansion near Carrolton, Mississippi. A chief of the Choctaws, LeFlore was one of the great cotton planters of the South. He had 15,000 acres of cotton land in Mississippi and vast holdings in other places. LeFlore was elected to the Mississippi Legislature but was a staunch Union sympathizer throughout the Civil War. A city and county in Mississippi are named in his honor.

BIRTHPLACE: Massey, Oklahoma, November 2, 1912.

MARRIED: Edna Hogner. CHILDREN: William, Fred Jr.

EDUCATION: Bacone Junior College; Haskell Institute; National Law School.

HONORS: Outstanding American Indian, Annual American Indian Exposition (1956).

MILITARY SERVICE: U.S. Army, 1945-56.

WILLIAM E.S. FOLSOM DICKERSON (CHOCTAW) TEACHER/AUTHOR

Mr. Dickerson has been a teacher in Texas public schools for 30 years. With retirement, he turned to writing in the hope that he could play a part in the elimination of prejudice and superstition in thought and action among people.

His research on Indians has taken him to every major tribe in the country and he has written more than 50 published articles on Indian treaties and other subjects.

He is the author of two books which enjoy a steady sale, and has others to come.

BIRTHPLACE: Choctaw Nation, Oklahoma, December 16, 1898.
MARRIED: Alice Good. CHILDREN: Lane, JoAnn, Edwin.
EDUCATION: University of Texas (B.A., Summa Cum Laude, M.A.).
HONORS: Phi Beta Kappa.
MILITARY SERVICE: U.S. Army, Infantry, World War I.
AUTHOR: *The White Path* (Naylor, 1965); *Cliff Dwellers* (Naylor, 1968).
ORGANIZATIONS: Texas State Teachers Association.

ROSEBUD YELLOW ROBE FRANTZ (DAKOTA-BRULE) AUTHOR

The eldest daughter of the well-known Chauncey Yellow Robe, Mrs. Frantz is also descended from Iron Plume and Sitting Bull, famous leaders of the Dakota tribe.

For twenty years, Mrs. Frantz directed "The Indian Village," a recreational project conducted by the Long Island State Park Commission. The schools of Long Island and New York City participated, and children were taught about Indians through story hours, games, songs and hand crafts. An art exhibit was an annual feature.

Mrs. Frantz has also appeared on CBS national radio network, in her own scripts. She appeared on radio and TV in a promotional tour for 20th Century-Fox and has appeared on NBC-TV numbers of times.

Especially interested in new art forms evolving from the contemporary environment, Mrs. Frantz also has an excellent collection of pottery including many fine Indian bowls.

BIRTHPLACE: Rapid City, South Dakota, February 26, 1907.
MARRIED: Alfred A. Frantz. CHILDREN: Tahcawin de Cinc-Mars Moy.
EDUCATION: University of South Dakota.
HONORS: Prize winning short stories at Scottsdale Indian Arts Exhibition.
AUTHOR: *Album of the American Indian.* (Franklin Watts, 1969).
ORGANIZATIONS: Forest Hills Woman's Club.

CLYDE W. PENSONEAU (KICKAPOO-SHAWNEE) GOVERNMENT ADMINISTRATOR, RETIRED

Mr. Pensoneau began a career in the Indian Service as a farm aid on the Uintah and Ouray Reservation. He was promoted to farm agent and then to agricultural extension agent, with assignments covering several reservations. In 1954, he became superintendent of the Hopi Reservation, and then was moved to Washington as Agriculture Extension supervisor.

Since he wished to work more directly with Indian people, he requested a transfer to the field, and was appointed Assistant Area Director of Community Service at Gallup. He returned to the superintendency of the Hopi Agency in 1965. This service was cut short by serious injury suffered in an accident. His interest in Indian matters is intense, however, and he hopes to return to work with and for his people.

BIRTHPLACE: Jones, Oklahoma, February 15, 1914.
MARRIED: Irene Duff. CHILDREN: Ralph, Eugene.
EDUCATION: Oklahoma State University (B.S.).
HONORS: Distinguished Service Award, Department of the Interior (1970).
ORGANIZATIONS: Masons; Scottish Rite; Shriner.

ROBERT C. GILLESPIE (DAKOTA-CHEYENNE) DIRECTOR, INDIAN HEALTH SERVICE, STATE OF CALIFORNIA

Robert Gillespie is responsible for the coordination of the health needs of Indians of California. He works with all state, county and private agencies concerned with the health of Indian people.

His long experience in the health field has included positions as executive director for a rehabilitation center, associate director of a children's hospital, assistant hospital administrator for a 600-bed hospital, and group leader and community organizer for Chicago's famous Hull House.

He is a great-grandson of the famous chief and warrior, Young Man Afraid of His Horses.

BIRTHPLACE: Oglala, South Dakota, July 1918.
MARRIED: Mary. CHILDREN: (10).
EDUCATION: Ohio State University, School of Social Administration (B.S.); University of Minnesota; (M.P.H.); Northwestern University Graduate School of Hospital Administration.
PROFESSIONAL PAPERS: Article in textbook used in colleges and universities.
AUTHOR: Three books on Indian Arts and Crafts.
ORGANIZATIONS: American Hospital Association; Elks; National Congress of American Indians.

RICHARD G. ZEPHIER (DAKOTA-YANKTON) TEACHER

In 1804, while Lewis and Clark were encamped among the Yanktons, a child was born in the camp. Captain Lewis wrapped the child in the American flag and declared it to be "an American."

Growing to manhood with the tradition of this christening upon him, Struck-by-the-Ree took pride in his Americanism and was a strong friend of the whites. He kept his tribe from joining the hostiles at the time of the Sioux uprising in Minnesota and actually threw a cordon of his warriors across South Dakota as a barrier between the hostiles and the white settlements.

Richard Zephier, who is a history teacher in an Oregon high school, is a descendant of Struck-by-the-Ree. His father, Alvin Zephier, pulled himself up by his boostraps to become an educator after starting out in life as a day laborer. He instilled in his children the desire to be a part of "shaping things." He made certain that each of them received college educations.

During his last three years in college, Richard worked as a psychiatric aide in a state hospital. In addition to teaching history he is also a coach, and has had two champion teams.

BIRTHPLACE: Wagner, South Dakota, December 7, 1938.
MARRIED: Carol Robbins. CHILDREN: Kira, Richard.
EDUCATION: Yankton College (B.A.); Northern State College.
SCHOLARSHIPS: United Scholarship Service; State Indian Scholarship.

280

ATLEE A. DODGE (ME-NOMINEE) TRIBAL AND CIVIC LEADER

Atlee Dodge is the son of a long-time Menominee tribal leader. As one who has been most active in tribal and state affairs, he continues in the pattern set by his father, Mitchell.

Atlee is one of the original incorporators of the Menominee Indian Tribe of Wisconsin, Inc., which serves to hold intact the Menominee tribal cultural heritage as identified by several treaties. This highly important group, of which Mr. Dodge is secretary and registered agent, has already won a landmark decision relative to hunting and fishing rights. The Menominee tribe is independent of federal supervision and has established its reservation as a county in Wisconsin.

Mr. Dodge is employed as a right-of-way agent for the highway division of the State. He has qualified as an expert witness in four counties before Courts of Record. He also has the responsibility over management and operation of Menominee tribal assets which include the tribal lumber mill and 230,000 acres of land with substantial forests, 80 lakes and more than 300 miles of trout streams. He is a salesman for the development company which through sales of lake properties is expected to increase the tax base of Menominee County to exceed 25 million dollars in a ten-year period. Mr. Dodge is a licensed Wisconsin real estate broker and a licensed private pilot.

In 1969, he was a candidate from the 7th Congressional

District for the seat vacated by Melvin Laird, now Secretary of Defense. Although he was defeated in this try, there is no doubt but that he will run again.

BIRTHPLACE: Keshena, Wisconsin, April 10, 1931.
MARRIED: Mary Elizabeth Powless. CHILDREN: Leah Sue.
EDUCATION: Oshkosh State University; University of Wisconsin (B.S.).
MILITARY SERVICE: U.S. Air Force -Korean Conflict.
ORGANIZATIONS: Menominee Loan Fund (past secretary); Wisconsin State Employees Association (past president); American Right-of-Way Association; Menominee Enterprises, Inc. (executive committee); American Legion; Menominee County Republican Party (past secretary).
SPECIAL ACTIVITIES: Governor's Interstate Indian Council.

JAMES J. WILSON, III (DAKOTA-OGLALA) EDUCATOR

Until 1969 Dr. Wilson has been Chief of the Indian Division of the Office of Economic Opportunity. This included responsibility for Community Action Programs and special field programs as they affected Indians. Previous to this, he was a teacher of education and psychology at Chadron State College, and on the faculty of Arizona State University where he worked in the area of Indian education and community development.

BIRTHPLACE: Pine Ridge Reservation, South Dakota.
CHILDREN: (7).
EDUCATION: Reservation high school; Northern State Teachers College (BS); Arizona State University (MA, Ed.D.).

BETTY MAE TIGER JUMPER (SEMINOLE) TRIBAL CHAIRMAN

Mrs. Jumper is the first woman in the history of her tribe to be elected chairman of the tribal council, the highest position that can be held.

When she was five, her family moved to the Dania Reservation (now Hollywood Reservation) which was then the beginning of Indian land held in trust by the Government for the Seminoles.

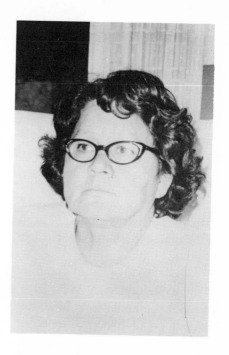

She was determined to go to school, and though this was strongly opposed by her grandmother, she prevailed upon her mother to let both she and her younger brother attend. School opened a whole new world for her, and she quickly adapted to the different way of life. Later, she and a cousin were the first Florida Seminoles to graduate from high school. Because of this "path breaking," many Seminole young people are going on to college and into the business world today.

After graduation, Mrs. Jumper was a public health nurse in Oklahoma. She then returned to Florida as a public health nurse covering three reservations more than 100 miles apart. Her services were also available to the Miccosukee Indians living along the Tamiami Trail. This was not an easy assignment for the Seminoles were still hostile to any "white man's ways."

In 1957, the Seminole Tribe was organized and for the first

time leaders were elected by the vote of the people. Mrs. Jumper was vice-chairman of the Council for two years and a member of the board of directors before she was asked to run for Chairman.

The Council is the governing body of the Tribe. Mrs. Jumper presides over this powerful four-man group that decides on programs for the welfare and betterment of the people. Aside from capably handling the myriad of business details that confront her, she spends much time in humanitarian service. She regularly visits with older people, sympathizing in their own language with their dismay over the changes of the 20th century, especially the changes so apparent among the young people.

"I can understand," she says, "for I remember back to the violent opposition in my family when I went to school. The elders said I had broken tribal law. The gap between the old and new ways of life is dramatic. It is also a challenge."

BIRTHPLACE: Indiantown, Florida, April 27, 1923.

MARRIED: Moses Jumper (one of only two Florida Seminoles to serve in World War II). CHILDREN: Moses Jr., Boettner, Scarlett.

EDUCATION: Cherokee Indian School.

AUTHOR: Historical Seminole Pageant (also director).

DAVID L. SPARVIER (OJIBWAY-CREE) LIBRARIAN

David Sparvier was a constant run-away from school because he understood only half of what was said. English was not taught nor was it heard, so that by the time some of the children reached fourth grade, the language was beyond their comprehension. They stayed in the fourth grade until they were old enough to leave school.

David's mother died when he was thirteen. He then left school and went to work in a lumber yard. After spending two years in a sanitorium he entered high school, where he gained pride and confidence in himself, and the incentive to continue his education.

Higher schooling was generally a happy experience for him except for one unfortunate experience with a bigoted professor, and an embarrassing course on French Canadian history. David says, "I shall never forget this episode as long as I live." However, it awakened in him the need to seek accurate information about the Indians of the Americas and keep correct the consistent misinterpretation and wrong presentation in books, mass media, films and TV, and also in the public school systems.

He studied to become a librarian, for he thought that this kind of training would be useful in helping bring about a revised interpretation of his people.

His first position was as a cataloguer for a provincial library; and as a library assistant on a bookmobile. He is presently head of the library service to Indians and Metis (mixed-blood Indians) for the regional library division of the Province of Saskatchewan. His duties are to promote library service throughout the province, to participate in conferences particularly geared to the culture and welfare of Indian people, and to prepare special book lists concerned with their history, among other activities. Saskatchewan is the only Canadian province to have an overall program to serve people of Indian ancestry jointly with other residents through a system of regional libraries.

BIRTHPLACE: Cowessess Reservation, June 11, 1938.
MARRIED: Jean Quewezance. CHILDREN: Arden.
EDUCATION: Indian residential schools; University of Ottawa (B.A.); University of Toronto (B.L.S.).
SCHOLARSHIPS: Indian Affairs Branch.
ORGANIZATIONS: Saskatchewan Library Association (president); Regina Friendship Centre (president); Canadian Association for Adult Education.

WILBUR W. DIXON (NAVAJO) TEACHER-ADMINISTRATOR

Wilbur Dixon, formerly director of the public services division of the Navajo Tribe is Equal Employment Opportunity Representative for the reservation. He is also a construction estimator and expediter. He has been an athletic coach, a principal, and is a teacher of mathematics at Many Farms High School.

BIRTHPLACE: Shiprock, New Mexico, April 6, 1927.
MARRIED: Ella Damon.
EDUCATION: Navajo Methodist Mission High School; McMurry College (B.S.); Northern Arizona University (M.S.); Utah State University (Ph.D., pending).
ORGANIZATIONS: Lions; Window Rock Teachers Association (past president).

FRANK PERATROVICH (TLINGIT) STATE LEGISLATOR

Frank Peratrovich has done many things in his life, but in his home state of Alaska he is identified with politics. A top football star in his youth, he was a banking and cost accounting major in college.

Frank's father was a Yugoslav who came to Alaska from San Francisco on a sailing vessel to oversee the construction of a cannery in the village of Klawock. This was the first cannery ever built in Alaska. After his marriage, Frank and his wife operated their own cannery. A family brand label featuring a picture of the Peratrovich's is on display in the State Museum in Juneau.

The couple also started a general store in Klawock, which they still operate. Through a number of off-and-on terms, Frank was mayor of his native village.

In 1944, he first ran for state office and won a seat in the House. In 1946 he ran for the Senate and has since been a member of the upper chamber except for one term. He was elected president of the Senate in 1961 and served in that capacity longer than any other senator.

Senator Peratrovich was chairman of the Democratic Party of Alaska in 1963. He has always championed minority groups and is respectfully recognized for the fine things he has accomplished for his own people.

BIRTHPLACE: Klawock, Alaska, April 12, 1895.

ROY PERATROVICH (TLINGIT) DISTRICT SUPERINTENDENT, BUREAU OF INDIAN AFFAIRS

Roy Peratrovich has served more than 30 years in the territorial government of Alaska and in the Bureau of Indian Affairs. Until his appointment as BIA District Superintendent, he was head of the BIA Tribal Operations.

Roy's father came to Alaska to supervise the opening of a cannery and was the first person to teach the Tlingits how to make fish nets. Roy was the first Alaskan, Indian or non-Indian, to have received a fellowship from the United Nations to study fisheries and cooperatives. He was assigned to the University of Nova Scotia for this study.

In his work with the territorial government, he was tax collector for the territory; chief enforcement officer for the territory; and director of land registration for the territory.

BIRTHPLACE: Klawock, Alaska.
MARRIED: Elizabeth Jean Wannomober (dec.). CHILDREN: Roy, Jr., Civil Engineer, Highway Planner for the State of Alaska; Frank, Employment Assistance Officer, BIA; and, Loretta Marie.
EDUCATION: Normal School.
SCHOLARSHIPS: John Hay Whitney Foundation Fellowship. United Nations Scholarship.
ORGANIZATIONS: Alaska Native Brotherhood (executive committee; past president five terms).

289

WOODROW W. CRUMBO (POTAWATOMI) ARTIST *

One of the top Indian artists of modern times, Woodrow Crumbo grew up in a traditionalist home and was a ceremonial dancer while still a boy.

At the end of the third grade, his schooling was interrupted for nearly ten years. During that time, a government worker encouraged him, with several other boys, to paint. She got them painting materials and found a market for their work.

"Some of us were so small that we sat on gallon buckets and used the backs of chairs for easels," Woody says.

In college during the depression years, his skill at dancing helped to provide his bread and butter. He organized and trained a student dance group which became popular entertainment. After graduation he continued to dance in Indian ceremonials. He also toured the country with the composer Thurlow Lieurance as an interpretative dancer.

Crumbo's life work began to take form when he became art director at Bacone College. He also became artist-in-residence at the Gilcrease Foundation. While at Bacone he designed a stained glass window based on a Delaware tribal design. The design was similar to one on a pouch given to William Penn by the Delaware Indians.

"Woody" Crumbo assisted in the planning of the first annual

exhibition of Indian Art at Philbrook Art Center in Tulsa. This is an annual event of great importance in the promotion of Indian art talent. Mr. Crumbo has been a vital force in the stimulation of creative production among Indians of all tribes.

Specializing in Indian costumes and culture, he has also explored Egyptian, French, English, Dutch and contemporary schools of art. He expresses himself in a variety of mediums with an unusual flare and sparkle, but always adhering to the authentic and legendary in Indian subject matter.

"Half of my life has passed in trying to complete the pictorial record of Indian history, religion, customs, ways of life and philosophies," the artist says. "I now have a graphic record that a million words could not tell."

BIRTHPLACE: Lexington, Oklahoma, January 31, 1912.
MARRIED: Lillian Hogue. CHILDREN: Minisa; Woody Max.
EDUCATION: Fort Sill and Chilocco Indian Schools; American Indian Institute (scholarship). University of Wichita; University of Oklahoma. Studied art under several well-known teachers. .
HONORS: Julius Rosenwald Fellowship (1945-1946).
MILITARY SERVICE: Aircraft designer, World War II.
EXHIBITIONS: More than 200 in Europe and North and South America; eight one-man shows; numbers of awards. Eleven public collections; nine private collections.
WORK PUBLISHED: *Pictorial History of Indian,* Oliver LaFarge (1956); *3rd Annual Indian Week Brochure,* Tulsa, (1938); *Tulsa Sunday World Magazine,* (December 7, 1952); *Sooner Magazine* (november, 1954); *Oklahoma Today* (1958); *Life International* (March 16, 1959). A movie script based on one of his paintings, is under contract.

∗ *See art section*

MARIA TALLCHIEF (OSAGE) BALLERINA

Maria Tallchief began as a child, and studied under the great Nijinsky in preparation for the career that was to take her to the pinnacle of her profession and to international fame.

Her first ballet lesson was when she was three; her debut in classical ballet was in the Hollywood Bowl at the age of fifteen.

After high school, Maria joined the Ballet Russe de Monte Carlo. Her first big opportunity came at the end of the season when, as an understudy, she danced the premier role in a Chopin concerto. Shortly afterward, she made her New York debut in the same role.

When she had advanced to ranking soloist, she joined Balanchine's Ballet Society, now the New York City Ballet and established herself as the equal of top dancers both here and abroad. When she became prima ballerina she was the first American dancer to achieve this title, and one of the world's greatest dancers. She has appeared in most countries of Europe, Latin America, and Japan and in all of the principal cities of this country.

All of this accomplishment came after great personal sacrifice and struggle. She would work herself to exhaustion; she suffered the jealousies of her fellow dancers; she filled countless hours with practice sessions. Tormented with shyness she changed herself into a woman of authority and radiance by sheer self-discipline - one who stood alone, unmatched by any other ballerina. She lived only to dance.

Professionally, Maria endowed the arts with a splendor that had not been seen in ballet before her time. She has also presented an outstanding image of the American Indian in mid-twentieth century. Of her many great roles, the greatest was *The Firebird* and for her exquisite performance in this ballet she will never be forgotten.

BIRTHPLACE: Fairfax, Oklahoma.
MARRIED: Henry Paschen, Jr. CHILDREN: Elise.
EDUCATION: Public schools.
HONORS: Special ceremony, Osage Nation, name of Princess of Two Standards given; "Woman of the Year," Woman's National Press Club (1953); "Maria Tallchief Day," Fairfax, Oklahoma (1953); Indian Council Fire Achievement Award and honorary life membership (1967); Oklahoma Hall of Fame (1968); and many others.

MARJORIE TALLCHIEF (OSAGE) BALLERINA

Marjorie Tallchief, the sister of Maria Tallchief, has carved out a distinguished career on her own. The two sisters studied, as children, under Nijinsky.

Marjorie became a member of the American Ballet Theatre and at 19 became a ballerina with the Grand Ballet of the Marquis de Cuevas in Monte Carlo. She was the first American dancer to become a *Danseuse Etoile* with the Theatre National de L'Opera de Paris, and the first American to dance at the Bolshio Theatre in Moscow.

Marjorie Tallchief is said to be one of the most versatile of the great ballerinas. As a guest star with the Harkness Ballet Company, she created the title part of *Ariadne* and the main part in *Amor Brujo* (1965).

She has danced leading roles in both the traditional classical and contemporary repertoires. She has danced twice at the White House for President Johnson and danced before President Kennedy and President deGaulle during the Kennedy's visit to France. She has danced also for Nikita Khrushchev, the Queen of Holland, Kind Beaudoin of Belgium, the Prince of Monaco, and Princess Margaret of England.

BIRTHPLACE: Denver, Colorado.
MARRIED: George Skibine. CHILDREN: Alexandre, George (both students of ballet).
EDUCATION: Public schools.
HONORS: Order of Nisham Iftikar, Tunisian Government, among many others.

294

JESS T. TOWN (CHOCTAW) AREA FIELD REPRESENTATIVE, BUREAU OF INDIAN AFFAIRS

When Jess Town attended Chilocco Indian school, it was a vocational institution and he was trained in shoe repair and leathercraft. In recognition of his work, he received an outstanding tradesman award. He followed this trade for a year and then was recommended for a shoe and harness-maker job at the Phoenix Indian School.

Soon after starting on this position, he was inducted into the Army. Upon his return from service, he worked as a clerk-typist and went to night school to prepare for more challenging positions.

Since 1951, Mr. Town has been with the BIA in several situations and in various parts of the country. Increasing responsibilities led him to his present assignment through which he administers the BIA program on 30 reservations in Southern California. He has taken a new approach in his relationships with tribal chairmen. He does not invite them to meetings, but waits for them to initiate and to ask him to join them in their meetings.

BIRTHPLACE: Talihina, Oklahoma.
MARRIED: Jane Olney. CHILDREN: Wynona, Ramona, Athena, Jesse, Alan, Nathan.
EDUCATION: Chilocco Indian School; Gregg Business College; Phoenix College;
MILITARY SERVICE: U.S. Army, 1952-54.
ORGANIZATIONS: American Legion.
SPECIAL ACTIVITIES: Y-Indian Guides; Boy Scouts of America; Little League Baseball.

295

YEFFE KIMBALL (OSAGE) PIONEER SPACE PAINTER *

Long a successful painter of Indian themes, Miss Kimball began fifteen years ago to pioneer in space-oriented art. Her paintings of Lunar Concepts and Outer Space progress from flat to full round. She uses a unique acrylic medium mixed with pure pigments which convey the fire and the bursting forth of time, eons ago.

Her prophetic statements and pictures relative to these yet unexplored areas drew the attention of the National Aeronautic and Space Administration who commissioned her to paint *Lunar Terminator* which toured the country under the auspices of the Smithsonian Institution.

Miss Kimball has a reputation as an innovator in the use of acrylic resins and sculpture-painting. Some of her paintings of animals represent a sophisticated development of primitive Indian paintings. In some paintings, she uses Indian art in a manner not unlike that which European artists have drawn from primitive African sculpture.

BIRTHPLACE: Mountain Park, Oklahoma.

MARRIED: Dr. Harry Slatin.

EDUCATION: Private instruction in France and Italy.

EXHIBITIONS: More than 100 major exhibitions; more than 70 one-man shows.

COLLECTIONS: More than 200 public and private collections.

AWARDS: Several firsts, among others.

HONORS: *Who's Who in American Art; American Indian Painters.*
PUBLISHED WORKS: *Book of Knowledge* (1957);
AUTHOR: *The Art of American Indian Cooking* (Doubleday, 1956).
ILLUSTRATOR: Keech (1940); Brindze (1951); Gallenkamp (1954); Leekley (1965); World Book of Knowledge (1957-58).
ADVISOR: Americana Foundation; Young America Films.
ORGANIZATIONS: Art Students League (vice-president); Arrow, Inc., (vice-president); Arts of Indian America (board).

* *See art section*

GEORGE MORRISON (CHIPPEWA) ARTIST, ASSOCIATE PROFESSOR OF ART *

George Morrison has distinguished himself by establishing one of the most outstanding records of any Indian painter.

Since 1964, he has been Assistant Professor of Art at the Rhode Island School of Design. He has been a teacher of special classes in painting, drawing and related subjects at various art schools. In September, 1970, he became associated with the newly formed Department of Indian Studies at the University of Minnesota with the title of Visiting Professor of Indian Studies and Studio Arts. He teaches a new course in Indian art history and will teach graduate students in painting.

BIRTHPLACE: Grand Marais, Minnesota, September 30, 1919.
MARRIED: Hazel Belvo. CHILDREN: Briand.
EDUCATION: Minneapolis School of Art; University of Aix-Marseille, France.
SCHOLARSHIPS: Women's Club Scholarship; Vanderlip Tranvelling Scholarship; Bernay's Scholarship; Consolidated Chippewa Tribal Scholarship; Fulbright Scholarship to France; John Hay Whitney Foundation Fellowship.
EXHIBITIONS: More than 150 group and invitational exhibitions throughout the world; more than 50 public and private collections.

AWARDS: A number of first awards and purchase awards.
ORGANIZATIONS: Audobon Artists; Federation of Modern Painters and Sculptors; Museum of Rhode Island School of Design; American Federation of Teachers; Providence Art Club.

* See art section

WALTER A. SOBOLOFF (TLINGIT) MINISTER

The Reverend Dr. Soboloff is one of Alaska's most distinguished men. He has been minister of the Memorial Presbyterian Church in Juneau for more than 20 years and has held various offices in the Church organization. Among these are moderator and state clerk for the Alaska Presbyter and moderator of the Washington Synod. He has served chaplaincy in both houses of the State Legislature.

Dr. Soboloff is a consultant for the Ford Foundation's educational program at the University of Alaska, and has been Assistant Director of Training for the VISTA II project in the southeastern part of the State. He is chairman of the State Board of Education and a lecturer on Tlingit culture at the Juneau-Douglas Community College, among his many other civic activities.

BIRTHPLACE: Juneau, Alaska, November 14, 1908.
MARRIED: Genevieve Ross. CHILDREN: Janet, Sasha, Ross, Walter, Jr.
EDUCATION: Sheldon Jackson Junior College; University of Dubuque (BA); Dubuque Theological Seminary (BD).
HONORS: Honorary LHD., University of Alaska (1968); Sheldon Jackson Jr., College Citizenship Award (1965); University of Dubuque, honorary D.D. (1952).
MILITARY SERVICE: Alaska National Guard - 19 years (Chaplain, Major).
ORGANIZATIONS: American Legion; Shrine; Lions; Alaska Native Brotherhood (past Grand President; Grand Secretary).
SPECIAL ACTIVITIES: National American Indian Workshop on School Affairs (instructor); State Education Commission.

HELEN WHITE PETER-SON (DAKOTA-OGLALA) ASSISTANT TO COMMIS-SIONER, BUREAU OF IN-DIAN AFFAIRS

As the first grandchild in an Indian family, Mrs. Peterson was the favored recipient of a treasury of tribal history and culture. Her grandmother often admonished her to "read, write and talk good so you can work among Indians." This advice was taken seriously. Her work among and for Indians brought Mrs. Peterson to the highest position held by a woman in the Bureau of Indian Affairs. She is the first woman, to be an assistant to the Commissioner.

Mrs. Peterson's first position after college was secretary to the head of the Education Department at Colorado State College. She served Nelson Rockefeller's national Office of Inter-American Affairs as director of the Rocky Mountain Council on Inter-American Affairs at the University of Denver Social Science Foundation. She then set up the Colorado Inter-American Field Service Program which later came under the Extension Division of the University of Colorado and which was concerned with the problems of Spanish-speaking groups. As part of this program, she organized some 20 Latin American Community Service Clubs which in turn created the Latin American Education Foundation in Colorado.

In 1949, Mrs. Peterson was sent as an adviser to the United States Delegation to the Second Inter-American Indian Conference in Peru. She authored a resolution on Indian education which was one of the few resolutions that the United States delegation got through at that international meeting.

In 1948, Mrs. Peterson was appointed director of the newly-created Mayor's Committee on Human Relations, and she set up that agency for the Denver city government. In 1953, she was appointed executive director of the National Congress of American Indians and held that position until 1961.

She was reappointed director of the Denver Commission on Community Relations in 1962 and has been executive director, American Indian Development since 1968.

In her various career positions, Mrs. Peterson has lectured widely; written many articles; served on boards of organizations and foundations; and worked to establish university classes in human relations. She has served as consultant to a number of cities in the area of race relations and minority group problems.

BIRTHPLACE: Pine Ridge Reservation, South Dakota, August 3, 1915.

MARRIED: Richard F. Peterson. CHILDREN: Robert.

EDUCATION: Chadron State Teachers College, (B. Bu. Ed. Cum Laude); Colorado State College; University of Denver Law School; University of Colorado (Denver).

HONORS: Outstanding Contribution in Human Relations Award, Denver Cosmopolitan Club; "Dolls for Democracy Award," Anti-Defamation League; Outstanding American Indian, American Indian Exposition, Anadarko; nominated for first annual Eleanor Roosevelt Award.

ORGANIZATIONS: NAIRO; Commission on Religion and Race, National Council of Churches; National Congress of American Indians; Opportunities Industrialization Center (board); Denver West Side Health Board (past treasurer); Intercultural School of the Rockies (board); Intercultural Advisory Committee to the Colorado State Department of Education; White Buffalo Council of American Indians; Delta Kappa Gamma.

300

JAMES L. SIMPSON (ATHAPASCAN) EDUCATIONAL ADMINISTRATOR

Resident director of Ketchikan Community College, one of Alaska's seven community colleges, James Simpson has come a long way from the orphanage which was his childhood home.

His educational career might have ended in the Indian school where he learned welding, but - World War II intervened - and he was drafted. The GI Bill helped him continue his education and, he says, "I had an insatiable desire to learn."

To complete his master's thesis and continue toward a Ph.D., James built his own home and then mortgaged it for schooling money.

In pursuing his own education, he formed the opinion that Western standards are being imposed on Alaska Natives without giving them a choice in the matter. He would like to see a sort of sliding scale of education that offers two ways of life with the free choice of which one to follow.

"Textbooks should also be redesigned taking into consideration the Native environment," Mr. Simpson says. "Textbooks have talked about things that the Native never sees or will never use. They should be taught some of the things their parents did in order to survive, and that will benefit them in their present ways of life."

At the same time, Mr. Simpson also believes that many young Natives, who may want to follow the Western mode of life, are being deprived of an opportunity to fit themselves into those standards because they are not being exposed to opportunities to do so. He is also disturbed to see hunting and fishing laws enforced on Natives who have survived off the land for centuries.

"Imposing Western standards on the older generation of Natives," he says, "disorients them from a way of life they've always known. Consequently, they lose their motivation to continue life in the way they know best."

BIRTHPLACE: Anchorage, Alaska, September 7, 1924.
MARRIED: Gloria Otness. CHILDREN: Ronald, James, Terry.
EDUCATION: Chemawa Indian School; Lewis and Clark College (B.S., M.Ed.); University of Washington (Ed.D.).
SCHOLARSHIPS: Kellogg Fellowship.
MILITARY SERVICE: U.S. Army, World War II, three years, Europe.
ORGANIZATIONS: Tongass Historical Society (first president).

ELSIE GARDNER RICKLEFS (HOOPA) TRIBAL LEADER

When she was a little girl, Mrs. Ricklefs cried to go to school. Throughout her life, schooling and education have remained important. She sees education and fuller participation in political life as major goals of Indian people.

When she graduated from high school she planned to become a doctor so that she could work among her people. She was a pre-med major in college, however, she did not become a doctor, but married one, instead.

Mrs. Ricklefs taught nursery and pre-school children for six years in several large cities. She continued to teach while her husband was completing his medical education.

As the first woman chairman of the Hoopa Tribal Council she helped her community build a hospital on the reservation when the Indian Hospital was closed down. She also helped set up the Klamath-Trinity Credit Union for her community and served as treasurer and general manager for several years.

Mrs. Ricklefs speaks her native language and frequently appears before school and other groups in native costume in a program on the culture of her people.

In 1967, with her husband, Mrs. Ricklefs travelled around the world visiting 17 countries in Europe, Africa, Mexico and Canada. From these travels she stored up information and ideas that would be helpful for her own people.

BIRTHPLACE: Korbel, California, February 2, 1920.
MARRIED: Dr. Ricklefs.
EDUCATION: Hoopa Indian Boarding School; public high school; University of California, Berkeley (AA).
ORGANIZATIONS: Humboldt-Del Norte Tuberculosis Association; National Congress of American Indians (regional vice-president).

HAL L. MULDROW (CHOCTAW) INSURANCE EXECUTIVE; MAJOR GENERAL, U.S. ARMY RETIRED

Before going into the insurance business, Mr. Muldrow was a director of athletics and athletic coach. He has had his own insurance agency since 1932.

Mr. Muldrow is the grandson of Osborn Fisher, who came over the Trail of Tears in the Indian Removal of 1832, who is recognized as having been a great Choctaw leader, representing his people as a member of the Choctaw legislature, as tribal treasurer, and spokesman in Washington.

After graduation from ROTC as a Cadet Colonel, Mr. Muldrow was commissioned as a second lieutenant in the field artillery. Seventeen year's later as a member of the 45th Division he held the rank of lieutenant colonel.

In World War II, Mr. Muldrow served overseas as a battallion commander of field artillery. Returning to the United States, he was appointed a brigadier general and then a commanding general. He next served in Korea as brigadier general in command of the 45th Division Artillery and later as major general commanding the Division. He retired from the army in 1960 after having served as commanding general of his division longer than any commanding general in the history of the division.

General Muldrow has been decorated many times for gallantry in action. On the beachhead at Salerno, under most difficult and dangerous conditions, he proved his iron courage and intrepid leadership. The Germans had laid a trap on the beach onto which the Allies poured. The battle waged for many hours, and at times the troops were closer to the enemy than to their own units. They were driven into a pocket between two rivers, at the extremity of which Muldrow's artillery stood without infantry as front cover.

As the artillery batteries were ordered to move back, Muldrow sighted enemy tanks moving toward them. He stripped his gun crews to the bare minimum needed to fire the pieces and ordered artillery fire at point blank range. The remaining men were given rifles and machine guns and ordered to execute infantry action which forced the enemy back. This was at the very heighth of the crisis when Muldrow's artillery units were the only forces facing the oncoming German tanks and highly-skilled infantry fighters. The German spearhead was not only stopped, but was driven back and enveloped by one whose entire training and experience was in artillery. Muldrow had enough military sense and courage to plan and direct a successful infantry maneuver within a few short minutes.

In the Sicilian Campaign, Major Muldrow went through enemy artillery fire with a portable transmitter to set up an observation post and relay field data back to his battallion. Orders, relayed from his forward position, assisted in large measure in forcing the enemy retreat and thus enable American forces to successfully advance.

General Muldrow also participated in the Naples-Foggia, Anzio, Rome-Arno, Southern France, Rhineland, Ardennes Alsace, and Central Europe campaigns.

BIRTHPLACE: Tishomingo, Oklahoma, May 31, 1905.
MARRIED: Clara Mae Bell.
EDUCATION: University of Oklahoma (BS).
HONORS: Distinguished Service Citation, University of Oklahoma

(1951-youngest person to be so honored); Special Service Award, Norman Chamber of Commerce; Outstanding Citizen's Award, U.S. Chamber of Commerce (1958); Merit Award, American Legion (1963); Distinguished Service Medal, Daughters of the Confederacy (1961); Beta Gamma Sigma (honorary).

MILITARY SERVICE: U.S. Army, World War II - Korea. (Silver Star Medal for gallantry in action; Bronze Star Medal for meritorious service in combat; Oak Leaf Cluster for meritorious service in direct support of combat operations; American Defense Medal; EAME Theatre Ribbon with 8 bronze Service Stars and Bronze Arrowhead; Legion of Merit, Korea; United Nations Campaign Service Medal; Army of Occupation Medal, Japan; Korean Campaign Service Medal, 3 Bronze Stars; Korean Presidential Citation.

ORGANIZATIONS: 33rd degree Mason; Shriner; Norman Chamber of Commerce (president); Rotary Club (past president); Norman Municipal Hospital (president); Oklahoma University Memorial Union (board of governors); Oklahoma University Alumni Association (past president).

NORA GUINN (ESKIMO) DISTRICT JUDGE

Mrs. Guinn, for 26 years, has been a public servant and benefactor. She is the only woman Eskimo judge in the State of Alaska, holding the highest position in the Alaska court system ever to be held by one of her people.

Judge Guinn began her public service career shortly after her marriage. In the tiny village of Tununak on the Bering Sea, she delivered babies, dispensed medicine and cared for the sick and injured.

When the family moved to Bethel, she served two terms in the Bethel City Council and was an assistant U.S. Commissioner for two years prior to Alaska statehood. She was later appointed Deputy Magistrate.

Speaking several Eskimo dialects fluently, Judge Guinn has an unique way of conducting her court. She does not wait for cases to come to her for adjudication. She frequently goes to the Eskimo villages and conducts entire court sessions in the language of her people. Her work does not end with the mere dispensing of a fine or sentence. She tries to find a way to prevent a recurrence of the problem.

Deeply interested in young people, Judge Guinn acts as a parole officer, gives counseling, speaks to school assemblies and to civic groups, and tries to improve the welfare of growing boys and girls.

Her district covers nearly 100,000 square miles and she travels frequently in small bush airplanes to dozens of remote villages. She has the respect and admiration of all with whom she comes in contact.

BIRTHPLACE: Akiak, Alaska, November 11, 1920.
MARRIED: Charles W. Guinn. CHILDREN: Susan Guinn Murphy, Charles, Jr.; John, Robert, Judy, Margaret, James, Shelby, Cindy.
ORGANIZATIONS: Veteran Woman's Auxiliary; Kuskokwim Valley Native Association (president).
SPECIAL INTERESTS: Education, health and welfare, mental health and retardation.

LEON LeCOEUR (HURON)ARTIST

Leon LeCoeur is a descendant of Chief Fleeting Cloud and of Chief Silent Cloud, and of French ancestors who were among the first settlers of Fort Detroit.

When he was seven, an accident caused the loss of speech. His parents were killed in the same accident and Leon grew up in numerous orphanages. When he learned to speak again through musical therapy, he had developed a talent for art, poetry and music. He creates through many avenues now, but painting is the preferred outlet for his talent.

Art critics have spoken of him highly. The *Chicago Tribune* said: "... not since Picasso has a more definitive style and school of art been seen." The *Chicago Daily News* referred to him as an artist "who thinks and not just paints."

BIRTHPLACE: Hazel Park, Michigan, 1924.
MARRIED: Nini Doktor.
MILITARY SERVICE: U.S. Navy, World War II, two years.
HONORS: "Artist of Year," American Education Association.

DEB J. VICTOR (CHOCTAW) SCHOOL SUPERINTENDENT

Mr. Victor has a long and distinguished record of service in educational activities. He has worked with Indian people of various communities in order to get their approval and cooperation for setting up school sites throughout the Southwest. He has worked with families on homesteads in all levels of community life. In addition, he has worked in education, with under-privileged people and their children for more than twenty years.

Among the many schools that he has opened and established is the first large elementary boarding school for the Bureau of Indian Affairs on the Navajo Reservation. He organized and was responsible for setting up the curriculum and other facets of the program for this school which accomodates 1,000 pupils.

He had this same responsibility for the Many Farms High School, the first federal high school on the Navajo Reservation. He was involved from the very beginning in the planning of the school which has an enrollment of 1,024 students. As Coordinator of the Navajo Community College and the Navajo Tribe, he has arranged for them to have the use of the high school facilities. He has also been the Coordinator and cooperative liaison person for the Area Education Division for the Rough Rock Demonstration School since its inception. This school was created with the cooperation of Arizona State University. In 1944, he partici-

309

pated in the Navajo Education Emergency Program - a program in which trailer schools were set up in strategic locations on the reservation. These provided schooling sites for children who would otherwise have had none.

Mr. Victor has also had experience as superintendent of bordertown dormitories and initiating public relations to assist school officials carry out educational programs for the bordertown students whose educational needs range from third grade through high school. He has supervised adult education programs for many years and was one of the first to conceive the idea of college level training for Navajo Instructional Aides.

He has encouraged his teachers and supervisors to introduce English as a Second Language teaching program. He established such a project for the entire school system at Chinle, Arizona. The success in this district brought about the acceptance of the ESL Program in all Navajo Area Schools.

Although his primary work has been in education, Mr. Victor has assisted Indian families from all stations of life in each community where he has been active.

BIRTHPLACE: Garvin, Oklahoma, May 2, 1911.

MARRIED: Lucy Watson. CHILDREN: Deb, Jr.

EDUCATION: Oklahoma State University (B.S., M.S.); Northern Arizona University; Arizona State University.

HONORS: Blue Key; Alpha Zeta; Dean's Distinguished List of Students; Kappa Delta Pi; "Big Man on the Campus," Oklahoma State University (1939) Phi Delta Kappa; "Citizen of the Year," Farmington-Shiprock, New Mexico; Order of the Red, Red Rose, Oklahoma School Men's Association; Order of the Arrow, Boy Scouts; Silver Beaver Award, Boy Scouts (1970); Certificate of Recognition, New Mexico College of Agriculture; *Who's Who in American Education; Community Leaders of America.*

MILITARY SERVICE: Oklahoma National Guards, 1927-36. (War Service Certificate received for being retained in civilian Government service for the duration of World War II to perform duties essential to the successful prosecution of the global conflict).

ORGANIZATIONS: National Education Association; Arizona School Administration Association; San Juan County Cooperative Project of Educational Administrators (past president); American Management Association; American Association of School Administrators; United States Civil Service Examiners (board); Lions (past president; board); 32nd degree Scottish Rite Mason.

SPECIAL ACTIVITIES: Navajo Area Curriculum Balance Committee; Navajo Area Committee for TESL; Red Cross (chairman); March of Dimes (chairman); Boy Scouting for the past 29 years in various positions; troops organized in all Navajo reservation schools; Girl Scouts, past 21 years; State Chief, Indian Clubs of Oklahoma Colleges; Director of Training Union and several committees, Baptist Mission, Shiprock, New Mexico.

SIDNEY M. CARNEY (CHOCTAW-CREEK) GOVERNMENT ADMINISTRATOR

When the Senecas lost out in their battle against the construction of Kinzua Dam, in which more than 9,000 acres of Seneca lands were taken for the construction work, Sidney Carney was assigned by the Bureau of Indian Affairs to work with the Tribe in the resolving of the resultant problems.

For the Senecas, he explored the possibility of acquiring new lands to be exchanged for those flooded, and reviewed ways in which the Indians could share in the benefits of a recreational potential brought about by the dam reservoir. He also investigated and determined special damages sustained by the Senecas with the take-over of their lands.

Carney, who is now Area Director at Anadarko for the Bureau of Indian Affairs, was specially cited for his work with the Senecas with a superior service award from the Department of the Interior for "the highest qualities of public service."

ARLEIGH HILL (SENECA) MUSEUM ASSOCIATE

When he was a schoolboy, Mr. Hill read in a history book that Indians were "barbarous, savage, and heathen." This made an indelible impression on him and he decided to study and investigate his heritage.

This incident was followed by another almost as traumatic. A Sunday School superintendent, in speaking to an almost entirely Indian congregation, referred to the Iroquois Indians as "pagans and heathens."

"Since then," Mr. Hill says, "I have studied the history of my people and have found that the so-called heathens had a belief in a Creator -a Supreme Being - and that they gave thanks for everything to this Creator."

Mr. Hill, who is Associate in Indian Arts and Crafts for the Rochester Museum and Science Center, has made it a lifetime pursuit to eradicate erroneous concepts about Indians through intelligent communication and personal example.

Arleigh Hill's grandfather migrated to Canada with Joseph Brant, the Mohawk leader in the American Revolution, on the English side. His father was secretary of the Hereditary Chief Council, Indian ambassador and interpreter.

As a young man, Arleigh was an industrial worker and a professional lacrosse player. He holds a number of lacrosse trophies.

312

BIRTHPLACE: Grand River Reservation, Ontario, Canada, June 5, 1909.

MARRIED: Henrietta Arazy. CHILDREN: Maxwell, Joyce.

EDUCATION: Public schools; museum courses.

HONORS: Citation, Police Athletic League of Rochester (1959); Civil Defense Citation (1945); Citation of Merit, Rochester Museum of Arts and Sciences (1959); Honorary name, Seneca Indians, Turtle Clan (1951).

ORGANIZATIONS: Neighborhood Indian Society (past president); Stadium Club of Rochester.

SPECIAL ACTIVITIES: Consultant on Indian programs for radio and television; research and writing on Indians.

ALLEN QUETONE (KIOWA) INTERGOVERNMENTAL RELATIONS OFFICER, BUREAU OF INDIAN AFFAIRS

Mr. Quetone has the responsibility for maintaining liaison with other federal and state agencies concerned with Indian Affairs. He was formerly superintendent for the Horton Indian Agency. He holds a B.B.S. degree from Oklahoma City University and he is newly appointed to his present position.

FRANCIS QUAM (ZUNI) PHARMACIST

Francis Quam was the first Indian to graduate from the University of Cincinnati in the 110-year history of that institution.

He is the first Zuni pharmacist and probably the first Indian to enter this profession.

He has been stationed as staff pharmacist on the Pine Ridge Reservation, and as Chief Pharmacist on the Turtle Mountain Reservation. He is presently Deputy Chief, Alaska Native Hospital Anchorage.

BIRTHPLACE: Zuni, New Mexico, November 14, 1939.
MARRIED: Cecelia M. Wilkie. CHILDREN: Cindy, Lori Ann.
EDUCATION: University of Cincinnati (B.S.).
ORGANIZATIONS: American Pharmacists Association; Knights of Columbus; Commissioned Officers Association PHS.

OSCAR HOWE (DAKOTA-YANKTON) ARTIST AND PROFESSOR OF ART *

A whole volume could be written about Oscar Howe who casts a tall shadow in his profession. He is the artist laureate of South Dakota and artist-in-residence and Professor Of Fine Arts at the University of South Dakota.

Howe is a descendant of Yankton chiefs, one of whom was noted for his gift of oratory. Another Chief distinguished himself at the time of the Santee Uprising and received a plaque from the government in appreciation of his services.

As a boy, Oscar was poor, ill and totally frustrated. While in school, he developed a disfiguring skin disease so severe that he suffered social isolation. Even his own brothers avoided him. In addition he contracted trachoma, a painful eye condition that nearly blinded him. This most unhappy boy tried to end his life and was sent home as "hopeless."

After months of intense care, Oscar was able to rid himself of the skin disease. His eyes, too, were healed, but the deep psychological wounds were much more difficult to eradicate.

Returning to school, he was encouraged to take up art and this was the torch that would make up for all that he had suffered within himself-and at the hands of others. His works met with instant success and before he graduated his paintings had been exhibited across this nation and in London and Paris as well. Many individual pieces found their way into private collections and were reproduced in various magazines.

When he returned to his reservation home, the young artist once again became despondent. There was little sympathy or interest in his work from his own peers. In desperation he accepted a position as art instructor at Pierre Indian School. The school job gave him the opportunity to leave his reservation home, even though it returned him to the scene of his first unhappiness.

In 1940, he was assigned to the South Dakota Artists Project. One of his assignments was to paint the dome of the Carnegie Library at Mitchell. He was also given the task of painting for a new auditorium ten large murals in oil depicting the history of the Missouri River Basin.

As a corporal in Germany, in World War II, Oscar Howe met the girl who became his wife. Her trip to America was financed by his first national award. An assignment to illustrate a two volume book on Indian costumes paid for the birth of their daughter.

Continuing his studies at college, Oscar had won a Distinguished Award before he received his undergraduate degree. As an artist he is indefatigable and spends every minute of his free time in creative work. Each year, he designs the decoration of the panels for the Corn Palace in Mitchell, depicting life-size scenes carried out in corn in its natural colors. His paintings would be at home in any contemporary show, even though they are distinctively and uncorruptedly Sioux in every motif and symbol.

BIRTHPLACE: Joe Creek, South Dakota, May 13, 1915.
MARRIED: Adelheid Hampel. CHILDREN: Inge Dawn.
EDUCATION: Dakota Wesleyan University (B.A.), University of Oklahoma (M.F.A.); Honorary Doctor of Humanities Degree, South Dakota State University (1968).
HONORS: Honored guest, Ralph Edwards *This is Your Life* TV program (1969); Fellow, International Institute of Arts and Letters (1960); Certificate of Appreciation, Indian Arts and Crafts Board (1962); Award of Recognition, Foundation of North American

Indian Culture; represented State of South Dakota in exhibit "Fifty Artists from Fifty States" circulated by American Federation of Arts (1966-1968) Waite Philips Outstanding Indian Artist Trophy (1966); *Who's Who in South Dakota; Who's Who in American Art; Indian Painters.*

EXHIBITIONS: More than 100 here and in U.S. Embassies in Europe; 25 one-man shows; numerous private and public collections.

AWARDS: Five grand awards; five first awards, among many others.

ILLUSTRATOR: *Legends of the Mighty Sioux* (Albert Whitman, 1941); *The Little Lost Sioux* (Albert Whitman Co., 1942); *Bringer of the Mystery Dog* (Haskell Institute, 1943); *North American Indian Costumes* (published in France, 1952).

WORKS PUBLISHED: *Design* (cover, March, 1941); *School Arts Magazine* (November, 1936; October, 1938); *Indians at Work; Art Education Today* (1937); *Time Magazine* (July 1947); *Oklahoma Today* (1958); *Indian Art of the United States* (1941); *A Pictorial History of the American Indian* (1956); (The artist has been featured in 29 publications).

✱ *See art section*

JOE S. SANDO (PUEBLO-JEMEZ) EDUCATOR

When Joe entered school, his English was limited. This was a severe handicap and prevented his mixing with his classmates. Because he was small and young, he was unable to make football or basketball teams until his senior year. He vowed that he would go to college and play for he was "football-minded."

Without guidance, he enrolled as a freshman and worked in a cabinet shop repairing furniture to help with his expenses. He did get to play football, but left school at the end of the first semester to enlist in the Navy. He worked up from Seaman to Petty Officer Second Class. His ship took part in the invasion of the Gilbert and Marianna Islands.

He re-entered college with a place on the football team still a prime ambition. He succeeded and became second-string varsity quarterback. His first job after college was with a prep school in Arizona. After eight years of working as a counselor in government schools, he entered graduate school. He majored in audiology and minored in speech pathology. During his employment as an audiologist in an Albuquerque clinic, he examined many future astronauts and test pilots.

In 1959, Joe was instrumental in starting an All-Indian Track meet at Jemez Pueblo. This meet has been held annually on Father's Day and has been a tremendous success. Many of the participants have been offered track scholarships at various Universities.

318

In 1969, Mr. Sando was selected, with nine other Indians, to visit New Zealand and observe and evaluate the Maoris of that country. The Maoris are the only ethnic group in the world who resemble American Indians in features, beliefs, attitudes and problems.

Currently chairman of the New Mexico Judicial Council which serves the State of New Mexico to improve the court and legal systems, he is also chairman of the All Indian Pueblo Housing Authority. Composed of 16 Pueblos, this is a more than two-million dollar project administered by Pueblo Indians for building modern homes. He is also chairman of the Educational Committee, All Indian Pueblo Council, which is involved in identifying Pueblo students as candidates for higher education.

In addition to his many other activities, he is doing research through which he hopes to prove that some of the Indian stories, or legends concerning Pueblo history are true. Also, he is working as biographer of outstanding Pueblo Indians under a Ford Foundation grant.

BIRTHPLACE: Jemez Pueblo, New Mexico, August 1, 1923.
MARRIED: Louisa Parker. CHILDREN: Deryn, Parker, Matthew.
EDUCATION: Santa Fe Indian School; Eastern New Mexico University (B.A.); Vanderbilt University (M.S.).
SCHOLARSHIPS: U.S. Children's Bureau.
MILITARY SERVICE: U.S. Navy, 1943-46.
ORGANIZATIONS: American Indian Historical Society; New Mexico Council of American Indians; National Congress of American Indians; Americans for Indian Opportunity (board); Northern New Mexico Economic Development District (board).

WILLIAM WAYNE KEELER (CHEROKEE) EXECUTIVE: PRINCIPAL CHIEF, CHEROKEE NATION

W. W. Keeler is often called the strongest leader of his tribe since John Ross unified the Cherokees after their removal from the east to Indian territory.

For many years, Keeler, who is of Cherokee extraction, has been active in welfare and educational work among restricted Indians. Keeler was appointed Principal Chief of the Cherokees in 1949 - a position he still holds. Serving as Principal Chief of the Cherokees under seven administrations, Mr. Keeler has accomplished many important things for his people. For one, he was instrumental in shaping legislation which resulted in the Cherokee Tribe gaining an award of $14,789,000 from the government for land sold by the Indians to the government 70 years ago.

He established, and is a trustee of the Cherokee Foundation, an organization to promote the welfare and culture of the tribe and to raise social and economic standards. He has also been active in the promotion of the Sequoyah Weavers, a group of Cherokee artisans whose looms produce some of the finest woolens in the world. He has brought industries for the employment of Indians to his area, and has initiated a number of other projects of economic benefits.

He has served on the Commission on the Rights, Liberties, and Responsibilities of the American Indian, which is sponsored by the Fund for the Republic, and is a member of the board of directors for the Center for Arts of Indian America. He received the 1957 All - American Indian award, presented annually to the outstanding American Indian, and was again similarly honored in 1961 at the American Indian Exposition. In February 1961, Keeler was named by the Secretary of the Interior to head a group to develop plans for reorganizing the Bureau of Indian Affairs.

In June 1962, Keeler was appointed by the Secretary of the Interior Udall as chairman of a three-man task force to study operations of the Bureau of Indian Affairs in Alaska, and to meet with native groups and discuss native land rights, problems of native fisheries, educational need of natives, and other related topics. He was chairman of the United States delegation to the Inter-American Indian Conference at Quito, Ecuador, in October 1964.

W.W. Keeler was elected chairman and chief executive officer of Phillips Petroleum Company on September 9, 1968, after serving as president and chief executive officer since July 10, 1967. He began his oil industry experience in 1924 at the age of 16 with summer vacation work in the company's engineering department. During succeeding summers he worked in the Burbank oil field of Oklahoma for the natural gasoline department and in the research department laboratories at Bartlesville, Oklahoma.

He was employed until 1941 at Phillips refineries at Kansas City, Kansas, and Odessa and Borger, Texas, as a chemist, process engineer, night superintendent, and chief process engineer. He was then promoted to technical assistant to the vice-president of the refining department, and in 1945 was made manager of the refining department. He became vice-president of the refining department in 1947. Four years later he was elected vice president, executive department, and to the board of directors of the company, and in 1954 was elected a member of the executive committee. He was named executive vice-president in 1956, and was elected chairman of the executive committee on April 14, 1962.

In August 1960, he headed the first U.S. Petroleum Industry Exchange Delegation on a 30-day tour of Russia and its oil industry. He has served as a member of the Military-Industrial Conference Committee.

In 1965 President Johnson appointed Keeler a member of the National Advisory Committee on the War on Poverty Program. In 1967 Keeler was appointed to the President's Committee on Economic Opportunity, and in 1968 Governor Hickel of Alaska appointed him chairman of a task force to find ways to improve the utilization of native labor within the state. He also is a member of the National Public Advisory Committee on Regional Economic Development, the Governor's Committee for Eastern Oklahoma Economic Development, and the board of directors of the Oklahoma Academy for State Goals.

BIRTHPLACE: Dalhart, Texas, April 5, 1908.

MARRIED: Ruby Hamilton. CHILDREN: William, Bradford, Richard.

EDUCATION: University of Kansas. (Registered professional engineer, Oklahoma).

HONORS: Sigma Tau (honorary engineering); honorary LL.D., College of the Ozarks (1961); honorary D. Eng., Colorado School of Mines (1961); Distinguished Alumni Service Citation, University of Kansas (1961) Indian Council Fire Achievement Award and honorary life membership (1963); Oklahoma Hall of Fame (1966); Golden Plate Award, American Academy of Achievement, as a "giant of accomplishment" (1969); Distinguished Service Citation, University of Oklahoma (1969); Legion of Honor, Order of DeMolay (1957); Outstanding Indian of Year, All American Indian Days (1957); Silver Beaver Award, Boy Scouts of America; Outstanding Indian Award, American Indian Exposition (1961); Outstanding Citizen Award, Oklahoma-Kansas Civitan International; "Significant Sig" Award, Sigma Chi).

ORGANIZATIONS: National Petroleum Council (several committees); National Petroleum Refiner's Association (trustee); American Petroleum Institute (executive committee); Independent Petroleum Association of America (director); Mid-Continent Oil and Gas Association; International Petroleum Exposition (director); Alumni Association, University of Kansas (past president); York Rite and 33rd degree Mason; Shriner; Royal Jester.

SPECIAL ACTIVITIES: First National Bank of Bartlesville (director); Agricultural Hall of Fame and National Center; Oklahoma state-wide committee, Living Legend Library; Gilcrease Museum (trustee) Institute of International Education (advisor, Southwest Regional Office); Bartlesville Chamber of Commerce (director); Boy Scouts of America National Council, and Cherokee Area Council (vice-president and director); Boy's Club, Bartlesville YMCA (vice-president); United Community Fund of Bartlesville (director).

FRELL M. OWL (CHERO-KEE) GOVERNMENT AD-MINISTRATOR, RE-TIRED

Frell Owl has devoted most of his life to building bridges of understanding between the Indian and white worlds. In recognition of this, he was awarded an honorary Doctor of Humane Letters degree from Dartmouth University at the 199th commencement exercises. The citation reads: "In this 200th year of the College, your life validates a reawakened Dartmouth purpose ... orphaned in boyhood and one of six children out of seven who went on to college on their own, you dedicated the privilege of your Dartmouth education to the service of those culturally bewildered American citizens who, as you put it, 'wear a shoe on one foot and a moccasin on the other.' For a third of a century, first as a teacher, and then as a leading administrator of Indian affairs, you worked to bridge the chasm between the Indian and the white man's world on which he had been required to depend as a stranger in his own land. Through it all-group frustration, personal perplexity, national dilemma--you never swerved from the goal of integration through the power of education. May this award of your College's honorary Doctorate of Humane Letters be a harbomger pf a tjord Dartmouth century committed in nothing less than the fulfillment of this goal everywhere."

After graduating from Dartmouth, Frell Owl joined the Bureau of Indian Affairs, first as teacher than as administrator. When he retired after 33 years, he was superintendent of the

Fort Hall Agency. He had been superintendent of several other reservations.

Now living on his home reservation, Mr. Owl is chairman of the Cherokee Planning Board, dedicated to the development of the reservation. He also owns and operates the Piney Grove Campground for tourists.

BIRTHPLACE: Cherokee, North Carolina, March 1, 1899.

MARRIED: Gladys D. Berry. CHILDREN: Mary Owl Melquist, Frela Owl Beck.

EDUCATION: Reservation school; Hampton Institute; Phillips Andover Academy; Dartmouth College (B.S.).

HONORS: Certificate of Superior Performance, Bureau of Indian Affairs (1960); Certificate of Meritorious Service, Department of Interior (1961); *Who's Who in the Midwest;*authorized by principal chief, Eastern Band of Cherokees, to present headdresses to Ambassadors from Japan, Denmark, Vietnam (1967, 1970).

ORGANIZATIONS: Rotary Cherokee Lions Club (charter member, past president); Cherokee Historical Association, Inc. (trustee); Cherokee Chamber of Commerce (past vice-president, board).

SPECIAL ACTIVITIES: North Carolina Education Advisory Committee to Appalachian Regional Commission; Cherokee Constitution Committee (past chairman); Neighborhood Facilities Committee; *Cherokee One Feather,* tribal newspaper; Cherokee Commission on Law and Order; Community Relations Committee, organized by National Park Service.

W. DAVID OWL (CHERO-KEE) MISSIONARY

Reverend Owl, now retired, has been a missionary to the Seneca Indians on the Cattaraugus Reservation for 45 years. Prior to this, he was a missionary for the American Friends Service Committee among the Osages and religious and physical education director at Haskell Institute. His religious work began among the Pimas. Once he determined to enter the ministry, he never wavered from this decision, although his education was obtained with considerable sacrifice and a heavy burden of responsibility.

In his pastoral work, David has steadfastly urged his Indian parishoners to share in the advantages, skills and responsibilities of their white neighbors.

"It is in our youth that the hope for the future development of our people rests," Mr. Owl says. "It is unfair to pass on, or to burden them, with the hurts and heartaches, the prejudices which have hampered older people and kept them from becoming full citizens of the land.

"All Indians must experience something of the grandeur, potential and satisfaction of living in the clear atmosphere of a true democracy. It is to this end that Indians must set their goals. This is not only our task but our great privilege."

326

BIRTHPLACE: Cherokee, North Carolina, July 11, 1893.

MARRIED: Janie Crow. CHILDREN: Betty Owl Nephew, David Jr.

EDUCATION: Reservation School; Hampton Institute; Springfield College (B.Hu.); Rochester Divinity School (B.D.).

SCHOLARSHIPS: Baptist Missions Scholarship.

HONORS: Indian Council Fire Achievement Award and honorary life membership (1942); Peter Doctor Memorial Award for Distinguished Service (1955).

MILITARY SERVICE: U.S. Army Field Artillery, World War I, one year (first sergeant) Kansas National Guard (first lieutenant).

ORGANIZATIONS: Kiwanis; Iroquois Temperance League (chaplain).

SPECIAL INTERESTS: Reading and writing Cherokee.

RONALD G. CARRAHER (COLVILLE) ARTIST

Presently art instructor at San Jose State College, Ronald Carraher has had a varied art career. He has been an assistant in the University of Washington art gallery; and an assistant professor of design, Rhode Island School of Design. He has studied photography and has produced educational films. He has been an art editor and an illustrator.

BIRTHPLACE: Colville Indian Reservation, Omak, Washington.

EDUCATION: University of Washington (B.A.); San Jose State College (M.A.).

SCHOLARSHIPS: University of Washington.

HONORS: *American Indian Painters.*

MILITARY SERVICE: U.S. Army, World War II.

EXHIBITIONS: More than 15 major exhibits, including Palace of the Legion of Honor, Winter Invitational, San Francisco; Pacific Arts Association Invitational; exchange exhibit with Japan.

AWARDS: More than six, including two purchase awards and a Grand Award.

THOMAS SEGUNDO (PA-PAGO) TRIBAL COUNCIL CHAIRMAN

Tom Segundo planned on becoming an engineer. He was working toward that end as a supervisor for a ship-building company when he returned to his reservation for a vacation.

At home he found an appalling situation. The land was gripped by drought, cattle were dying, and thousands of horses had been killed to conserve precious forage and water. The people were in an equally bad way.

Borrowing a truck, Tom began to haul hay onto the reservation. He bought it as cheaply as he could and sold it for barely enough to cover expenses. He drove day and night and blew out one to three tires every day.

Then he took note of other pressing problems. Scores of boys just out of the army were at loose ends. There was little work. Tom organized athletic activities, borrowing from the tribal loan fund. He developed a football team which went through its first season undefeated. Enough money was earned to pay back the loan and to buy some equipment - and delinquency among the young people began to fall off markedly.

The tribe began to realize that they had a natural leader. They elected him chairman of the tribal council - the youngest Indian in the country to hold such a position. He was also the youngest man ever to be chosen as a leader by his tribe.

Once in office, Segundo set about to strengthen district councils, and to streamline and codify the Papago law. He imposed a tax upon traders and drew up the Papago Development Plan which called for many constructive changes.

Tom served as tribal chairman for seven terms. Then he enrolled for university studies in law and social science so that he might work for his people with even greater adequacy. This was far from easy, for he had a large family to support and had to earn a living as he went along.

Now Tom is back with the Papagos again, serving once more as tribal chairman. He is one in whom the instinct for dynamic, functioning democracy burns fiercely. He has set upon a long-range program which will take years to complete - but which is going forward, step by step toward final emancipation.

BIRTHPLACE: Sells, Arizona.
MARRIED: Flora Hendricks. CHILDREN: Florine, Maxine, LaNova, Muriel, Charmaine, Thomas Jr.
EDUCATION: Reservation Schools, University of Chicago.
HONORS: Indian Council Fire Achievement Award and honorary life membership (1952).

AHAB SPENCE (CREE) HEAD, CULTURAL DEVELOPMENT DIVISION, DEPARTMENT OF INDIAN AFFAIRS, GOVERNMENT OF CANADA

Dr. Spence is the son of a nomad trapper who neither spoke nor understood English, but who realized the value of education. He encouraged his son to learn a new way of life in a new environment. Dr. Spence has the distinction of being the first Canadian Indian ever to receive an honorary Doctor of Laws degree from a Canadian University.

Dr. Spence's education began at an Indian residential school 300 miles from his home. Later, he went to live in a minister's home and attended a non-Indian school. He became interested in the missionary field and set his goals in that direction.

For twenty-five years he served as a missionary and teacher in Indian communities of northern Saskatchewan. In that period, he rose from this position to that of Archdeacon and member of the general synod of the Anglican Church of Canada. He continued to study, taking five university courses by correspondence.

In later years, he held the position of Provincial Chairman of Indian Education for the Saskatchewan Home and School and Parent-Teachers Federation. He was also National Chairman of its Committee on Indian-Eskimo Education. In 1963, he became principal of the Pelican Indian Residential School and two years later was Liaison Officer for the Saskatchewan Region of the Indian Affairs Branch. He was appointed to his present position in 1968.

When he was principal at Pelican Lake, he commented: "I have automatically relinquished the title of 'Archdeacon' and once more become a human being."

Dr. Spence firmly believes in the importance of encouraging Indian people to achieve a high degree of education. He sees education as the key factor in improving the lot of his people, and uses every opportunity to emphasize this point. He recognizes that it is difficult to motivate Indians to accept the white man's education. As long as they followed their traditional occupations of fishing, hunting and trapping, education wasn't needed.

But now," he stresses, "Indians must adjust to the new day and the first step is to seize every educational opportunity that is open."

BIRTHPLACE: Split Lake, Manitoba, Canada, July 1, 1911.
MARRIED: Elizabeth Bear. CHILDREN: Janet Spence Fontaine, Byron William, June, Bruce, Barry.
EDUCATION: Emmanuel College (Lic. Theo.) University of Saskatchewan (B.A.).
HONORS: Honorary LL.D., University of Saskatchewan (1964).
MILITARY SERVICE: Supplementary Chaplain, RCAF.

GILBERT S. MONTURE (MOHAWK) INTERNATIONALLY KNOWN MINERAL ECONOMIST

Seldom has one individual led so noteworthy a life and been in so many far-away places as Gilbert Monture. He is a leading authority on the world's available minerals.

Dr. Monture is a direct descendant of Chief Joseph Brant who helped Great Britain maintain her hold on North America until defeated by the colonists.

Getting an education for Dr. Monture was not easy, even though he was a superior scholar. Dr. Monture taught school on his home reserve until he could enter college. His father was a sailor-turned "hard luck farmer" and the Monture family had many struggles to survive. Gilbert walked five miles each way to attend high school and his college studies were interrupted by military service.

After the war, Monture first worked as a journalist, and then became an editor for the Mines Branch of the Canadian Department of Mines and Resources. In this capacity, he read every report that was put out on mining and metal industries.

An old injury made it impossible for him to return to active military duty in World War II, but he was of tremendous importance in another kind of service. Loaned to the Department of Munitions and Supply as chief executive assistant to the metals controller he showed that he could assess Canadian resources with uncanny ability. He subsequently became Canadian Executive Officer of the Combined

Production and Resources Board in Washington. His services were of such value that he was made an officer in the Order of the British Empire. Later, he was appointed Chief of the Mineral Resources Division, responsible for everything affecting the development of Canadian mineral resources.

In postwar years, Dr. Monture revealed an additional talent for diplomacy at the technical level. He worked for Canada, the Commonwealth, NATO, and the United Nations on some 20 committees and economic missions over the world. He served with a team of NATO experts who worked out a plan for the allocation of strategic materials within the Free World. He helped survey world resources of iron ore for the United Nations; gave technical mining advice to the governments of Malaya and Indonesia; helped Jamaica and Afghanistan revise their basic mining legislation; and went to Bolivia as a consultant to the United Nations Technical Assistance Group.

Dr. Monture's outstanding service to Canada, both in war and peace, and to the world at large, has brought him many honors. He is now associated with a Canadian minerals development firm.

BIRTHPLACE: Six Nations Reserve, Ontario, Canada
MARRIED: Elva Penwarden. CHILDREN: Barbara Monture Malloch.
EDUCATION: Reservation and public schools; Queen's University (B.S.).
HONORS: Honorary Doctor of Science degree, University of Western Ontario; Indian Council Fire Achievement Award and honorary life membership (1957) among many others.
MILITARY SERVICE: Canadian Army, World War I (Lieutenant); Commissioned officer, Royal Canadian Engineers.
ORGANIZATIONS: Canadian Institute of Mining and Metallurgy; American Institute of Mining and Metallurgy; Indian-Eskimo Association (honorary president).

EDWARD McGAA (DAKOTA-OGLALA) ATTORNEY

Edward McGaa is a descendant of two warriors who were known for their bravery in the Custer Battle. Ed, himself, is a courageous warrior. Serving with the Marines in Vietnam, he flew 110 combat missions and was awarded eight air medals among other recognitions.

He has also been honored by the Oglala Sioux for participating twice in the Sun Dance ceremony. This is an ancient rite of thanks to the Great Spirit. It tests the valor of the dancers who are fastened to the Sun Dance pole by ropes skewered through the loose skin of the breast. They dance for four days or until the ropes break through.

At first considering a military career, Ed decided to enter law school on his return from Vietnam, thinking that this would be the best way he could serve his people. He believes that he will have a harder fight than any he experienced in service to overcome reservation poverty and to encourage his people to acquire higher education. After his graduation from law school he was appointed Legal Specialist, National Indian Leadership Training Program, sponsored by Navajo Community College.

BIRTHPLACE: Pine Ridge Reservation, April 16, 1936.
MARRIED: Kathryn Doblar.
EDUCATION: St. John's University (B.S.); University of South Dakota Law School (Juris Prudence).

334

SCHOLARSHIPS: Donner Scholarship; Joel McCrea Indian Scholarship. (Both were specially created and he was the first to receive these).

MILITARY SERVICE: U.S. Marine Corps, 1953-55, Korea; 1960-67, Vietnam. Eight Air Medals, Vietnam Cross of Gallantry, Presidential Unit Citation. (Major, USMC Reserves).

SPECIAL INTERESTS: Presenting the truth of Indian culture as learned from the old people; speaking for Indian rights; teaching Indian costume and dance at the University of South Dakota.

ARTHUR D. AMIOTTE (DAKOTA-OGLALA) ARTIST

Arthur Amiotte descends from the Minniconjou chief, Standing Bear, who toured Europe with Buffalo Bill's Wild West Show, and from Antoine Janis, one of the first fur traders in the Upper Missouri area.

Arthur, who has developed a painting style bordering on cubism, was started on his art career by Oscar Howe (see biography). He is presently an art instructor in a Sioux City, Iowa high school and lectures on Dakota history, legends, lore and religious beliefs.

BIRTHPLACE: Pine Ridge, South Dakota, March 25, 1942.

MARRIED: Amelia Wohlers.

EDUCATION: Northern State College (B.S.).

SCHOLARSHIPS: State Indian Scholarship; Bureau of Indian Affairs; Schwarz Art Education.

HONORS: National Honor English Fraternity; National Honor Education Society; International Men's Professional Educators Fraternity; *Who's Who in American Universities and Colleges; American Indian Painters.*

EXHIBITS: More than ten major exhibits; more than four one-man shows; more than ten public and private collections.

AWARDS: More than five awards.

GEORGE M. COCHRAN (CHEROKEE) ARTIST

Without formal training of any kind, George Cochran has developed as a portrait artist of considerable skill. His work has appeared in leading newspapers and magazines, and he has done portraits of many famous persons.

At a government school, he learned to be a barber. This, he says, was because he and his father stopped on their way to the school to get haircuts. The school superintendent delegated George the task of cutting the hair of the other boys to look like his own.

Cochran ran away from most of the schools he attended. He tramped around the country and worked at odd jobs, knowing all the time that he wanted only to draw. Finally he settled down and opened up his own barber shop. He was successful, even though it was during the depression and he had a growing family to support.

Finding himself in Oregon after service in World War II, he decided to settle there. But as an Indian, he could not secure a license and so he became a farm laborer, working at any kind of "picking" he could get. One day, he drew some sketches of a lumber mill. The owner liked them so well that he purchased them. This started George on a drawing spree that lasted several years. He traveled about the country in an old Ford, peddling his pictures for what he could get. He sold his work for a dollar, for gas, for something to eat.

Later, he again tried for his barber's license. Friends helped him set up his own shop and he was instrumental in changing the law with respect to licenses for the benefit of Oregon Indians. In the time that the could take away from business, he drew a collection of Northwest Indian portraits and was commissioned by the Warm Springs Tribal Council to do 45 drawings and paintings. His oils hang in a number of government buildings.

Mr. Cochran has three famous ancestors. He is a descendant of Sequoyah, who invented the Cherokee alphabet; of General Stand Watie, Commander of Cherokee troops in the Confederate Army during the Civil War; and Houston B. Teehee, who was registrar of the United States Treasury.

BIRTHPLACE: Stilwell, Oklahoma.
MARRIED: Nell Hooks. CHILDREN: Joan Cochran Dow; Betty Cochran Lancaster; William, Thomas, Charles, Sue Nell, James.
EDUCATION: Haskell Institute; Chilocco Indian School.
MILITARY SERVICE: World War II-GI barber.
HONORS: *Who's Who in American Art; Who's Who in the West; International Directory of Arts.*
EXHIBITIONS: Many one-man shows.
AWARDS: Grand Award and many prizes.
ORGANIZATIONS: Cherokee Foundation, Inc., Indian Festival of Arts (board); Kiwanis; National Congress of American Indians; Oregon Archaeological Society (honorary life member).

JOAN HILL (CREEK-CHEROKEE) ARTIST *

Joan Hill is an artist of considerable stature. She is said to have won more awards than any other Indian woman in her field. She works in all painting and drawing media, ranging in many styles from representational realism, portraiture and traditional Indian painting through abstract expressionism, winning awards in each of these styles.

On her father's side, Joan is descended from chiefs, interpreters and scouts for the government. Her grandfather was chief of the Creeks, a member of the House of Kings and the House of Warriors. He was also prosecuting attorney, postmaster, president of the Creek Board of Education, U.S. Deputy Marshall and captain of the Lighthorse Indian Police.

On the Cherokee side, there were also chiefs and leaders. In the Civil War, the two family lines fought on opposing sides.

Miss Hill, who was an art instructor in the Tulsa schools, decided to become a full-time artist in 1966. In the few short years since then, she has gained national recognition and received great acclaim for her excellent work.

BIRTHPLACE: Muskogee, Oklahoma
EDUCATION: Northeastern State College (B.A. (Ed). Private study with internationally known artists. Art Travel Study in eleven countries.

* *See art section*

338

HONORS: *Outstanding Young Women of America* (1965); *Leadership Index, A Who's Who in Oklahoma* (1964); *American Indian Painters* (1968); *American Indian Paintings of the Southwest and Plains Areas* (1968); *Phi Theta Kappa* (honorary scholastic).

EXHIBITIONS: More than two hundred here and in American embassies abroad; 16 one-man shows;

COLLECTIONS: 50 private and 300 public collections.

AWARDS: 82 awards, of which 59 are from national competitions. These include two grand awards.

PUBLISHED WORKS: Frontispiece painting, *Sam Houston with the Cherokees;* cover drawing, *A History of the Baird Scales Family; Southwest Review* (cover); *Poetry of Alexander Lawrence Posey* (frontispiece portrait and illustrations); *Life International,* November, 1969.

ORGANIZATIONS: Muskogee Art Guild (art director); National League of American Pen Women.

SPECIAL ACTIVITIES: Art and book collections; music; photography.

DONALD D. ROSS (DA-KOTA-BRULE) EDUCA-TIONAL ADMINISTRA-TOR

Donald Ross is director of Indian Studies at Huron College, For the past several years he has been director of the Indian Projects of the Teacher Corps for the University of Nebraska.

His career in education began as an English teacher at the Oglala Community School on the Pine Ridge Reservation.

Mr. Ross interrupted his college career to join the Navy for the Korean Conflict. He was stationed on Guam, and served on two destroyers and a destroyer tender.

With money from the GI Bill, a loan and a scholarship, he was able to assist himself through his undergraduate studies. The incentive came through his realization that man, as an individual, needs a reaffirmation of faith, and a purpose and goal that relates to others.

With his schooling completed, he taught, supervised, headed a department, and was a school principal with the Bureau of Indian Affairs. As an educator he has recently been involved in a new area of Indian education - that of preparing prospective teachers for work with Indian children enrolled in federal and public schools.

In his work with teachers, he has found that those instructing Indian children have little understanding of the problems of their students that are related to biculturalism and bilingualism. He has developed a special interest in this and has developed an extensive bibliography and chronology for those studying Amerindian history and culture.

BIRTHPLACE: Mission, South Dakota, July 18, 1929.
MARRIED: Willene DeRoin. CHILDREN: Deborah, Sheila, Randall, Harriet, Joseph.
EDUCATION: Haskell Institute; Dakota Wesleyan University; University of Kansas (BS.Ed.); Chadron State College (MS.Ed.Adm).
SCHOLARSHIPS: Illinois Federation of Women's Clubs.
MILITARY SERVICE: U.S. Navy, four years, Korean Conflict - Korea, Japan, Okinawa, Hong Kong, Taiwan, Hawaii.
ORGANIZATIONS: Veterans of Foreign Wars; American Legion (past post commander); National Congress of American Indians; South Dakota Education Association; National Education Association.

HARRY RAINBOLT (DAKOTA-OGLALA) ACTING EXECUTIVE ASSISTANT, BUREAU OF INDIAN AFFAIRS

Mr. Rainbolt has held a number of supervisory management posts in the BIA's field and headquarters office. He is a new appointee to an executive key position with the BIA staff.

CECIL CORBETT (NEZ PERCE-CHOCTAW) DIRECTOR, COOK CHRISTIAN TRAINING SCHOOL

During the years he attended college, Mr. Corbett worked as a highway rodman, inspector, instrument man, and chief of a surveying party.

After completing theological training, he was stationed at Flandreau Indian School. In 1961, he accepted a pastorate among the Pimas and four years later was named director of program assignment at Cook Christian Training School. In that period, he conducted a study of Indian missions for the National Indian Goals Committee. This report was supported by many of the denominations which have historic work among Indian people. He was also Field Associate for Indian Work for the United Presbyterian Church. He became Director of Cook Christian Training School in 1968.

BIRTHPLACE: Cherokee, North Carolina, March 4, 1931.
MARRIED: Irene Blatchford. CHILDREN: Esther, Ruth, Paul.
EDUCATION: Huron College (B'A.); University of Dubuque Theological Seminary (B.D.).
SCHOLARSHIPS: Nez Perce (Broncheau) Scholarship; Board of National Missions.
HONORS: Honoris Causa, Doctor of Divinity, Huron College (1966).

ERNEST CHILDERS (CREEK) RETIRED ARMY OFFICER, GOVERNMENT EMPLOYEE

Colonel Ernest Childers began his military service in 1937 when he enlisted in the Oklahoma National Guard. In 1940, he was mobilized with the 45th Infantry Division and received basic training at Fort Sill. When the division took part in the initial assault on Sicily, he was First Sergeant of Company C, 180th Infantry. He went ashore in the third wave at Blue Beach.

In the fighting on the island, several officers became casualties and Childers took over as one of the platoon leaders. As a result of his performance in combat, he received a battlefield appointment to second lieutenant.

The unit left Sicily for Italy to take part in the Naples-Foggie Campaign. On September 22, 1943, Lt. Childers undertook the courageous actions that earned him the Congressional Medal of Honor. The accompanying citation reads:

"For conspicuous gallantry and intrepidity at risk of life above and beyond the call of duty in action on 22 September, 1943, at Oliveto, Italy. Although Lieutenant Childers previously had just suffered a fractured instep, he with eight enlisted men, advanced up a hill toward enemy machine-gun nests. The group advanced to a rock wall over-looking a corn field and Lieutenant Childers ordered a base fire laid across the field so that he could advance. When he was fired upon by two enemy snipers from a nearby house he killed both of them. He moved behind the machine-gun nests and killed all occupants of the nearer one. He continued toward the second one and threw rocks into it. When the two occupants of the nest raised up, he shot one. The other was killed by one of the eight enlisted men. Lieutenant Childers continued his advance toward a house further up the hill and, singlehanded, captured an enemy mortar observer. The exceptional leadership, initiative, calmness under fire, and conspicuous gallantry displayed by Lieutenant Childers were an inspiration to his men." In addition to the Medal of Honor, Childers received five other decorations. Over a period of 20 years with the Army, he served in the capacity of Commanding Officer of company size units, Staff Officer in Logistics, Supply Instructor, Procurement, Ordnance, Budget and Fiscal Officer, and Training Officer in the Army Ground Forces Operations. His overseas assignments include North Africa, France, Germany, Austria, and Korea. Other commands were Panama, and Alaska. He also toured this country on a Savings Bond speaking tour during World War II.

Rising through the enlisted ranks, he attained the rank of Lieutenant Colonel in 1965. With retirement from the Army, he accepted an appointment with the Job Corps Coordination for which he is a coordinator for civilian conservation centers.

BIRTHPLACE: Broken Arrow, Oklahoma.
MARRIED: Yolanda LaDema. CHILDREN: Yolanda, Ernest.
EDUCATION: Chilocco Indian School; Army Ground Forces School Order of Battle Course; Infantry School Advanced Infantry Course; several college level courses in various subjects.

VINE DELORIA, SR. (DA-KOTA-YANKTON) ARCH-DEACON (RETIRED)

Reverend Deloria's father was a chief who became a missionary-priest in charge of the entire Standing Rock Reservation. He was responsible for the conversion of many thousands of his tribe to Christianity. There is a carved figure of him in the "Ter Sanctus" reredos back of the Great Altar in the Episcopal Cathedral in Washington, D.C.

In his boyhood, Vine attended a military academy where he rose to Cadet Colonel. When he later graduated from college he worked in Colorado mines and then was boy's adviser at an Indian school. Volunteering for the Episcopal ministry, he completed the theological course in three years. His ordination to deaconate and priest took place in his father's church, where Vine had been both baptized and confirmed.

Reverend Deloria served the Indian mission field until 1951 and was at one time in charge of the eastern half of the Pine Ridge Reservation. As superintending presbyter, his field was nearly as large as the state of Connecticut and had more than 800 communicants.

For a number of years, Vine was rector of Trinity Church in Denison, Iowa. Then he was appointed to the National Council staff of the Episcopal Church (1954) as Assistant Secretary to the Division of Domestic Missions. He was in charge of all Indian missions work. His appointment was the first time in history that the Church had named an Indian to a national executive post.

For reasons of health, Reverend Deloria returned to Iowa and then, at the persistent urging of the office of the Bishop of South Dakota, he became archdeacon of the Niobrara Deanery to work again among the Indians of South Dakota. He travelled over the entire state, visiting annually as many as 87 churches on the reservations and several congregations in towns and cities.

BIRTHPLACE: Wakpala, South Dakota, October 6, 1901.
MARRIED: Barbara S. Eastburn. CHILDREN: Vine, Jr., Barbara Deloria Sanchez; Philip.
EDUCATION: Kearney Military Academy; Bard College (B.A.); General Theological Seminary (B.D.).
HONORS: Indian Council Fire Achievement Award and honorary life membership (1954); Honorary D.D., Bard College (1954).

VINE DELORIA, JR. (DAKOTA-YANKTON) AUTHOR

With the publication of his first book, *Custer Died For Your Sins*, "young Vine," to distinguish him from his equally distinguished father, skyrocketed to national prominence and on to the best seller lists. His book is now in its sixth printing and interest in it continues to mount.

Vine, at one time, was executive secretary of the National Congress of American Indians. He resigned to enroll in law school. His first position was as a staff associate for the United Scholarship Service in Denver where he developed a placement program to place Indian students in independent schools in New England.

Since the publication of his book, he is very much involved in personal appearances, interviews, and with other writing.

BIRTHPLACE: Martin, South Dakota.
EDUCATION: Iowa State University (B.S.); Lutheran School of Theology (B.D.); University of Colorado Law School (LL.B.).
HONORS: Anisfield-Wolfe Award in Race Relations.
SPECIAL ACTIVITIES: Southwest Intergroup Relations Council (board).

ELLA DELORIA (DAKOTA-YANKTON) ANTHROPOLO-GIST

Ella Deloria is a distinguished anthropologist whose works on her people are considered "the" authority.

In college preparatory school, her excellent scholastic reports attracted the attention of a philanthropist who provided her with a college scholarship. She specialized in anthropology, linguistics and ethnology, but for a period after graduation she taught and was a national health education secretary for the YWCA, serving Indian schools and reservations.

In 1929, Miss Deloria was appointed research specialist in Indian ethnology and linguistics in the Department of Anthropology, Columbia University. She was co-author, with the noted Dr. Franz Boas, of two works on Dakota linguistics prepared for the technical use of scholars.

Miss Deloria has served on survey committees of Indian communities, and was the only woman and only Indian on the Navajo Enquiry party of four experts, sponsored by the Phelps-Stokes Fund (1944). A signal honor, at that same time, was the invitation to speak before the American Philosophical Society founded by Benjamin Franklin. This is a goal to which every struggling scientist aspires but seldom achieves.

To help in an emergency, Miss Deloria was principal of St. Elizabeth's Mission School for a three-year period, where she learned her own ABC's. With the appointment of a permanent principal, she left to complete a number of manuscripts on Dakota material. She still lectures on her people and is looked upon with great respect.

BIRTHPLACE: Wakpala, South Dakota.
EDUCATION: Oberlin College; Columbia University (B.S.).
HONORS: Special diploma, Columbia Teachers College; Indian Council Fire Achievement Award and honorary life membership (1943).
AUTHOR: *Speaking of Indians* (Friendship Press, 1944) and many articles and professional papers.

FRITZ SCHOLDER
(LUISENO) ARTIST

Critics call Fritz Scholder one of the leading "new Indian artists." He did not grow up in an Indian environment and it was not until he began to get seriously interested in art that he also became interested in his Indian heritage.

After earning his M.F.A. degree Fritz was Instructor of Advanced Painting and Art History at the Institute of American Indian Arts. After five years of teaching, he went on an extensive tour of Africa and Europe. He lectured on Indian art at the University of Leiden for the Dutch Society De Kiva, among other appearances.

On his return to New Mexico, Fritz purchased an old adobe house and began to paint full time. His first one-man show in New York City met with critics acclaim and his paintings were called "Indian Protest Art," "Pop Indian," and "New Indian Art." They are a blend of traditional and contemporary art. According to Vincent Price, noted connoisseur of primitive and Modern Art, Scholder "approaches tradition . . . with all the modern stops pulled out, and he succeeds in making arresting music of it."

Another art authority says: ". . . the Indian painter has labored under an articicial dictum for years regarding a so-called Indian style, created in the 1930's by a non-Indian. The non-Indian artist over-romanticized the Indian, the Indian artist became caught in a tourist pleasing cliche. This is the quandary in which the Indian has been caught for well over 35 years. Fritz Scholder has taken a warrior's leap out of it."

BIRTHPLACE: Breckenridge, Minnesota, October 6, 1937.

MARRIED: Romona Attenberger.

EDUCATION: Wisconsin State University; Sacramento City College (A.A.); Sacramento State College (B.A.); University of Arizona (M.F.A.).

SCHOLARSHIPS: John Hay Whitney Foundation Fellowship.

HONORS: *Who's Who in American Art; Who's Who in the West; International Director of Art; Prize Winning Paintings;* and *American Indian Painters.*

EXHIBITIONS: More than 20 major exhibits, including the Edinburgh Art Festival, Berlin Festival, Museum of Arts, Buenos Aires, National Library, Santiago, Chile, and the art museum in Barcelona.

COLLECTIONS: More than ten public and private collections.

AWARDS: Three purchase awards, two Grand Awards, among many others.

WILMA L. VICTOR (CHOCTAW) EDUCATIONAL ADMINISTRATOR

When Miss Victor was appointed Superintendent of Intermountain Indian School (1964) she transferred from a position as the first academic director of the Institute of American Indian Arts. There, she had served on the initial team which prepared and implemented the arts-oriented program of this outstanding Indian school.

Miss Victor began her career in the Bureau of Indian Affairs schools in 1941 as a teacher on the Navajo Reservation. She has risen to the status of top ranking woman educator in the BIA. Her success has made her nationally recognized in the entire field of education.

At Intermountain School, which has 2,100 students, she has developed a special program for the Navajo youngsters who come there with little or no formal schooling. Because of her exceptional creative and executive ability in the administration of this unique and complex school situation, she is one of six women in Government circles who have received the Federal Woman's Award.

Miss Victor's years of service for Indian youth has made her keenly aware of the challenges and opportunities facing them. She has personal concern for each one of her students and sets high standards for them, bringing an inspiring enthusiasm to her work.

In demand as a speaker at educational conferences, Miss Victor was keynote speaker for the first National Indian Workshop on School Affairs (1969) and for a conference of school administrators in Canada. She addressed the National Education Association at the 20th anniversary of the White House Council on Rural Education; the DAR national convention; and special conference of universities and education groups.

BIRTHPLACE: Idabel, Oklahoma.

EDUCATION: University of Kansas; University of Wisconsin (Milwaukee) (B.S.); University of Oklahoma (M.Ed.); Utah State University (doctorate pending).

HONORS: Federal Woman's Award (1967); "Distinguished Service Citation," University of Oklahoma - for sustained record of outstanding service to Oklahoma and Nation (1969); Sustained Superior Performance Award, Bureau of Indian Affairs; one of "Seven Women of Seventies," *Salt Lake City Tribune; Who's Who in America; Who's Who in American Education; Who's Who of American Women; Dictionary of International Biography.*

MILITARY SERVICE: U.S. Army, Women's Army Corps, 1943-46 (First Lieutenant); WAC Service Ribbon; American Theatre Campaign Medal. Victory Medal.

SPECIAL ACTIVITIES: American Association of School Administrators; Utah Governor's Advisory Committee on Women's Programs; Utah TB and Health Association (director); Utah State Conference on Social Welfare; Council for Exceptional Children; BIA Advisory Committee for Title III of Elementary and Secondary Education Act; KCPX (TV) News Special Advisory Board.

MURRAY WHITERABBIT (WINNEBAGO) EMPLOYMENT ASSISTANCE TECHNICIAN

Mr. Whiterabbit began his employment with the Bureau of Indian Affairs in 1950 as a procurement clerk. He transferred to the employment assistance branch in 1958 and was promoted to his present position of employment assistance technician in 1960.

He was brought up in the Winnebago tradition by his grandmother who constantly advised him to get as much education as possible. That is the only way for Indian survival and well-being in the future, she told him. He is now president of the Ashland, Wisconsin, Board of Education and is vice-president of the Unified School District No. 1. He has been instrumental in inaugurating a credit course in Indian history and culture at the Ashland High School. He also promoted the employment of a Youth Counselor in the Ashland school system to work exclusively with Indian youth and parents.

Mr. Whiterabbit is active in Indian and community affairs. As a member of the Great Lakes Inter-Tribal Council Education Committee he is concerned with upgrading educational curricula and opportunities for Indian students in local school districts as well as on the state level. He is a co-founder of this Council.

He is a member of the Winnebago Claims Committee and co-chairman of the committee to plan the disposition of the award when it becomes final.

Among his civic activities, he is Disaster Chairman of the Ashland County Chapter, American Red Cross.

BIRTHPLACE: Black River Falls, Wisconsin, August 20, 1918.

MARRIED: Valborg Ahlin. CHILDREN: Ronald, Sharyn, Marlene.

EDUCATION: Winnebago Indian Mission School; public high school; Madison Business College; University of Wisconsin.

HONORS: Honor Award for Commendable Service, Department of the Interior (1969).

MILITARY SERVICE: U.S. Army (Rangers), 1942-44 Silver Star, Purple Heart, Combat Infantry Badge.

ORGANIZATIONS: Veterans of Foreign Wars (past commander); Winnebago Veterans (past Commander); Celebrations, Inc., (president).

SPECIAL INTERESTS: Builder of model airplanes; Wisconsin Council of Churches for Wisconsin and Upper Michigan Synod (lay delegate); Lutheran Church in America (vice-president and church council member).

NATACHEE SCOTT MOMADAY (CHEROKEE–CHOCTAW) TEACHER, WRITER

Natachee Momaday is decended from a Cherokee woman who married a French physician; from Samuel Scott, a member of the House of Burgesses of Virginia; and, from General Charles Scott of Revolutionary War fame. General Scott was also the fourth governor of Kentucky.

Natachee has studied both art and journalism and has written numerous articles on art subjects. Her art includes oil paintings, water color and pastel, and silver jewelry.

As a teacher, she has dedicated her life to helping young Indians understand that they can keep the best of their own culture while selecting and adapting the best of others.

BIRTHPLACE: Fairview, Kentucky.
MARRIED: Al Momaday. CHILDREN: N. Scott.
EDUCATION: Haskell Institute; Crescent Girl's College (B.A.); University of California (Los Angeles); University of New Mexico.
AUTHOR: *Owl in the Cedar Tree* (Ginn, 1965); two other books in writing; more than 50 published short stories.
HONORS: African Women Educational Award (1969); Outstanding woman writer, New Mexico Press Women Zia Award (1969).
ORGANIZATIONS: Daughters of American Revolution; United Daughters of Confederacy; Delta Kappa Gamma; American Pen Women; International Press Women; New Mexico Pen Women (art chairman).

N. SCOTT MOMADAY (KIOWA) UNIVERSITY PROFESSOR, AUTHOR

Dr. N. Scott Momaday is the only Indian to win the Pulitzer Prize. He grew up on several reservations, and is now an associate professor of English and Comparative Literature at the University of California

After his graduation from college, Dr. Momaday taught in a school on the Jicarilla reservation. With the winning of a creative writing scholarship, he attended Stanford University for his master's degree. Other scholarships and fellowships assisted him to complete study for his doctorate in English and American literature.

The Pulitzer prize boom, *House Made of Dawn,* tells the tragic story of a young Indian's efforts to readjust to civilian life after World War II. The book is patterned after other Indians known to the writer; he, himself, escaped the harshness related in the story.

A second book by the same author - *The Way to Rainy Mountain* - is a beautifully written retracing of the 300-year old migration of the Kiowa tribe. The author worked with older people of the tribe, recording their memories of the trek that has survived only as oral history among the Kiowa people.

His second book, *The Way to Rainy Mountain,* is really two books in one - partly tribal history, and partly the writer's memories and comments. This book is illustrated by his father, the noted artist Al Momaday, and is described as "prose poetry, sensitive, aware, lovely and philosophical."

In the years ahead, Dr. Momaday plans to write many more books. Especially interested in preserving Indian legends and folktales, he considers it vital to collect this material because "each generation moves further away from the traditions."

BIRTHPLACE: Lawton, Oklahoma, February 27, 1934.
MARRIED: Gaye Mangold. CHILDREN: Cael, Jill, Brit.
EDUCATION: University of New Mexico (AB); Stanford University (AM., Ph.D.).
SCHOLARSHIPS: Wallace Stegner Creative Writing Scholarship; John Jay Whitney Foundation Fellowship. Guggenheim Fellow.
HONORS: Pulitzer Prize (1969).
AUTHOR: *House Made of Dawn* (Harper & Row, 1968); *The Way to Rainy Mountain* (University of New Mexico Press, 1969).

AL MOMADAY (KIOWA) ARTIST, SCHOOL PRINCIPAL

Al Momaday's grandfather was the first Indian judge when the Kiowa Agency was established. When he was young, Al heard many awesome tales from his grandfather, thus his first art attempts were sketches of the scenes so vividly described.

Also, he sketched and painted from memory, the dances and costumes of the Indians of the southern plains.

Al Momaday is a distinguished artist and a distinguished teacher. At Jemez Pueblo, where he is principal of the day school, he has initiated a program of arts and crafts that has brought international recognition to the school. One of the first parent groups for the discussion of problems and programs within the Pueblo School was started by Mr. Momaday. He has given a progressive leadership in art and education to the community.

BIRTHPLACE: Mountain View, Oklahoma, July 2, 1913.
MARRIED: Natachee Scott; CHILDREN: N. Scott.
EDUCATION: Bacone College; University of New Mexico; University of California (Los Angeles).
HONORS: Outstanding Indian Artist, Dallas Exchange Club, (1956); Outstanding Indian Artist, Western (N.Y.); Art Association (1956); Outstanding Indian Artist Hollywood Arts Festival (1962); *Who's Who in New Mexico;* honorary plaques, New Mexico Arts and Crafts Fair for outstanding exhibits; award, African Educators

for outstanding art work and public relations; Certificate of Appreciation, Indian Arts and Crafts Board (1967).

AWARDS: Six Grand Awards among others.

PUBLISHED WORK: LaFarge (1956-1960); Pierson and Davidson (1960); Haskell Institute (9160); Willoya and Brown (1962); *Tulsa Magazine* (May, 1948); *The Lutheran* (May 28, 1958); *Indian Life* (1960).

COMMISSIONS: Altar plaques, St. Luke's Lutheran Church, Albuquerque (Indian designs representing symbols of the Christian Church (1958).

ORGANIZATIONS: Artist's Equity; Southwest Indian Arts; New Mexico Indian Art Commission (past chairman).

GEORGE D. SCOTT (CREEK-SEMINOLE) DEPUTY DIRECTOR OF EDUCATION PROGRAMS

Formerly educational director of the Chicago American Indian Center, he has also been consultant to the National Education Association and the U.S. Office of Education. He holds an M.A. degree from the University of Chicago. He is one of fifteen newly announced appointments to the BIA.

LLOYD HOUSE (ONEIDA-NAVAJO) AD-MINISTRATOR, LEGIS-LATOR

Lloyd House, from a state where no Indian had ever been elected to public office, was the first in 55 years of statehood to become a State Senator. Of the total vote in his legislative district, the Indian vote is less than three percent.

All of Mr. House's early education was in federal Indian boarding schools. His higher education was interrupted by his enlistment in the Marines for duty in Korea. All of his four brothers were also members of the Marine Corps.

His first position was as a teacher-advisor in a federal Indian school. He resigned to work for the Social Security Administration as a resident representative to the Navajos. He translated a Social Security booklet into Navajo. Currently he is Director of Social Security for the Navajo Tribe, a program that he devised. During the first 2½ years of his administration, more than $170,000 was brought in for the Navajo self-employed.

Mr. House, who is fluent in four languages -English, Spanish, Apache, and Navajo-firmly believes that education is the solution to Indian problems.

BIRTHPLACE: Winslow, Arizona, October 24, 1931.
MARRIED: Victoria Monsegur. CHILDREN: Josephine, Electa, Margaret, Lloyd II.

EDUCATION: Indian boarding schools; Sherman Instutute; Bacone College; Marine Corps Institute; Northern Arizona University (B.S.).

SCHOLARSHIPS: Women's Federation; Navajo Tribal.

HONORS: Outstanding Performance Award, Social Security Administration.

MILITARY SERVICE: U.S. Marines, Korean Conflict, 13 months - 10 in combat zone.

ORGANIZATIONS: Veterans of Foreign Wars (Post Commander); American Legion; Marine Corps League.

SPECIAL ACTIVITIES: Native American Church; Window Rock P.T.A. (past president); National Deputy Chief of Staff, Veterans of Foreign Wars Headquarters.

JOHN BORBRIDGE (TLINGIT) EXECUTIVE

John Borbridge has been a tireless worker for the Native movement in Alaska and an outstanding leader in the battle for Native claims. He is presently serving as first vice-president of the Alaska Federation of Natives and president of the Central Council of the Tlingit and Haidas.

Under his leadership, the Central Council of the Tlingit-Haida Indians has been developing programs for the use of the award monies to advance the welfare of the two tribes. The programs include educational scholarships, care of the elderly, and community and industrial development.

BIRTHPLACE: Juneau, Alaska, 1926.

MARRIED: Emma Nicolet. CHILDREN: Charles, John, Linda, Sandra.

EDUCATION: Sheldon Jackson Junior College; Northwest Missouri State Teachers College; University of Michigan (B.A.).

ROBERT E. LEWIS (PUEBLO-ZUNI-CHEROKEE) GOVERNOR, ZUNI PUEBLO

Mr. Lewis was elected Governor of Zuni Pueblo in 1965. This was the first time a secret ballot was used in the tribal elections. It was also the first time that Zuni women were permitted to vote.

Governor Lewis, now serving his third term, is one of the outstanding Indian leaders. A tactful and diplomatic administrator, he is courageous in defending his viewpoints and has achieved a great deal for his people.

Among his major accomplishments are the completion of a number of modern new buildings; the establishment of a tribally-owned police department; a reservation sales tax; a skills survey of the people; the securing of funds for an industrial park; the reorganization of tribal structures; the purchase of land, planned and subdivided for the construction of mutual help homes; and, the establishment of two electronic firms with an employment potential of 500 Zunis.

He has also obtained a charter for a bank, approved by the State of New Mexico; expanded the high school; established an additional public elementary school; and, initiated vocational subjects in the high school curriculum.

Projects on which he is currently working are: an EDA application for airport improvements; a natural gas distribution system for the village; a shopping center; a storm sewer and drainage system; the paving of village streets; establishment of a volunteer fire department; and, the establishment of a public junior high school.

Heading the list of his personal goals and accomplishments in importance is the Zuni Plan - a compilation of 24 major short term goals designed to solve most of the immediate problems of the people.

BIRTHPLACE: Zuni, New Mexico, August 24, 1914.
MARRIED: Virginia Panteah. CHILDREN: James, Roberta, Margaret, William, Hayes, Robert, Stuart, Jean, Allen.
EDUCATION: Phoenix Indian School.
MILITARY SERVICE: 1942-1945.
ORGANIZATIONS: American Legion (past post commander).

ROBERT E. DOMINIC
(OTTAWA-CHIPPEWA)
COLLEGE INSTRUCTOR

Robert Dominic is the son of the president of the Northern Michigan Ottawa Association who successfully negotiated the settlement of a $10 million land claim for this tribe.

Young Robert has been interested in a teaching career in his special field of chemistry since college. He is a faculty member of Alpena Community College as an instructor in Chemistry.

BIRTHPLACE: Detroit, Michigan, August 15, 1941.

MARRIED: Linda Burrows. CHILDREN: Douglas, Cherie.

EDUCATION: North Central Michigan College; University of Colorado; Central Michigan University (B.S., M.S.).

SCHOLARSHIPS: United Scholarship Service; Bureau of Indian Affairs.

HONORS: Beta Beta Beta (honorary biological fraternity).

ORGANIZATIONS: American Indian Youth Council (charter member).

FRED IPALOOK (ESKIMO) TEACHER (RETIRED)

A dedicated teacher for the past 40 years, Fred Ipalook was honored following his retirement by some 2,000 people - the entire community of Barrow, Alaska. He was also presented the Distinguished Service Award of the Department of Interior, the Department's highest honor.

Fred went to school for the first time when he was six years old. He began to teach at the age of nineteen. He married at the same time, and had nine children. Now he must figure with a pencil to count his 19 grandchildren.

In 1934, Fred returned to his home village to teach and remained there until his retirement. Throughout the years, he was active in the civic affairs of the community. He had several terms as president of the Barrow Cooperative and guided that endeavor through its growing pains and frustrations. He was also trustee, pianist and elder of the Presbyterian Church.

Mr. Ipalook worked hard to break down the language barrier between teachers and pupils. He pioneered the development of a language log for use in teaching English as a second language and demonstrated outstanding ability in working with adults and children.

An outdoorsman, Mr. Ipalook still enjoys walrus and caribou hunting and fishing.

BIRTHPLACE: Barrow, Alaska.
MARRIED: Ruth Kudralook. CHILDREN: (9).
HONORS: Department of Interior Distinguished Service Award (1970).

ROBERT DOMINIC, SR. (OTTAWA) CHEMIST/ PHYSICIST

Mr. Dominic was a metallurgist for General Motors during World War II. He has also been a forestry technician and a baseball manager and commissioner.

In 1948 he organized the Northern Michigan Ottawa Association to prosecute the treaty claims of Michigan Indians. As Acting President, and with his wife as secretary, the two have managed to keep this important issue alive. The Association has enjoyed victory in two cases - with an award of $932,620.01 and $10,800,000.00 both cases decided in favor of the Ottawa-Chippewa tribes. Ten other claims cases are pending. These victories have been won in the face of seemingly insurmountable obstacles.

Mr. Dominic also works for the education, welfare, and employment of Indians. He organized the first All-State Indian Pow Wow in 1959 and is active in programs that "war on poverty."

BIRTHPLACE: Cross Village, Michigan, February 23, 1913.
MARRIED: Waunetta McClellan. CHILDREN: Robert, Michael (Chemist), David (pre-law student), Christine Dominic Merry, Dennis, Brian.
EDUCATION: Haskell Institute; Central Michigan University (B.S.).
MILITARY SERVICE: World War II.
ORGANIZATIONS: Ottawa-Chippewa Tribal Council (president);

Northern Michigan Ottawa Association (president); Michigan Indian Commission (past vice-president); Planned Parenthood Association (executive board).

SPECIAL ACTIVITIES: NEMCA, 13 county war on poverty programs (executive board); member of Overall Economic Development Programs, appointed by County Board of Supervisors.

CARL WOODRING (OSAGE) ARTIST

Carl Woodring was started on his career by the late Acee Blue Eagle. He first began to paint in 1956 and within a year was exhibiting throughout this country and Europe. A prolific painter in his early years, he did little work in 1964 and 1965, but has again taken up painting in earnest.

In that period when he "slowed down" he was an architectural engineer with a Tulsa firm. In addition to his painting, he has also done some sculpturing.

BIRTHPLACE: Arkansas City, Kansas, December 6, 1920.

MARRIED: Margaret (Div.). CHILDREN: Rose, David, Nikkie, Shawn.

HONORS: In one year, received more awards than any other artist entered in Philbrook exhibit.

MILITARY SERVICE: U.S. Air Force, World War II and Korean War, 11 years.

EXHIBITIONS: Fifteen major exhibits; three one-man shows; eight public and private collections. His paintings have hung at the Brussel's World Fair, Belgium; American Embassy, Paris; France; Office of the Lord Mayor, Mannheim, Germany; Parkland Hotel, London.

AWARDS: Two Grand Awards.

WORK PUBLISHED: *Oklahoma Today* (1959).

JACK C. MONTGOMERY (CHEROKEE) CONTACT OFFICER, VETERANS ADMINISTRATION

True heroes usually refuse to proclaim their bravery and usually do not aspire to any Hall of Fame. Yet, their deeds are so outstanding that they are naturally singled out for recognition.

Jack Montgomery, excelled in athletics in school, and had planned a career as football coach and teacher - but his life turned out differently.

With the outbreak of World War II, he entered service with the Oklahoma National Guard. In 1944, he was a lieutenant in command of an infantry platoon on Anzio Beach, Italy. Two hours before dawn, a strong force of Germans "dug in" and threatened the platoon's position. Crawling within grenade reach of the enemy, Montgomery killed eight Germans and captured four.

Returning to his platoon, Montgomery then called for artillery fire directed on a house where he suspected Germans were entrenched. Armed with a carbine, he braved the withering fire of riflemen and machine gunners and proceeded toward this building. Two enemy machine guns were silenced in the face of his furious assault, and seven of the enemy surrendered.

When the artillery barrage lifted, Montgomery ran fearlessly toward the strongly defended house. He exposed himself daringly to capture the remaining enemy and send them to the rear. His actions accounted for a total of eleven enemy dead, 32 prisoners, and an unknown number of wounded. That same night, Montgomery was struck by a mortar shell and seriously wounded.

For these deeds, Montgomery was awarded the Congressional Medal of Honor, the highest recognition this country can give. His citation says: "his selflessness and courage inspired his men to a degree beyond estimation."

After his honorable discharge from the Army, Montgomery was engaged in veterans work, and then requested active duty once more. He became an infantry school instructor and later athletic coach and recreation officer for the 51st Infantry in Trieste. He served 2½ years during the Korean Conflict.

BIRTHPLACE: Long, Oklahoma.

MARRIED: Joyce B. Magness.

EDUCATION: Chilocco Indian School; Bacone Jr. College; University of Redlands (BA).

SCHOLARSHIPS: Athletic scholarship.

MILITARY SERVICE: U.S. Army, World War II and Korea, 7½ years. (Congressional Medal of Honor; Silver Star; Bronze Star; Purple Heart with Oak Leaf Cluster; Combat Infantryman's Badge; Italian Military Cross of Valor.

ORGANIZATIONS: American Legion; Veterans of Foreign Wars; Disabled American Veterans; Military of the Purple Heart; 45th Infantry Division Association (national president).

BRUMMETT ECHOHAWK (PAWNEE) ARTIST *

Echohawk is an internationally known artist, a World War II combat veteran, an articulate author and an eloquent lecturer. He cannot recall a time when he was not drawing horses - he even drew them on the undersides of tables. Echohawk paints horses with skilled authority now, and is equally skilled in training them.

Brummett is the grandson of a Pawnee warrior who was a member of the Pawnee Scout Batallion during the Indian Wars of 1964-67. When the bombs fell on Pearl Harbor, Brummett was on duty with the National Guard. Called into the army, he was assigned to train others, for he was adept at hand-to-hand fighting. His training classes included a group of British Commandos.

Brummett served in some of the heaviest combat fighting in North Africa, Sicily, and Italy. In these battles, he performed all of the requirements as a traditional Pawnee warrior, and this fact has been acknowledged by the tribe. He was once wounded and evacuated to a hospital from where he went AWOL and made his way back to his unit. It was a difficult journey and held many strange experiences.

In a foxhole in Europe, near the end of the war, Brummett decided that he would become a trained artist. With the aid of his GI benefits, he attended the Chicago Art Institute, struggling with much self-discipline and faith through extremely lean years. His belief in himself was justified and his talent was soon established.

The artist has done illustrations for Chicago newspapers and for various magazines, and special covers for western magazines. He has sketched for film animation. His own line of Indian Christmas cards finds eager buyers. His paintings are in the classic tradition of the 18th century. He uses a variation of Van Gogh's palette knife technique.

An authority on the Custer Battle at the Little Big Horn, Brummett frequently lectures on this subject to enthralled listeners. He paints mainly on commission, and is presently at work on a series of Indian Nation landscapes.

BIRTHPLACE: Pawnee, Oklahoma, March 3, 1922.

MARRIED: Mary McInnes.

EDUCATION: Pawnee Indian School; Publis High School; Detroit School of Arts and Crafts; Art Institute of Chicago.

MILITARY SERVICE: U.S. Army, infantry, World War II, five years - Purple Heart with Oak Leaf Cluster; Bronze Star; Army Commendation Medal; Combat Infantry Badge, three battle stars, invasion arrowhead.

EXHIBITIONS: Many, including Pakistan, Indian; a number of permanent collections.

COMMISSIONS: Commissioned with Thomas Hart Benton to paint mural in Truman Memorial Library; Aluminum Company of America; *Western Horseman Magazine* (annual cover); Comic strip, "Little Chief" runs in *Tulsa Sunday World.*

WRITER: Writes and illustrates own articles on Indian subjects for various newspapers, including *London Sunday Mirror.*

ORGANIZATIONS: Pawnee Indian Veterans of Oklahoma (president).

* *See art section*

RUDOLPH C. GORMAN (NAVAJO) ARTIST *

The artist Gorman, better known as "R.C.," majored in literature and is a gifted writer. Painting, however, is his primary interest. In this field, he is well-established.

"R.C." is a definite part of two worlds - a summary of the culture learned at his grandmother's knee, while embracing the neo-culture of the 20th century. More than a talented Navajo painter, he is an artist of scope and promise. Although he often paints native subjects, his work is cosmopolitan in style and free of the traditional.

Using ink, oil, pastel, water color or acrylic, he paints more suggestively than realistically, and often in the fully abstract. He favors washes, bleeding colors, fade-outs, in a dynamic, but technically sound, art.

R.C." is a descendant of sandpainters, silversmiths, chanters and weavers on both sides of his family. His father, Carl, also an outstanding artist, encouraged him in his career when he made his first paintings with sand and rocks as a child. He lived in a hogan, herded sheep, and watched the medicine men as they went about their healing ceremonies or rites of blessing. Yet, very soon after leaving the reservation, he absorbed an articulate conception of international culture.

This young artist, solid Navajo one minute and mercurial and uninhibited the next, is rapidly emerging on the contemporary scene. With fantastic range and depth. He uses his art as a bridge between the two worlds to which he belongs. He continually searches for new directions and new dimensions - not with studied consciousness, but, because he is truly a creative artist. He operates his own gallery in Taos, New Mexico.

BIRTHPLACE: Chinle, Arizona, July 26, 1932.

EDUCATION: Arizona State College.

MILITARY SERVICE: U.S. Navy, 1952-1956.

HONORS: Recipient of the first scholarship given by the Navajo Tribe for study outside of the U.S., Register of United States Living Artists; American Indian Painters.

EXHIBITIONS: 30 exhibitions; 15 one-man shows; three two-man shows with his father; 47 private and public collections.

AWARDS: Grand Award and eleven other awards, three honorable mentions.

WORKS PUBLISHED: *South Dakota Review; Southwestern Indian Arts and Crafts; Southwest Indian Paintings; Southwestern Art; Western Review; New Mexico Magazine; National Geographic Magazine; Sunset Magazine; Orange County Illustrated* (cover). Written up in a number of publications.

✱ See art section

MARIAN DODGE LEE (NAVAJO) SCHOOL PRINCIPAL

A granddaughter of the great tribal leader, Henry Chee Dodge. Mrs. Lee has been a teacher in Indian schools for the past fifteen years. She is now principal of the 362-pupil Cotton- wood Day School.

Indians as well as other mi- nority groups are becoming more aware of their rights, Mrs. Lee says. She believes that more changes will take place within the next few years than took place in the past 100 years. These changes will be more rapid because Indians, themselves, are becoming concerned and involved, she points out.

"Today I see an awakening among Indians to the fact that things can be changed," Mrs. Lee says. "Indians can control their own destinies . . . they do have 'the right to be wrong,' if that be the case."

BIRTHPLACE: Crystal, New Mexico, January 18, 1934.
MARRIED: Patrick A. Lee. CHILDREN: Barbara, Susan, Leonard, Tiffany.
EDUCATION: Marygrove College (B.A.); Colorado State College (M.A.)
SCHOLARSHIPS: Marygrove College; Navajo Tribal Scholarship.

RUSSELL MOORE (PIMA) MUSICIAN

Russell ("Big Chief") Moore, jazz trombonist extraordinary, is in the first ranks of Indians in the arts, and is honored world-wide for his musical ability.

Russell's childhood was spent in an adobe house in a remote part of the Gila River Reservation. His earliest memory is of his grandfather singing Pima chants and songs.

Even before he went to school, Russell's musical inclinations were apparent. He loved to hear the marching band of the mission school, and imitated the tunes on a homemade instrument— a piece of pipe with holes in it. One of his favorite tunes was *Garry Owen,* the theme song of General Custer's regiment. He made so much noise with his pipes, that his parents hid them in order to have some peace and quiet.

At school, he was nicknamed "Muscle Roar" a turnabout of his name and a tribute to his music making. "I wanted to play *all* the instruments," he says. "I wanted to lead the band."

Because of the death of his father when he was eleven years old, Russell was sent to live with an uncle in Chicago. The uncle was a music teacher and he saw to it that the boy learned to play the piano as well as several brass instruments. Instruction on the trombone, for which he was to become famous, began in his teens after he enrolled in a government school. After graduation from this school he began his professional career.

His first step into the big time came when he joined Lionel Hampton's jazz band (1935). Later he played with other nationally-known groups. He toured from coast to coast as first trombonist with "Satchmo" Louie Armstrong and also played solo spots. When Armstrong's band broke up, Russell made his home in New York City, playing with many of the bigger night club orchestras. He also had his own bands in Philadelphia and in Columbus, Ohio.

Russell's reputation spread to Europe, Asia and Africa, Australia and New Zealand. He took part in the International Festival of Jazz in Paris (1949) and four years later organized a band of French musicians with whom he toured Italy, Switzerland, Belgium and North Africa. Then he spent a year in Paris appearing at well-known tourist night spots.

Rejoining Armstrong for another tour, Moore travelled Australia, New Zealand, Japan, Iceland and the Virgin Islands. He is featured in the Armstrong record album, *Hello Dolly,* and has appeared on major network TV shows. He has performed at the White House and played for the Inaugural Balls' of Presidents Kennedy and Johnson.

Fame has not caused this great musician to forget his own people. He is zealous in his efforts to encourage Indian students to make the most of whatever opportunities come their way.

Fame has not caused this great musician to forget his own people. He is zealous in his efforts to encourage Indian students to make the most of whatever opportunities come their way.

BIRTHPLACE: Gila Crossing, Arizona, August 13, 1912.
MARRIED: Ida Powlas. CHILDREN: Randall, Amy.
EDUCATION: Phoenix Indian School; Sherman Institute.
HONORS: Award, Pima-Maricopa Tribal Council (1966); Certificate of Appreciation, Secretary of Interior Udall, for achievement in the realm of music and for outstanding attainment as an Indian (1966); *Guide to Jazz; Encyclopedia of Jazz.*

JOHN RAINER (PUEBLO-TAOS) EDUCATIONAL ADMINISTRATOR

John Rainer comes from a closely knit family group, resistant to outside influences. He did not speak English until he was thirteen and throughout his youth had to struggle to maintain a balance between two cultures. His schooling was secured in the face of bitter hostility from the Taos people.

Although John's family were unable to assist him financially, they did support him in his struggle for self-determination. Much pressure was brought upon his family to bring John back to the traditional ways of life, and his father was denied many honors that were his due.

Wanting to return to his people as a teacher, John completed his college studies. A strong believer in education, he has sent all three of his children through college.

Now the owner of a cattle ranch and a mercantile store at his home pueblo, John has been a teacher and principal in Indian schools. He has been executive secretary of the National Congress of American Indians and chairman of the All-Indian Pueblo Council. He was also director of the Ute Rehabilitation Program. He has been active throughout his life in affairs pertaining to Indians and is greatly respected in his native state.

Formerly Executive Director, New Mexico Commission on Indian Affairs, John is currently Director, National Indian

Scholarship Program sponsored by the Donner Foundation at the University of New Mexico. The program is for graduate students only.

BIRTHPLACE: Taos, New Mexico.

MARRIED: Wynema Freeman. CHILDREN: Ann (Master's degree, anthrolology, Harvard). John, Jr. (Master's degree, Brigham Young University); Howard (M.A., Brigham Young University).

EDUCATION: Santa Fe Indian School; Bacone Junior College; University of Redlands (B.A.); University of Southern California (M.A.).

SCHOLARSHIPS: John Randall Haines Scholarship; John Hay Whitney Foundation Fellowship.

HONORS: *Who's Who in New Mexico.*

ORGANIZATIONS: Lions; National Congress of American Indians (vice-president); Governor's Interstate Indian Council (chairman); Taos Municipal School Board (vice-president); American Indian Development, Inc. (board); U.S. Civil Rights Commission Advisory Board for State of New Mexico; Taos Pueblo Cattle Association (secretary-treasurer); Small Business Administration Council for New Mexico.

JOHN C. RAINER, JR. (PUEBLO-TAOS) EDUCATOR

John Rainer, Jr., a recent graduate from Brigham Young University starts a faculty position this year as counselor and teacher to the Indian Student body. The University has an Indian student population of more than 300 from 64 tribes and 27 states. BYU has an outstanding program in Indian education.

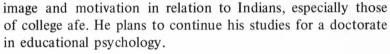

John has been working with proglems of the self-image and motivation in relation to Indians, especially those of college afe. He plans to continue his studies for a doctorate in educational psychology.

BIRTHPLACE: Taos, New Mexico.
MARRIED: Verenda Dosela.
EDUCATION: Brigham Young University (B.A., M.A.).

ANNIE DODGE WAUNEKA (NAVAJO) TRIBAL LEADER

Annie Dodge Wauneka, who dresses in traditional native costume, 18 years ago became the first woman elected to the 74-member Navajo Trival Council. In running for her second term, she competed against her own husband; and, was re-elected to her third term again running against one male opponent.

Before becoming a councilwoman, Mrs. Wauneka was an active community worker. She was instrumental, among other things, in revising the special Navajo grazing regulations, a task that took eight years to accomplish.

As Chairman of the Tribal Council Health Committee, Mrs. Wauneka has energetically campaigned for better Navajo health. She speaks out vigorously for improvements in health conditions and travels the length and breadth of the vast reservation speaking to Navajo people on health matters. She visits patients in hospitals, bringing them messages of cheer and comfort. Her activities permit her to work with physicians in the production of health movies, acting in some of these as well.

Mrs. Wauneka made so strong, and such a unusual impact in her efforts, that she was soon appointed to other health committees, both local and national. She has traveled extensively in connection with this work. Her own radio program on health education, is broadcast entirely in the Navajo language.

One great obstacle that Mrs. Wauneka had to overcome was the hostility toward white man's medicine by traditional Navajos. First, she gained the trust of the medicine men, teaching them in their own words the miracles of modern science. Next, she tackled runaways from tuberculosis clinics on the reservation, explaining to them that they were exposing others to the dread disease.

Tuberculosis is now virtually eliminated as a major health problem among the Navajo, and Mrs. Wauneka is given great credit for helping accomplish this goal. Not only did she assist in bringing about an appreciable decrease in mortality rate from tuberculosis, but also in the mortality rate from dysentery, a serious ailment among Navajo children. She has influenced many reluctant Navajos to turn to white doctors for medical attention.

In 1963, Mrs. Wauneka was singled out by President John F. Kennedy to receive the Presidential Medal of Freedom, given to persons who made outstanding contributions to the security of national interest or world peace, cultural or other significant public or private endeavor.

Mrs. Wauneka is the daughter of Henry Chee Dodge who was the first chairman of the Navajo Tribal Council and an outstanding leader in behalf of his people.

BIRTHPLACE: Navajo reservation.
MARRIED: George Wauneka. CHILDREN: Georgia Wauneka Plummer; Henry, Irma, Franklin, Lorencita, Timothy, Sallie, George, Jr.
EDUCATION: Albuquerque Indian School.
HONORS: Josephine B. Hughes Memorial Award, Arizona Press Women (1958); Outstanding Worker in Public Health, Arizona Public Health Association (1959); Indian Council Fire Achievement Award and honorary life member (1959).

MARGARET BEAUCHAMP BREUER (ARIKARA) TEACHER

Mrs. Breuer has been a teacher in Indian schools since 1943. She has taught as many as three generations of students.

She, with her sister, are the first two Indians from the Fort Berthold Reservation to graduate from public school. Further education was gained only through great determination and sacrifice. Her parents, both missionary teachers, could give little help. While still taking her college work, Mrs. Breuer was both teaching and raising a family.

With marriage, hard times were to continue. The first home, built from logs and chinked and plastered with a clay-mud mixture, was struck by lightning and burned to the ground. Her first teaching position was an answer to many prayers, for the toes were out of the homemade moccasins the family wore. The position as substitute teacher was fifty miles from home, but Mrs. Breuer was so grateful for the opportunity that she went "with a song of praise and thankfulness." Since then, she has traveled to remote areas to teach, going by horseback, wagon, truck, tractor, car and even on foot.

The family lived through drouth, sickness and other calamities, by "faith, planning, and our own efforts," Mrs. Breuer says.

"I am not the product of my own making, but of what others have planned and sacrificed for," she states. "I humbly thank them for their part in my life. There was always someone with a helping hand when I needed it."

Mrs. Breuer has been a vital factor in developing and improving race relationships. In 1949, during the North Dakota blizzard, she played an heroic part in getting the sick to hospitals, signalling relief planes and aiding the distressed.

BIRTHPLACE:Armstrong, North Dakota, August 16, 1906.
MARRIED: Henry Breuer. CHILDREN: Peter, Bernard, H. Almit.
EDUCATION: Valley City State Teachers College; North Dakota State Teachers College (B.S.)
HONORS: North Dakota Mother of the Year (1958); Superior Performance Award, Department of Interior, Bureau of Indian Affairs (1969).

CONSTANCE HARPER PADDOCK (ATHABASCAN) CHIEF CLERK, HOUSE OF REPRESENTATIVES, ALASKA

Mrs. Paddock is the first Alaskan Native to hold the position of chief clerk of the Alaskan House of Representatives. Her duties are numerous and she often puts in twelve hours a day.

Mrs. Paddock started to work for the Legislature in 1957 as assistant chief clerk. She later became secretary to the Secretary of State.

One of ten children, all of whom are living, Mrs. Paddock comes from an interesting family. Her paternal grandfather pioneered the way into the Yukon. His son was the first to raise the American flag on top of Mt. McKinley, the highest peak in North America. Her mother spoke with a Virginia accent, because her second grade teacher was from that state. A firm believer in getting an education she was proud that she had two children who were college graduates.

BIRTHPLACE: Nenana, Alaska, June 18, 1920.
MARRIED: Thomas O. Paddock. CHILDREN: Tom Jr., Maxine Paddock Reichert (first Alaskan Indian to be awarded a degree (psychology) from Reed College), Anna.
EDUCATION: Eklutna Vocational School; Haskell Institute (most outstanding graduate of her class).
ORGANIZATIONS: Alaska Native Sisterhood (past vice-president).
SPECIAL ACTIVITIES: Juneau-Douglas Community College (advisory board).

ESTHER BURNETT HORNE (SHOSHONE) TEACHER

Esther Horne comes from a family that really contributed to the history of our country. She is the great-great-granddaughter of Sacajawea, the girl guide of the Lewis and Clark Expedition, and granddaughter of Finn Burnett, the frontiersman who rode with Jim Bridger and who fought beside Chief Washakie.

Esther's career has been one of singular leadership and noteworthy contributions in her chosen field of endeavor. As an elementary and demonstration teacher with the Bureau of Indian Affairs she exemplified for more than thrity years, the highest type of teaching, both in the classroom and in associated areas of education. With rare ability, she has enriched the academic, social and cultural needs of hundreds of Indian and non-Indian children.

A highly creative teacher, Mrs. Horne emphasized the virtues of Indian culture by teaching Indian values and the contributions of Indians to civilization. With her husband, she assisted many disadvantaged Indian children by giving them a home and helping them continue their education. She has been completely dedicated to the development of youth and continues to contribute to Indian education and to education in general. She organized the first Indian Girl Scout troop in the United States and has worked actively with Scouts throughout her life.

"As a teacher, I have directed my efforts towards the dignity of the individual Indian student, helping him to create within himself a feeling of security and confidence so that through his own efforts he can be just as successful as anyone from any other race in the American scene," Mrs. Horne says.

In 1965, Mrs. Horne was Good Will Ambassador to nine European countries in a positive effort to promote travel in Indian areas and invite new interest in Indian arts and Crafts.

BIRTHPLACE: Fort Washakie, Wyoming, November 9, 1909.
MARRIED: Robert Horne. CHILDREN: Yvonne Horne Barney, Diane Horne Kjelbertson.
EDUCATION: Haskell Institute; Valley City State Teachers College; Moorehead State College; University of New Mexico.
HONORS: Outstanding Teacher's Award, Department of Interior (1957); named Honorary Lt. Governor of Oklahoma (1959); First Master Teacher in Bureau of Indian Affairs (1963); Woman of the Year, Seratoma (1965); Community Excellence of Service Award, Wahpeton, North Dakota (1965); Distinguished Service Award in Education, Department of the Interior (1966); Model for Sacajawea bust for North Dakota Historical Museum (1950); Jefferson Peace Medal from Lewis and Clark Sesquicentennial Committee cast in same mold as one given to Sacajawea (1956).
AUTHOR: Three historical pageants; many articles in newspapers and magazines.
SPECIAL ACTIVITIES: Guide of Lewis and Clark Sesquicentennial Expeditions (1955-56); Governor's delegate, White House Conference on Youth (1960); Consultant, Indian Affairs, Girl Scouts of America; Consultant on Indian Affairs and Education, at large.
ORGANIZATIONS: Indian Council Fire; National Congress of American Indians; V.F.W. Auxiliary; North Dakota Federated Women's Clubs (Indian Affairs chairman); National Indian Workers Committee, Episcopal Church.

HAZEL POLING (OTTA-WA) ADMINISTRATOR, INDIAN HEALTH SER-VICE

When she was a slip of a girl, Mrs. Poling came from a small Michigan village to report for work as a clerk-typist in the Bureau of Indian Affairs.

When the responsibility for Indian health was transferred to the Public Health Service, she went along, and rose to the position of administrative assistant.

Mrs. Poling is one who has contributed something of value to others. Remembering her own lost feelings when she first came to Washington, she won the approval of her supervisors and initiated a recruitment program. She staffed the offices of the Division of Indian Health with efficient young Indian people and opened career opportunities for them. Many have gone on into the administrative field from the start she gave them.

Mrs. Poling is proud of the fact that her first two recruits are still in government service, and both have worked their way up to the top. She has spent more than 30 years with the government, after graduation from Haskell Institute.

In 1964, Mrs. Poling received the coveted Oveta Culp Hobby Award of the Public Health Service. The citation reads: "for her untiring efforts in bringing competent young Indian people into the Federal service, in assisting them to adjust to the non-Indian world and the work environment, and thus promoting benefits to both the Indian population and the government."

388

Actually, these comments merely scratch the surface, since it in no way indicates the hours of counselling, the friendly interest, the sympathetic attention, and the "taking in" of the lonely youngster away from home for the first time.

Mrs. Poling arranges transportation for those who she has selected to come to Washington, meets the recruits at the station or airport, assists them in finding living quarters, and usually hosts their first social event, perhaps a cookout in her back yard. As if they were her own children, she gets them off to a good start, and is ready with a helping hand if, and when it is needed. Since she started her recruitment program, more than 200 students from nearly 35 tribes and 20 states have traveled the same route that Hazel Poling did, from a small village or reservation to Washington and the Indian Health Service.

BIRTHPLACE: Frederick, Michigan, June 5, 1920.
MARRIED: Carleton C. Poling. CHILDREN: Virginia Poling Stacey.
EDUCATION: Haskell Institute.
HONORS: Oveta Culp Hobby Award (1964); Superior Service Award, Public Health Service (1964); Indian of the Year Award, American Indian Society of Washington (1968).

ROE B. LEWIS (PIMA-PAPAGO) EDUCATIONAL COUNSELOR

Dr. Lewis, by training, practice and spirit, is essentially an educator. He is the first Indian to be ordained as a minister in the United Presbyterian Church and to have a complete college and theological seminary education. He also has the distinction of being the first Indian Minister in his Church to receive a Doctor of Divinity degree.

Dr. Lewis is the son of an Indian missionary. His father died when Roe was a small boy, and Roe, who showed strong religious inclinations, then determined to prepare for the ministry.

In college, he majored in education. His first employment was at Phoenix Indian School where he organized and developed a modern school of agriculture. Later he went to the Pima-Maricopa reservation as school principal.

Dr. Lewis completed theological training with special attention to rural sociology and economics. He became associated with Cook Christian Training School where he organized the Department of the Rural Church, and then, for awhile, was pastor of the Central United Presbyterian Church in Phoenix.

Since 1956, Dr. Lewis has been a member of the staff of the Board of National Indian Missions, United Presbyterian Church, as an educational counselor for Indian youth. He acts as a friend and adviser to scores of young people during their high school, college and graduate years, seeking always to guide them in their vocational and educational endeavors. He is a strong and active protagonist for the opening of educational doors and the support of educational opportunities for all Indian people.

BIRTHPLACE: Pima Reservation, Arizona.

MARRIED: Sarah Simmons. CHILDREN: Robert, Rodney, John.

EDUCATION: Tucson Indian School; University of Arizona; Arizona State College (B.A.); San Francisco Theological Seminary (B.D.).

HONORS: Indian Council Fire Achievement Award and honorary life membership (1966); Dubuque University, honorary doctorate (1966).

ORGANIZATIONS: Southwestern Regional Conference (first Indian elected president); National Fellowship of Indian Workers (past president).

SPECIAL ACTIVITIES: Cook Christian Training School (board); Commission on Indian Ministries, National Council of Churches; Ministries with Indians of the Board of National Missions, United Presbyterian Church (advisory board).

LEAFORD BEARSKIN (WYANDOTTE)

Leaford Bearskin entered military service immediately following his graduation from high school. He has made it a lifetime career.

After basic training, he was first assigned to Alaska as a crew chief in World War II. He then entered flying cadet school and, after receiving his pilot wings entered heavy bombardment training. He was sent to New Guinea as an Aircraft Commander on a B-24 Liberator Bomber. Altogether, he flew 46 combat missions in heavy bombers.

He was next assigned to train heavy bomber crews in various phases of warfare before going to Japan as a ground force officer. He was a squadron commander in the Berlin Airlift of 1948, flying 29 missions in this project. Next, he was Squadron Commander, Director of Material and Deputy Commander at a fighter base in Georgia. From this base he participated in the first flight of jet fighter aircraft across the Pacific. He was Air Base Group Commander in support of this flight.

After completing a staff logistics course, he was assigned to a Squadron Commander's position in Korea. His next assignment was as Squadron Commander and Assistant Headquarters Commandant at Strategic Headquarters, Omaha, with the rank of Lieutenant Colonel.

From 1960-63, Colonel Bearskin was employed by Federal

Civil Service as Chief, Vehicle and Aerospace Ground Equipment in the First Strategic Aerospace Division at Vandenberg Air Force Base. There, he was responsible for the supervision of the utilization and maintenance of automotive equipment and for testing, monitoring and analyzing ground handling equipment for the Atlas, Titan, and Minuteman missile weapons systems.

For the next three years, he was at March AFB as Chief, Traffic Management Branch, Directorate of Transportation, Headquarters 15th Air Force. With his promotion to Deputy Director in 1966, he was responsible for the monitoring and development of transportation systems in support of all Fifteenth Air Bases.

Today, Colonel Bearskin is Deputy Director, Directorate of Logistic Plans in the same headquarters. He is second in charge of a plans organization which supervises the planning and operation of material requirements to support war plans for bomber and missile weapons systems located throughout the western states and in several overseas locations. He has completed 31 years of government service, including his military career.

BIRTHPLACE: Wyandotte, Oklahoma.
MARRIED: Peggy Vernon. CHILDREN: Nancy, Ronald.
HONORS: Distinguished Flying Cross; Air Medal; Air Force Outstanding Unit Award; Good Conduct Medal; Presidential Unit Citation; Medal for Humane Action; Asiatic Pacific Campaign (with 4 battle stars); American Campaign Medal; American Defense Service Medal (one bronze star); Occupation Medal (Japan); World War II Victory Medal; United Nations Service Medal; Air Force Longevity Service Award (with 3 bronze Oak Leaf Clusters). Air Force Reserve Medal; three outstanding efficiency ratings; several commendations for "outstanding accomplishments."

ALVIN W. BEARSKIN (WYANDOTTE) AERO-SPACE ENGINEER

Very few people in the world can say that materials with which they worked landed on the moon. As aerospace technician (flight systems) for NASA, Alvin Bearskin evaluated the design and operational function equipment that was taken by the astronauts on moon landings. His concern is with experimental craft, making certain that they are built correctly, function and operate perfectly. They must fit into the spacecraft system, and the system in the spacecraft must be at the peak of perfection. His work takes him all over the country.

Alvin suffered from two bouts of polio when he was a child - at eight months, and again at twelve. Each time, he had to learn how to walk anew. In spite of this, and a shoulder disability, he grew to normal manhood. Between high school and college, he was employed in road construction work, handling all types of heavy duty equipment. In college he lettered in football.

His college training was gained with the help of the GI bill, and with both he and his wife working to defray expenses. He is now a registered aerospace and architectural engineer in several states, with plans to return to college to complete studies for his Master's Degree.

BIRTHPLACE: Wyandotte, Oklahoma.
MARRIED: Mae Wilson.

EDUCATION: Oklahoma State University (B.S.).

MILITARY SERVICE: Army Engineer Corps, World War II, 5½ years - American-European Theatres; Korea (Good Conduct Medal). (In military service he participated in Operation Eager Beaver, which was a cold weather test of men and equipment in the northern Yukon. Temperatures fell to -56).

ORGANIZATIONS: Local, State and National Professional Engineers; Masons (Master; Consistory; Commandery).

LELAND S. BEARSKIN (WYANDOTTE) AIR FORCE MAJOR (RETIRED)

Leland Bearskin, was the first Indian to land an aircraft on the Antarctic Continent, when a Captain and Command Pilot with the UU.S.A.F. His squadron was then engaged in the Air Resupply of scientific stations in that area. He was involved in two phases of the project - known as Operation Deepfreeze. Once, a storm forced him to make an emergency landing with his C-124 crew and passengers. He came down on the edge of the Antarctic after a resupply drop had been made to a scientific station at the South Pole.

Leland first enlisted in the Field Artillery after graduation from high school. He later transferred to the Air Force and was promoted to Flight Officer after completing basic training. He was commissioned Second Lieutenant a year later.

During World War II, he flew C-47 "Gooney Birds," on troop drop and aerial resupply missions in Europe and North Africa. In the Korean Conflict he was pilot for high ranking officers of all services in the Far East, including flights within South Korea. He was an aircraft commander on numerous Arctic resupply drops including the well known DEW line supply. He participated in Exercise Arctic Night, a paratroop drop on Greenland Icecap in 1956 as an aircraft commander. He flew in the Gyroscope Operation between Pope Air Force Base and Japan when an airborne division from this country traded places with a similar division in Japan.

Leland Bearskin "dropped the South Pole" on the Antarctic mission of 1956. The pole was a section of bamboo painted with orange and black stripes. A large reflective globe was mounted at the top. The South Pole station reported that the "pole hit squarely on the geographical South Pole" which was marked by a "T."

On a mission to New Zealand, Leland presented a war bonnet to the Maori natives as a good will gesture from North American Indians. The bonnet had accompanied him on 17 missions over the South Pole and Marie Byrd Land Stations. He also presented an Oklahoma state flag, carried on these same missions, to the Governor of Oklahoma.

He retired from the Air Force in 1961 with the rank of Major.

BIRTHPLACE: Wyandotte, Oklahoma.
HONORS: Air Medal with 5 Oak Leaf Clusters; Outstanding Unit Award; Good Conduct Medal; American Defense Medal; American Theatre Medal; European African Middle Eastern Theatre Medal with 7 major battle stars; World War II Victory Medal; National Service Defense Medal; United Nations Service Medal; Korean Service Medal; Air Force Reserve Medal; Air Force Longevity Service Medal with 3 Oak Leaf Clusters.

WILLIAM J. MUSSELL, JR. (SALISH) SPECIAL ASSISTANT, MINISTER OF INDIAN AFFAIRS OF CANADA

Like his paternal grand-father, Mr. Mussell has been chief of his tribe.

In high school he was an outstanding student and athlete. As a leading, all-around athlete, he won a number of awards and also a sportsmanship trophy. He was among the top ten students all during high school. He was class president from second grade through the twelfth grade.

Throughout his lifetime Mr. Mussell worked exceedingly hard. As a child he did seasonal work along with his family. In a succession of jobs he managed to earn money - by delivering papers; in retail stores; and as a waiter and a cook. He also worked in a pulp mill; a dairy; as a law clerk; and as a research assistant. These varied work experiences taught him the value of perseverance and industriousness. The wide variety of his relationships with other people taught him the importance of working amicably with others.

William and his brother were the first Indian children to attend public school from their community. He was the first from his community to graduate from a University. At the time he was elected chief of his band, he was the only chief in Canada with a university degree. Before he was elected, his mother had served two terms as chief, an unusual accomplishment for an Indian woman.

While still a university student, Mr. Mussell became a member of the executive board of the North American Indian Brotherhood. This position took him to many Canadian reserves and as a result of his work, the organization prepared briefs to the government recommending changes in Indian Affairs administration.

Mr. Mussell has also been treasurer and president of the Vancouver Indian Centre. He served two years as a probation officer and two years as a parole officer. He was appointed to his present position as Special Assistant to the Minister of Indian Affairs, in 1969.

"It was the encouragement of the elders to do well, and the desire to show that Indian people can compete and do well and at the same time serve their people, that spurred me on," Mr. Mussell says. He looks upon his present position as an opportunity to help Indians in a more effective way.

BIRTHPLACE: Sardis, British Columbia.

EDUCATION: University of British Columbia (B.A., B.S.W., Secondary School Teacher's Certificate).

SCHOLARSHIPS: Canadian Legion, British Columbia government; UBC Special Bursary.

AUDRA MARIE PAM-BRUN (BLACKFEET) NURSE

Audra Pambrun is director of Community Health Aides, Blackfeet Community Action Program. She is responsible for the promotion of health and medical care among the 7,000 Blackfeet Indians on their 1,500,000-acre reservation. She drives 2,000 miles a month to counsel and help Indians and non-Indians in their homes.

In addition, Miss Pambrun, who is the second of her tribe to wear a nursing cap, was instrumental in establishing Montana's first suicide intervention crisis center in an effort to reduce the suicide rate among young Blackfeet Indians. This is 47 percent higher than the national rate.

"As a child, I lived with the poverty, the discrimination, the discouragement, and the despair so prevalent today among teenagers," Miss Pambrun says. "Suicide occurs primarily among age groups 12 to 21 years with 15 to 17 being the critical age group. Suicide among Indians in the past was never a problem - but time after time I hear a potential suicide relate that he cannot cope with the conflict between his Indian culture and the so-called mainstream American culture that surrounds him."

For her services in behalf of her prople, Miss Pambrun was honored with a citation by the American Medical Association at their 1970 convention. Earlier, she was selected from 39 state finalists as America's most BE-INvolved Nurse and honored by the American Nurses Association and Schering Laboratories.

BIRTHPLACE: Browning, Montana, January 10, 1929.

EDUCATION: Columbus School of Nursing; University of California, Los Angeles and Berkeley.

ORGANIZATIONS: American Nurses' Association; Montana Nurses' Association; American Suidiology Association; Royal Neighbors of America (Oracle).

SPECIAL INTERESTS: To help young Indian men and women into professional careers.

FLORE LEKANOF (ALEUT) DEPUTY DIRECTOR OF COMMUNITY SERVICES, BUREAU OF INDIAN AFFAIRS

Formerly executive director of Alaska State Community Action, and a former teacher in Alaskan schools, he holds an M.A. in education from the University of Washington. He is newly appointed to his present post.

EDWARD M. RED OWL (DAKOTA-SANTEE) MISSIONARY BENEDICTINE MONK

Brother Red Owl entered the Blue Cloud Abbey in 1962 and has made his final commitment to monastic life. He is Associate Director of the American Indian Culture Research Center at the Abbey, and Executive Secretary, Tekakwitha Conference, an organization of Roman Catholic Missionaries of the Midwest. He is a frequent lecturer on Sioux culture, history and psychology. He also serves as advisor and consultant to various educational and other conferences related to Indian affairs.

He is convinced that "the current Indian generation has the duty and the obligation to establish themselves as equal citizens and to assert themselves articulately and aggressively so as to contribute the richness of their heritage to a society that direly needs enrichment."

Devotion and commitment to this task has been his consuming passion, Brother Red Owl says.

BIRTHPLACE: Santee Indian Reservation, Nebraska, December 21, 1941.
EDUCATION: St. John's College Prep School; St. John's Junior College; Conception College; St. John's University.

ALONZO T. SPANG, SR. (NORTHERN CHEY-ENNE) EDUCATIONAL ADMINISTRATOR

Currently Dean of Student Personnel Services at Navajo Community College, Alonzo Spang was one of the first persons to be hired for the college staff. The college is the only one located on an Indian reservation and controlled by Indians. He gave up a secure position to accept the challenge of helping build a firm foundation for a totally new concept in Indian education.

Before accepting this position, Mr. Spang was Director of Cook Christian Training School. His appointment to that position marked a turning point in the school's history. Mr. Spang was the first Indian and the first non-ordained person to head the school as Director.

Mr. Spang is the first member of his tribe to obtain a Master's Degree and to be in a doctoral program. He still speaks his native language and acts as consultant to his tribe on educational matters. In 1965, the tribe honored him by making him a chief. His grandfather, on his mother's side, was a medicine man.

During his undergraduate days, Alonzo worked his way through college. It took him six years to graduate and for two years during this period, he taught school. His wife helped him through school, and "without her understanding and encouragement, I would not have gained as much as I have," he says.

Throughout his career, Alonzo Spang has been very much involved in various consulting roles on "disadvantaged peoples." He speaks out strongly for Indian involvement and control in all facets of life and is in demand as a speaker at conferences, Indian and non-Indian sponsored, across the country. At one time, he was Project Director of the Indian Community Action Program at Arizona State University. He directed a program which served approximately 50 tribes in seven states - a total of 175,000 Indians.

BIRTHPLACE: Lame Deer, Montana, December 17, 1933.
MARRIED: Clarice M. Daniels. CHILDREN: Jeneen, Alonzo, Jr., Lyndon, Kirk.
EDUCATION: Eastern Montana College (B.S.); University of Montana; University of Chicago; Arizona State University (M.A. Ed.D., pending).
SCHOLARSHIPS: Montana Academic Scholarship; John Hay Whitney Foundation Fellowship.
HONORS: Outstanding Contribution to Indians Award, Scottsdale All-Indian Celebration (1969).
ORGANIZATIONS: National Council of Churches, Division of Indian Work (past vice-president); Kappa Delta Pi; Masons.
SPECIAL ACTIVITIES: Presbyterian Church (several committees); Ganado Learning Center (board). Cook Christian Training School (trustee); Episcopal Training Program (board); Masons; Kappa Delta Pi.

HOWARD ROCK (ESKIMO) EDITOR, TUNDRA TIMES

Mr. Rock's last name is derived from his father's name, "Weyahok," which means "rock" in Eskimo.

In 1935, Howard worked his way to Seattle on a government supply ship for schools and hospitals located in Alaska. He went to Oregon and studied art under an artist friend. This man arranged for him to continue art study at the University of Washington. He remained there for three years.

Later, he found work with a jewelry store and designed ivory jewelry and other items engraved with Eskimo scenes. This work ended when he was drafted into the Air Force. He became a radio operator and though he asked to be stationed in Alaska, he was sent to Tunis, in North Africa, for a period of three years. An Eskimo in Africa was somewhat out of place.

When he was mustered out of service, Howard went back to his jewelry design. After sixteen years of this, he returned to his home village of Point Hope and began to paint oils of Eskimo scenes. His first one-man show was very successful.

Howard took part in village concerns, and during the course of a meeting held to discuss two projects that were causing his people great worry, he mentioned the need for an informative publication. It was again mentioned at a meeting of Eskimo leaders. A way was found to make the publication possible. Through the generous help of an interested friend, the paper - the *Tundra Times* was given birth on October 1, 1962.

Howard was immediately appointed editor, and though he had no experience in journalism, he did understand the problems of his people and was well able to articulate them. He soon began to learn the ropes of the newspaper business. The *Tundra Times* was an unknown quantity, he says, because "it was the first time anything like it had been attempted in Alaska." It was not long before the paper asserted itself authoritatively and both the *Times* and its editor began to receive awards in recognition of a "crusading spirit."

The *Tundra Times* is credited with turning national attention to the plight of the Pribilof Islanders and helping to secure a hearing for their grievances, among other major accomplishments.

BIRTHPLACE: Point Hope, Alaska, August 10, 1911.
EDUCATION: St. Thomas Mission School; government schools in Alaska.
MILITARY SERVICE: U.S. Air Force, 1943-45 - North Africa.

BILLY MILLS (DAKOTA-OGLALA) ATHLETE

Billy Mills, orphaned at the age of thirteen, was faced with many adolescent hardships. Finally, he was sent to Haskell Institute and it was there that he began to compete in sports. He was a three-time winner of the State two-mile cross-country championships, and a two-time winner of the State mile title. When he graduated, he was awarded a full athletic scholarship to the University of Kansas.

In college, he was often discouraged and tempted to drop out, but athletics helped to make life bearable and he "stayed with it." He won many distance races in collegiate competition and represented the United States in the Pan American games at Sao Paulo, Brazil (1959).

While in school, Billy enlisted in the Marine Reserve and was commissioned a second lieutenant upon graduation. At KU, Mills became the Big Eight cross country champion and led the Jayhawks to the NCAA championship. He also ran his first 10,000 meter race and set a conference record of 31 minutes.

In the Marines, he forgot about track and field. Promoted to first lieutenant, he began to think once more of running with the Olympic games to be held in Tokyo. A Marine officer encouraged him to run again and he won the inter-service 10,000 meter run in Germany in 30:08 and got his mile time down to 4:06.

He got down to the business of training for the Tokyo games a year before the games were to start. He ran twice a day, every day, for a total of 100 miles a week. Still not well known in the field of sports, he placed with the Olympic team (1964) and the rest of course, is sports history.

Running against 36 of the greatest distance men in the world, he charged down the track in the last 110 yards of the gruelling 10,000 meter run to set a new Olympic record of

28:24.04. He was the only American runner to win one of the distance races in the Olympic Games.

Billy's race was called the greatest upset in Olympic Games history. During the last 300 yards he was accidentally pushed by one of the runners and fell twenty yards behind, and he came from that far behind to win by .04 of a second.

The president of the International Olympic Committee said that in 50 years of watching the Olympics, "I never saw an American respond better to pressure." Billy himself said that he was determined to make an all-out effort, physically, mentally and spiritually. "Win or lose," he said, "I know that I will hold the key to success in life."

Since the Olympics, Billy has travelled to more than 50 countries and has taken at least one foreign trip every year for the past ten years. He has been in the insurance business, but is now with the Bureau of Indian Affairs as a Public Relations Officer.

BIRTHPLACE: Pine Ridge, South Dakota, June 30, 1938.
MARRIED: Patricia. CHILDREN: Christy, Lisa.
EDUCATION: Haskell Institute; University of Kansas (B.S.).
MILITARY SERVICE: U.S. Marine Corps, 1962-65.

MURIEL H. WRIGHT (CHOCTAW) HISTORIAN

Her role is a dual one in the contemporary life of Oklahoma, inasmuch as Muriel Wright both makes and preserves history. She is noted for her research and writings on the entire scope of the Oklahoma story and is editor of the *Chronicles of Oklahoma* published by the Oklahoma Historical Society.

Many of her numerous writings on various phases of Oklahoma life are used

as standard reference volumes and state adopted textbooks. Her several hundred articles on Oklahoma history, many of which have won national recognition, have appeared in newspapers and periodicals throughout the country. Special notices of her work appear in many authoritative historical volumes.

Miss Wright is also well-known in connection with the marking and preservation of Oklahoma historic sites.

Closely identified with tribal affairs, Miss Wright served for many years as secretary of the Choctaw Committee organized for welfare and educational purposes. As secretary of the Choctaw Advisory Council, she was instrumental in securing the preservation of the last capital of the Choctaw Nation as an historic site and education center. She was also directly involved in the compilation of a Chickasaw language dictionary.

Miss Wright comes from an historic Choctaw family and is also a descendant of the Mayflower Pilgrims. Her father, Dr.

E.N. Wright, was a prominent physician and surgeon. He was president of the Indian Territory Medical Association and initiated the founding of the Oklahoma State Medical Association a year before Statehood. His father was the Reverend Allen Wright, principal chief of the Choctaw Nation. He was an outstanding scholar and held many positions of trust. It was he who gave the state its name of Oklahoma.

BIRTHPLACE: Lehigh, Indian Territory.

EDUCATION: East Central State Normal College; Wheaton Seminary; Barnard College

SCHOLARSHIPS: Rockefeller Foundation Fellow.

HONORS: Distinguished Service Citation, University of Oklahoma and University of Oklahoma Association (1948); Oklahoma Hall of Fame (1950); Annual Matrix Award, Theta Sigma Phi (1941); "Woman of the Year," Business and Professional Women's Club (1950); Award, Soroptimist International (1953); Award of Honor, Oklahoma Public Schools (1957); Honorary LHD, Oklahoma City University (1964); MacDowell Club Award (1948); National Award Camp Fire Girls, one of four women in United States who have done most for youth (1968); Alpha Gamma Delta Distinguished Citizen Award for Outstanding Achievement and Community Service (1970); *Oklahoma, A History of the State and Its People; American Women: Oklahoma, Yesterday, Today and Tomorrow; Who's Who in Oklahoma; A Handbook of Oklahoma Writers; First Families of America; Handbook of American Genealogy.*

AUTHOR: *The Story of Oklahoma* (1949); *Our Oklahoma* (1949); *Our Oklahoma: A History of the State and Its People* (1929) (co-author); articles on Oklahoma, Encyclopedia Britannica (1943-1963); article on Oklahoma, Encyclopedia Britannica, 1968 200th continuous publication anniversary edition (1968).

ORGANIZATIONS: Mayflower Descendants; Daughters of American Revolution; Colonial Dames of XVII Century; United Daughters of Confederacy; National League of American Penwomen (past president, Oklahoma branch); Oklahoma State Writers; Oklahoma Poetry Society; Delta Kappa Gamma; Alpha Gamma Delta; Theta Sigma Phi; Oklahoma City Civil War Round Table (past president); American Association State and Local History.

LUCILLE WINNIE (SEN-ECA-CAYUGA) AUTHOR

Lucille Winnie grew up on several reservations and went from her last place of residence to carve out a career in the larger society about her.

For a time she was a teacher in Indian Service schools. She left teaching to work in Washington in an executive role in the fast-growing aviation industry. She was often the only woman passenger on many of the early airline flights which are now a part of aviation history.

In World War II, she set up and supervised the travel section for the War Production Board. The work became so demanding that it was taking toll of her health, so she went to work for an advertising newspaper as Copy Desk Clerk, and later in charge of the Advertising Copy Desk. After the war, she worked for the Veterans Administration and then spent three years in Hawaii.

On her return to California, she accepted a position with a federally controlled radio-TV station, working in the technical laboratory. She was promoted to network traffic controller, a job she considered to be one of the biggest challenges of her working life.

Various positions followed this experience. She was then assigned to work on the Catawba project in South Carolina. In this project, the Catawba tribe were emancipated from federal and state control and placed on their own. Miss

Winnie was in charge of the vocational and college programs that were organized for the tribe.

Her next important assignment was on the Northern Cheyenne Reservation to develop an arts and crafts program. Now retired, Miss Winnie has set her fascinating life story down in a book that makes equally fascinating reading.

BIRTHPLACE: Oklahoma, March 27, 1904.

EDUCATION: Reservation Schools; Haskell Institute; Michigan Central College; New York State University (Buffalo); University of California (Los Angeles); University of Hawaii.

AUTHOR: *Sah-Gan-De-Oh, the Chief's Daughter* (Vantage, 1969).

GERALD TAILFEATH-ERS (BLOOD) ARTIST

Gerald Tailfeathers has been painting the history of his people since he was ten. He has completed an estimated 400 pen and ink drawings, and oil and tempera paintings since he began his professional career in 1959. He has recently taken up sculpturing.

Attempting to become an artist was very difficult, Gerald says. It required years of sacrifice and many hours of strain and sweat. A scholarship to art school finally launched him on his way. He spent five years in serious study.

The following five years he worked as a display artist, and the next ten years as a draftsman and architect. In his art, Gerald specializes in the buffalo hunting Indians of the Plains, somewhat in the style of Remington.

BIRTHPLACE: Blood Reservation, February 13, 1925.
MARRIED: Irene Goodstriker. CHILDREN: Sherry Lynn, Pamela.
EDUCATION: Banff School of Fine Arts; Southern Alberta Institute of Technology.
HONORS: Invited to do a design for the Indians of Canada Pavilion, Expo '67, Montreal.
EXHIBITIONS: More than 10 major exhibitions; many public and private collections; several one-man shows.
ILLUSTRATIONS: *White Calf* and *White Peril* (children's books); *Western Horseman* (cover); *The Horse in Blackfoot Indian Culture* (cover).

JANIS HERMAN DUKE-POO (DAKOTA-BRULE) SOCIAL SERVICE WORK-ER IN CHILD WELFARE

Mrs. Dukepoo's father worked for the Smithsonian Institution and she learned much about her Indian heritage while taking part in anthropological "digs."

She is presently liaison social worker with the Bureau of Indian Affairs, and concerned with Indian children living in foster homes.

BIRTHPLACE: Igloo, South Dakota, January 9, 1944.
MARRIED: Frank Dukepoo. CHILDREN: Christine.
EDUCATION: Arizona State University (B.S.).
SCHOLARSHIPS: United Scholarship Service; Bureau of Indian Affairs.

FRANK C. DUKEPOO (HOPI-LAGUNA) GENETICIST

Frank Dukepoo is one of the first two Hopi Indians to have a Ph.D. degree. His goal is to teach zoology at the college level in an institution with a large number of Indian students. Prior to completing work for his doctorate, he was an assistant zoology teacher and laboratory instructor at Arizona State University.

BIRTHPLACE: Parker, Arizona, January 29, 1943.
MARRIED: Janis Herman. CHILDREN: Christine.
EDUCATION: Arizona State University (B.S., M.S., Ph.D. (1970).
SCHOLARSHIPS: Arizona State University (2); *Arizona Republic* Newscarrier Scholarship; United Indian Scholarship Service; Bureau of Indian Affairs Scholarship; John Hay Whitney Opportunity Fellowship; Ford Foundation Advanced Study Fellowship.
SPECIAL ACTIVITIES: Playing the saxaphone in bands. He is a former director of the Salt River Indian Band and presently plays with a Latin orchestra night club group.

415

FRED BEAVER (CREEK-SEMINOLE) ARTIST *

Fred Beaver has been painting professionally and consistently winning awards since 1946. He specializes in Seminole Indian subjects.

Fred lost all of his family when he was a boy. Without this support, he was barely able to complete school. Graduating in the depression years, and again without help or encouragement, he could not pursue an art career. Instead, he entered the Indian Service and was employed at the Five Civilized Tribes Agency.

While in high school, he learned to play the piano at an old Indian church near his home. He walked four miles to the church to learn the fundamentals of music from a self-instruction book. Later, he sang for chapel services and with church choirs, and for awhile had his own radio program.

While in military service, Fred had an opportunity to study voice and now is in demand as a singer. He has sung on major radio shows and given many concerts.

When he first began to paint, he entered one small work in the annual show at Philbrook Art Center. This won an honorable mention and gave him his start. Since then, he has won numerous awards, has exhibited in major galleries and has had many one man shows. He has also served as judge for important exhibitions.

416

BIRTHPLACE: Eufaula, Oklahoma, July 2, 1911.

MARRIED: Juanita Brown.

EDUCATION: Haskell Institute.

MILITARY SERVICE: Air Force, World War II, three years North Africa, Sicily, Corsica, Sardinia.

HONORS: Oklahoma All-State football and basketball (1930-31); Waite Phillips Outstanding Indian Artist Trophy, Philbrook Art Museum (1963).

EXHIBITIONS: More than 100 in 34 states and the District of Columbia.

COMMISSIONS: Thunderbird Restaurant and Motel, Oklahoma City, Oklahoma; Seminole Arts & Crafts Center, West Hollywood, Florida (murals).

PUBLISHED WORKS: *Newsweek* (September 4, 1950); American Indian Exposition Program booklet cover (1956); *Museum News,* Anadarko, Oklahoma, cover (June, 1962); *Orbit Magazine, Sunday Oklahoman,* May 10, 1964; January 23, 1966).

* *See art section*

LUCY SQUIRREL GEORGE (CHEROKEE) CRAFTSMAN *

Mrs. George is a maker of fine baskets of honeysuckle - a craft, now rare, but once practiced by her tribe.

During the depression years, Mrs. George found it necessary to supplement her family income. Other Cherokee women were making and selling baskets for income, but unfortunately, Mrs. George had not been taught basketweaving by her mother.

Most of the Cherokee weavers used rivercane or white oak. There was only one woman in the area who wove with honeysuckle vines. Mrs. George felt that it would be a sales advantage to use a material not in general use.

With no teachers available, she had to teach herself. Using only the knowledge that she gained from friends who used white oak splints she adapted this knowledge into a new basketry form. It was not long before she had acquired an impressive skill and began the creation of a wide variety of basketry forms. Through her own creative ability, she added new esthetic dimensions to the art of basketweaving for the Cherokees.

When the Cherokees opened their own crafts cooperative, Mrs. George's interests in basketmaking were challenged to new heights of individual design. Her honeysuckle baskets, perfectly constructed through forty years of successful weaving, have won numerous prizes at the Cherokee annual fairs, at exhibitions in many states and abroad. The rich designs of the baskets, both decorative and utiltarian, make each piece a collector's item.

In the last several years, Mrs. George has begun to demonstrate her weaving and to teach younger Cherokees the skill of her nimble fingers. This year, she was honored with her first one-man show.

BIRTHPLACE: Cherokee, North Carolina, November 17, 1897.
MARRIED: Jacob George. CHILDREN: Ammons, Sherman, Katie, Newman, Alfred.

✱ See art section

FRANK J. SELF (CHOCTAW) MAJOR, U.S. AIR FORCE RETIRED

When he was 16, Frank Self ran away from school, but 29 years later he was honored as an Outstanding Alumnus.

Twelve years of his life were spent in an orphanage and then he entered Haskell Institute. It was in 1938 that he ran away, because his dreams of becoming another Jim Thorpe were shattered because of an injury. Returning to Haskell in 1946, he graduated with honors after eight years spent as a wanderer and in the services of the Army and Navy.

Enrolling as a pre-medical student, Major Self decided to become a teacher, for his experiences in World War II had convinced him that education was the key to a successful life. He returned to Haskell to teach, but with the country again at war, he entered the Air Force.

With his retirement in 1968, he entered the Southwestern Baptist Theological Seminary to prepare for the ministry.

BIRTHPLACE: Hugo, Oklahoma, May 11, 1922.
MARRIED: Delores Weber. CHILDREN: Karen, Sarah, John.
EDUCATION: Haskell Institute; Eastern Oklahoma A&M Junior College; Oklahoma State University (B.S., 1949; M.S., 1951).
HONORS: Outstanding Alumnus, Haskell Institute (1957).
MILITARY SERVICE: U.S. Army-Navy, World War II; Air Force, 1952, - Japan, Formosa, Hawaii, Okinawa, Midway, Korea.

KAY CURLEY BENNETT (NAVAJO) AUTHOR

In 1968, Mrs. Bennett was named New Mexico "Mother of the Year." A year later, she was appointed to the State's Commission on Human Rights by the governor.

Mrs. Bennett was born in a hogan on the Navajo Reservation. She was named Kaibah by her mother, but later shortened this to Kay.

After World War II, she became a teacher-interpreter at Phoenix Indian School, and held this position for seven years. In 1951, she sang in public for the first time, and since has entertained at numerous ceremonials and charity events. She is noted not only for her singing, and recordings of Navajo songs, but also for her collector's item, "Navajo dolls." She is the author of two books - one, the story of her own life, and the other a saga of the Navajos.

In a precedent-making move for a Navajo woman, she ran for County Assessor on the Republican ticket in 1968 but was unsuccessful. It is her conviction that Indians should become involved in civic and political affairs.

BIRTHPLACE: Sheepsprings, New Mexico.
MARRIED: Russell Bennett.
HONORS: New Mexico "Mother Of The Year" (1968).
AUTHOR: *Kaibah* (Westernlore); *A Navajo Saga* (Naylor).

INA BEAUCHAMP HALL (ARIKARA) TEACHER; COMMUNITY LEADER

Mrs. Hall was a delicate child and, even though she suffered a stroke while in high school, she graduated. She was the first person of Indian blood to graduate from that school.

Until her marriage, she taught school. After her marriage she managed a ranch with her husband while raising nine children.

To help with expenses, she accepted a "temporary" teaching position. She improved this school, organized the first 4-H Club and the first PTA, and made the school a center for community activities. At the age of 41, she started to attend summer sessions at a teacher's college. Seven years later, after much hard work and difficulty, including the death of her husband, and the loss of her home, she secured her teaching certificate.

Continuing to teach, she became a school principal, and initiated many improvements and advancements for the benefit of the pupils. She next accepted an appointment with the North Dakota State Extension Service as extension agent for her reservation. In this capacity, she started thirteen, 4-H Clubs, four Homemakers Clubs and four Community Development Clubs. She raised the money to establish a community center and worked to obtain better housing for the reservation Indians.

It would be difficult to list all of the wonderful service rendered by Mrs. Hall in her lifetime. She served three terms on the North Dakota Commission on Adult Education; organized and wrote the curriculum for the first arts and crafts training schools which served as models for other reservations, and started the annual reservation fair, among numerous other activities.

Somehow, she was able to buy another home and to send all of her children to college. She has been a pillar of strength in times of sorrow and need, and a friend to Indian and non-Indian alike.

BIRTHPLACE: Fort Berthold Reservation, March 4, 1905.
MARRIED: Edward Hall. CHILDREN: Adeline, Marjorie, Celeste, Edward, Jr., Donald, Beda, Beverly, Robert, Darrold.
EDUCATION: Dickinson State Teachers College.
HONORS: North Dakota "Mother of the Year," (1966).

HAROLD D. COX (CREEK) ASSOCIATE COMMISSIONER FOR SUPPORT SERVICES, BUREAU OF INDIAN AFFAIRS

As INDIANS OF TODAY went to press, this appointment was officially announced. Mr. Cox served 25 years with the U.S. Air Force. retiring in 1967 with the rank of Lieutenant Colonel. He has held budget and management posts with the Air Force in the Pacific, Berlin and NATO, and has been fiscal officer for the U.S. Office of Education.

HELEN MAYNOR SCHEIRBECK (LUMBEE) DIRECTOR, EDUCATION FOR AMERICAN INDIANS OFFICE, DEPARTMENT OF HEALTH, EDUCATION AND WELFARE

Mrs. Scheirbeck has worked extensively with Indian tribes and communities, Indian young people, Indian-interest organizations, and colleges and universities across the country. Most recently, she was associate director of the Office of Community Development, Bureau of Indian Affairs. Prior to that, she developed and directed the Center for Action on Poverty at the University of Wisconsin. This leadership training program for disadvantaged people served the entire country.

Previously, while participating in the Congressional Fellowship Program, she lived with the Menominee Indians in Wisconsin and studied the transition of a terminated tribe to county government. She also assisted the Menominees in the development of a coordinated anti-poverty effort.

Mrs. Scheirbeck has also been a consultant to the Office of Economic Opportunity, working with Indian tribes in the Midwest, Southwest, and Southeast. While on the staff of the Senate Sub-Committee on Constitutional Rights, she developed the hearings held throughout the country on the rights of Indians. This work culminated in the passage of the Indian Bill of Rights, a part of the Civil Rights Act of 1968.

BIRTHPLACE: Lumberton, North Carolina, August 21, 1935.
MARRIED: N.A. Scheirbeck (div.) CHILDREN: Mary Lorelei.
EDUCATION: Berea College (B.A.).
SCHOLARSHIPS: John Hay Whitney Foundation Fellowship.
ORGANIZATIONS: National Congress of American Indians; National Association of Indian Leaders; American Political Science Association.

ROBERT E. DREW (CREEK) CHIEF, OFFICE OF TRIBAL AFFAIRS, INDIAN HEALTH SERVICE

Mr. Drew is a health career specialist working almost continuously with the Indian Health Service. Early in his employment, he was a community health worker on the Pine Ridge reservation and a teacher in Bureau of Indian Affairs schools.

BIRTHPLACE: Eufaula, O-klahoma, June 12, 1922.
MARRIED: (divorced).
CHILDREN: Iris, Stanley, Priscilla, Michael.
EDUCATION: Bacone Junior College; Oklahoma Southeastern College (B.S.); Oklahoma State University (M.S.). (Football scholarships).
MILITARY SERVICE: U.S. Army (Infantry) World War II, five years. (Purple Heart, Silver Star).
ORGANIZATIONS: National Congress of American Indians.

BERTHA GEORGE (HAIDA) TEACHER AND CERTIFIED DENTAL ASSISTANT

When Bertha George graduated from high school she was the only Indian student among 532 seniors. Her primary education had been in her home village in Alaska.

Her first teaching position was with the Alaska Native Service, working among the Haida, Tlingit, Tsimpsheans, Aleuts and Eskimos. In some of these remote village schools, she taught home economics, including sewing and knitting.

For one year, she was in charge of a new dental fluoride team which traveled all over Alaska. She arranged the itinerary, travel and living quarters. From this work, an interest developed and she later took training for her certificate as a dental assistant. With this achieved, she was employed by the Public Health Service traveling with their Mobile Dental Trailer and working among Indians in the Olympic Peninsula of the State of Washington.

At one time, Bertha taught in the PHS Adult Education Program in the hospital at Mt. Edgecumbe, Alaska. She taught patients in the hospital to speak English, to read and to write. She was also an information specialist in the Alaska exhibit at the Seattle World's Fair. (1962) She is currently a teacher in the Social Studies Resource Center of a Seattle High School.

BIRTHPLACE: Hydaburg, Alaska.

EDUCATION: Bellingham Teachers College; Central Washington State College; Seattle Dental Assistant College.

ORGANIZATIONS: Alaska Native Sisterhood (past Grand Vice-President and secretary); Business and Professional Woman's Club (secretary); Tlingit and Haida Organization (secretary); Seattle Teachers Association.

WAYNE TERRAPIN (CHEROKEE) COMMERCIAL ARTIST

Wayne Terapin had no formal art training until he entered college, although as a child he used to mold animal heads from clay along the creek banks near his home. He spent many hours drawing animals, too, and art was his favorite school subject. He especially liked to draw maps, but drawing was considered a waste of time and he was given no encouragement to pursue it.

During high school, he enrolled in an art class and his teacher wanted him to take up art seriously. This did not come about until he entered Bacone Junior College and began to paint under the supervision of Richard West (see biography).

Wayne began to find Indian art fascinating, and West taught him to realize that to truly paint his people, he must know and learn everything that he could about them. This launched a research program into Cherokee culture, legends and folklore. He has learned all of the traditional customs of his tribe.

BIRTHPLACE: Stilwell, Oklahoma, July 19, 1934.

EDUCATION: Bacone Junior College.

HONORS: National advertising award, U.S. Keds Shoe Company (1960); advertising art award, National American Wholesale Grocers Association (1969).

ALBERT M. HAWLEY (GROS VENTRE-ASSINIBOINE) EDUCATOR; GOVERNMENT ADMINISTRATOR *(Retired)*

Before going into the Indian Service, Mr. Hawley was a teacher-coach in public schools. He retired in 1966, from his position as superintendent of the Fort Apache Agency, but, he is still spoken of with respect, admiration, and affection.

While superintendent, he staked his entire career in the "water fight" between the White Mountain Apaches and the Salt River Users Association. When the Apaches, under his guidance, built the Smith Park Dam, the legal repercussions resulted in national headlines. In appreciation of his personal courage and efforts on their behalf, the Tribe re-named the Smith Park Project "Hawley Lake." He was also given honorary membership in the Tribe.

Reared on the Fort Belknap reservation, Mr. Hawley has spent 32 years in government service. Before his retirement, he was cited for "stimulating and inspiring the Indian people to use their initiative and ability; and for his help and participation in organizing community clubs, self-help housing programs, and his development and management of tribal enterprises."

BIRTHPLACE: Hays, Montana, April 13, 1906.
MARRIED: Lucille Talbot. CHILDREN: Joseph, Albert, Mary, Elizabeth.
EDUCATION: Haskell Institute; Davis and Elkins College (B.S., cum laude); Stanford University (M.A.).

427

HONORS: Distinguished Service Award, Department of Interior (1966); Distinguished Alumni Award, Davis and Elkins College (1968); Outstanding Haskell Alumni (1969).
MILITARY SERVICE: U.S. Navy, World War II, four years. (Commanding Officer, Lend Lease Battallion, Cabiness Field).
ORGANIZATIONS: National Rifle Association; Phoenix Rod and Gun Club; Arizona Rifle and Pistol Association.
SPECIAL ACTIVITIES: American Indian Athletic Hall of Fame (vice-president); Indian Advisory Board, Oshrin Hospital, Tucson (Tribal Relations Consultant).

HERSCHEL SAHMAUNT (KIOWA) TRIBAL RELATIONS OFFICER, BUREAU OF INDIAN AFFAIRS

Mr. Sahmaunt, who received his M.S. from Oklahoma University, organized the Southwest Oklahoma League for Indian Development. He was a staff member of the subcommittee on Indian Education of the U.S. Senate Committee on Labor and Public Welfare before his appointment to his present post.

EUGENE B. WILSON (NEZ PERCE) TRIBAL AFFAIRS OFFICER, IN-DIAN HEALTH SERVICE

As Tribal Affairs Officer in the Phoenix area of the Indian Health Service, Eugene Wilson maintains liaison with all of the tribes in its jurisdiction, and with governmental and private agencies concerned with Indian health.

Before joining the Indian Health Service he was a teacher, guidance officer and vocational counselor in Bureau of Indian Affairs schools, and a teacher-administrator in the Idaho public school system.

BIRTHPLACE: Kamaiah, Idaho, August 15, 1917.
EDUCATION: Sherman Institute; Bacone College (A.A.); University of Idaho (B.S.Ed.); University of Kansas (M.S.Ed.).
MILITARY SERVICE: U.S. Army Air Force, 1941-46 (Captain).

430

JOE DAN OSCEOLA (SEMINOLE) PRESIDENT, SEMINOLE TRIBE OF FLORIDA, INC

Joe Dan Osceola was the first Seminole to graduate from a public high school. He is a descendant of Osceola, the great leader of the tribe during the Seminole Wars.

Joe Dan has been raised in Seminole tradition, but attendance at college brought him to grips with the world outside of the reservation and gave him a good understanding of non-Indian people. He has the responsibility of giving a different kind of leadership than any other Seminole has demonstrated.

Well aware of this, Mr. Osceola believes that the landslide vote that elected him Tribal President signals a change in the attitudes of the older generation. "They've come to realize that we live in an inseparable world where we do the same kind of work, go to the same schools, see the same TV programs, and drive on the same highways," he says.

"Younger Indian generations are becoming less different than white children with whom they go to school," the Seminole leader states. "Mickey Mantle and the astronauts are heroes to Indian youths as well as they are to others."

Mr. Osceola says that his major goals will be to promote understanding and appreciation of his people and to improve their standards of living. As Tribal President, he presides over a $13-million business corporation that includes a cattle program; land development; a revolving credit system; a Seminole Village as a tourist attraction; a textile plant; an industrial plant; a woodcraft shop; and a camp ground.

Recently, the Seminoles were awarded $12,347,500 for land taken from them in the Seminole Wars. In a suit filed 20 years ago, the Seminoles had sought close to $50 million dollars. Mr. Osceola will now have the responsibility of deciding whether to appeal the suit, or to work out, with his people, a satisfactory allocation of these funds.

He is a son of Richard Osceola, one of the great leaders of the Seminoles during the 1920's-30's. It was through him that the Seminole Reservation was established.

BIRTHPLACE: Miles City, Florida, December 20, 1936.
MARRIED: Linda Tiger. CHILDREN: Brian, Wade, Gem, Jo-Lin.
EDUCATION: Public School; Georgetown College.
ORGANIZATIONS: Americans for Indian Opportunity (executive board); United Southeastern Tribes, Inc., (chairman); Lambda Chi Alpha.
HONORS: Commissioned "Kentucky Colonel" (1967); One of "Outstanding Young Men of America," Jaycees (1968).
SPECIAL ACTIVITIES: State of Florida, Commission on Indian Affairs (member); Seminole Tribe Economic Development Committee; South Florida Council, Boy Scouts of America (executive board); American Indian Tribal Leaders; Conference on Scouting (vice chairman).

FRANKLIN H. DUCHENEAUX (CHEYENNE RIVER DAKOTA) ACTING LEGISLATION OFFICER, BUREAU OF INDIAN AFFAIRS

An attorney, Mr. Ducheneaux is the son of a former chairman of the Cheyenne River Tribe. A 1968-69 Congressional Fellow, he has served as Congressional Relations Officer for the BIA and is one of 15 new appointees to the BIA staff as INDIANS OF TODAY went to press. He holds B.S., and J.D. degrees from the University of South Dakota.

NELLIE STAR BOY MENARD (DAKOTA-BRULE) ARTS AND CRAFTS SPECIALIST, TEACHER OF INDIAN CRAFTS

Mrs. Menard's vocational and avocational interests are in all phases of Indian arts and crafts. She is a recognized authority on the crafts of the Dakota people. Because of her excellence in feather work, she was chosen to make the twelve war bonnets that were on display at Expo '67 in Montreal.

Nellie is the originator of the War Eagle Dance Club for the promotion of Indian culture and traditions. This group is well-known throughout the country. She has been honored many times through special ceremonies, given only for a select few, by her people.

BIRTHPLACE: Rosebud Indian Reservation, June 3, 1910.
MARRIED: Clarence Menard. CHILDREN: Clarence, Jr., Michael, James, Stanley, Larry, Cornell, Martina, William, D'Arcy.
EDUCATION: Flandreau Indian School.
HONORS: Superior Performance Award, Department of the Interior, Indian Arts and Crafts Board (1962).
SPECIAL INTERESTS: Interpretation of Indian crafts and culture; encouragment of the talents of craft workers; installation and arrangement of museum displays.

MARCIA ANN BIDDLE-MAN (SENECA) FIRST LIEUTENANT, UNITED STATES MARINE CORPS

Lt. Biddleman is the highest ranking woman Marine on active duty. She has been in training at the U.S. Navy Aerographer's Mate School preparing to become the weather forecaster for the largest Marine installation on the East coast.

Marcia is an enlisted Marine. After "boot camp," she began training in aerography and for two years thereafter was the weather observer at Marine Corps Air Station in California. She was next a Drill Instructor and was selected from among non-commissioned officers to attend the Woman Officer Candidate Class. Commissioned a Second Lieutenant after graduation, she was immediately enrolled in the advanced Woman Officer Basic Course. Upon completion of that course, she received the signal honor of selection to receive the first WOBC leadership award ever given in the Marine Corps Association. She is the only Woman Marine Officer serving as Weather Forecaster.

Marcia's father and grandmother are members of the Wolf Clan of the Seneca Tribe. An ancestor was Clifford Shongo who was a medicine man and carver of false face masks used in ceremonials. She is tremendously interested in Indian customs and culture. With her family participating, a totem pole was carved and erected in the yard of the family home. The pole which took nearly a year to plan, carve, paint and erect tells the story of the family. It has been featured in a number of newspapers.

BIRTHPLACE: Titusville, Pennsylvania, December 7, 1945.
EDUCATION: Military training institutes.
SPECIAL ACTIVITIES: Sponsorship of two children through Christian Children's Home; choir singer, Methodist Church; counselor, Senior and Intermediate Methodist Youth Fellowship.

RONNIE LUPE (APACHE) TRIBAL LEADER

The White Mountain Apaches are said to have made greater progress in the past decade than any other group. A growing network of recreational facilities centered on 16 Apache-built lakes in the past year, alone, brought the tribe some $1.5 million in revenue. A $2 million year-round recreational facility is now being built. The tribe has established a forest products industry and has a thriving cattle business.

As chairman of the White Mountain Apache Tribal Council for three years, Ronnie Lupe was able to bring honor, dignity and national recognition to his progressive and forward looking people. He became known as one of the most dynamic leaders among younger Indians in the country.

Presently Legislative Coordinator for the Tribe Mr. Lupe acts in a liaison capacity between the Apaches and state and federal officials.

BIRTHPLACE: Fort Apache Reservation, 1930.
MARRIED: Vera. CHILDREN: (Five).
MILITARY SERVICE: U.S. Marines, Korea.
SPECIAL ACTIVITIES: Commission of Indian Affairs, Arizona (board); Arizona Regional Medical Program (regional advisory board); National Indian Education Advisory Committee, Bureau of Indian Affairs; Indian Development, District of Arizona (Board); candidate, Arizona State Senate (1970).

ARNOLD T. ANDERSON (IROQUOIS) BUSINESS EXECUTIVE, SCIENTIST

Born and brought up on the Six Nations Reserve in Canada, Mr. Anderson became one of the key members of the team of scientists that undertook the development of atomic energy in World War II.

He collaborated with Professor Albert Einstein and at the conclusion of the war was cited by the United States Government for his valuable services.

Mr. Anderson was unable to complete his university education because of the economic depression of that time and went to work with a sheet metal company. He continued to study at night, however, and became a highly qualified scientist, getting his degree at a later time.

In 1947, Mr. Anderson was employed as director of research for the Union Carbide and Chemical Company. He has fulfilled a number of management assignments and is now Manager of Urban and Public Affairs for the company's Chemicals and Plastics Group. He directs the equal opportunity program, coordinates all aspects of skills training, and assists with community relations and public affairs programs. He has an extensive background of interest and experience in minority group affairs.

BIRTHPLACE: Grand River Reservation, Canada, March 31, 1915.
MARRIED: Elsie Anderson. CHILDREN: Arnold, Jr.; Mark.
EDUCATION: McMaster University (B.A.).

MILITARY SERVICE: Canadian Army World War II, 5½ years.
PROFESSIONAL PUBLICATIONS: Many.
ORGANIZATIONS: American Chemical Society; American Institute of Chemical Engineers; Technical Association of Pulp and Paper Industry; Cellulose Division, American Chemical Society; Technical Libraries Association; Personnel Managers Association; Commercial Chemical Development Association; American Management Association (lecturer); American Association for the Advancement of Science; American Ordinance Association; National Congress of American Indians; The Wilderness Society; Instrument Society of America; Industrial Management Club (president); Chamber of Commerce (many committees, several chairmanships).
SPECIAL ACTIVITIES: Lutheran Church in America (lay reader); Red Cross; Community Chest; Boy Scouts of America; other church and community related activities.

ETHEL BRANT MONTURE (MOHAWK)
PUBLIC RELATIONS

Mrs. Monture has successfully sought participation in the mainstream of Canadian life. She is a lecturer, author, an expert on Indian culture, and a specialist in Iroquois history.

She is a great-great-granddaughter of Colonel Joseph Brant, the celebrated Mohawk chief who was commissioned for his part in the Pontiac War of 1763. Brant was one of the outstanding Indian leaders involved in the American Revolution, even though he fought on the side of the English. In return for these services Brant was given a tract of land six miles wide on each side of the Grand River in Ontario.

Mrs. Monture is now working on the Brant genealogy. Professionally, she reviews textbooks for bias against Indians for the Ontario Department of Education.

For eleven years, Mrs. Monture worked with the Canadian Council of Christians and Jews promoting better understanding of Indians. She has also been a hospital laboratory technician. Mrs. Monture has lectured widely on Indian affairs and has spoken for Indian rights before government bodies.

BIRTHPLACE: Six Nations Reservation, Ontario, Canada.
MARRIED: Wilbur Monture. CHILDREN: Cameron, Alice Monture Edward.
EDUCATION: Reservation and public schools.

438

WALTER RICHARD WEST (CHEYENNE) ARTIST

Richard West, for many years director of the art department of Bacone College, is in the foreground among Indian artists. He first began to develop his outstanding artistic ability in elementary school and has consistently progressed to fame and honor.

Mr. West is known for his traditional Indian paintings and for his portraits, abstractions, and other European-derived style works.

He is especially noted for a series of religious paintings showing Christ as an Indian.

BIRTHPLACE: Darlington, Oklahoma, September 8, 1912.

MARRIED: Maribelle McCrea (dec.). CHILDREN: Walter, Jr., James. MARRIED: Rene Wagner.

EDUCATION: Concho Indian School; Haskell Institute; Bacone Junior College; University of Oklahoma (B.F.A., M.F.A.); University of Redlands; Tulsa University.

HONORS: Honorary Doctor of Humane Letters, Eastern Baptist College (1963); Delta Phi Delta (honorary art); Outstanding Cheyenne of the Year (1968) Teacher of the Year Citation, Bacone College (1969); *Who's Who in American Art; Who's Who in the South and Southwest; Who's Who in Oklahoma; Personalities of the South; American Indian Painters.*

MILITARY SERVICE: U.S. Navy, World War II (Lieutenant) convoy duty on the Atlantic.

AWARDS: Three grand prizes among many firsts and others. Waite Phillips award and trophy, Philbrook Art Center.

SOLOMON COOK (MO-HAWK) EDUCATOR FARMER

As far as it is known, Solomon Cook is the only Indian teaching agriculture in New York State. He is also a guidance counselor. In addition to his teaching activities, he owns a large dairy farm with a herd of Holstein cows.

Dr. Cook worked his way through college, and he says to succeed one must be willing to work. He earned about 80 percent of his expenses as a baby sitter, dishwasher, waiter, janitor and office boy. With this income and borrowed funds, he completed the studies for his three degrees.

After military service, Dr. Cook taught horticulture at South Dakota State College where he was also engaged in research on vegetable crops.

BIRTHPLACE: Hogansburg, New York, January 8, 1920.

MARRIED: Mary Jacobs. CHILDREN: Michele Ann.

EDUCATION: Reservation school, public high school, Cornell University (B.S., M.S.A., Ph.D.).

MILITARY SERVICE: U.S. Navy, World War II -two years, South Pacific, Philippines, Okinawa, Japan (Philippine Liberation Medal; Victory Medal).

ORGANIZATIONS: Salmon River Teachers Association; Northern Zone Teachers Association; New York State Teachers Association; New York State Personnel and Guidance Association; American Dairy Association; Dairy Council of New York; Eastern Artificial Breeders Cooperative; New York State Holstein-Fresian Association; Holstein Fresian Association of America; American Indian Historical Society.

SPECIAL ACTIVITIES: Commission on Human Rights.

AGNESS SAVILLA (MO-HAVE) TRIBAL LEADER

Mrs. Savilla has dedicated her life in service to her own people, and to Indians in general.

For many years a teacher, she first taught on the Navajo reservation. Elected to the Colorado River Tribal Council in 1943, she was continuously on that body until 1968 when she retired from tribal politics. She is the only woman to have been a Tribal Council member. She continues to serve as Chairman of the Health, Education and Welfare Committee, having held this office since 1955.

A well-known tribal historian and genealogist, she has worked with a number of distinguished anthropologists in such studies. She is active, too, in developing the arts and crafts of the reservation. She has a special interest in neglected children and has raised a number of these as her own. She was influential in establishing the foster home operated and supported by the Colorado River Tribes.

BIRTHPLACE: Parker, Arizona.
MARRIED: William Savilla. CHILDREN: (1).
EDUCATION: Haskell Institute.
HONORS: "Arizona Fair Lady Award," *Arizona Republic* (1964); Special Service Award, Outstanding Arizona Indians, Phoenix Indian Basketball Association (1960); Citation of Merit for Outstanding Contribution in Encouraging Employment of the Handicapped, Social Advisory Group to Governor of Arizona.
ORGANIZATIONS: National Congress of American Indians (past regional vice-president); U.S. delegate to Inter-American Congress on Indians in Quito, Ecuador (1964).

ROBERT L. MILLER (SEMINOLE-CREEK) EDUCATOR

At one time, Robert Miller was the publisher of a weekly newspaper, and was engaged in that occupation for 26 years. He developed a program for Oklahoma veterans that included on-job training in the newspaper field.

Mr. Miller had been out of school for more than 20 years when he decided to return and complete courses required for a degree. Eight years ago, he was one of four men instrumental in starting a program for adult Indian education in Oklahoma. This adult Indian center is believed to be the first of its kind among colleges and universities. It led to the Indian Education Program in the Southwest Center for Human Relations Studies at the University of Oklahoma. Mr. Miller directs this program, and edits the *Indian Education* news letter which reports on activities within the program.

One of five Seminoles, Mr. Miller, serves on the Five Civilized Tribes Inter-Tribal Council. He worked for several years to obtain permission from the Bureau of Indian Affairs so that Oklahoma Seminoles could vote on their tribal constitution. The Seminoles are the only one of the Five Civilized Tribes to have a constitution and to elect tribal leaders. The Five Nations were abolished by Congress in 1906 after granting Oklahoma Statehood. The Seminole Constitution was adopted in 1969.

BIRTHPLACE: Wewoka, Oklahoma, November 11, 1908.
MARRIED: Juanita Allison. CHILDREN: Susan.
EDUCATION: Oklahoma State University (BA).
MILITARY SERVICE: U.S. Army, Field Artillery, World War II - 1942-1943.

CARL NELSON GORMAN (NAVAJO) ARTIST

Carl Gorman, a distinguished artist, is one of the first to lead Navajo artists in new directions. He believes in the traditional, but also in the adaptation of the traditional to the modern in any area of the arts.

One of the Navajo "code talkers" who served so valuably in World War II, Carl used money from the GI Bill to realize his dream of formal education. Since then he has been a technical illustrator for Douglas Aircraft, co-owner of a silk screen design company, manager of the Navajo Arts and Crafts Guild, and an instructor on Indian art at the University of California, Davis campus.

A member of the Black Sheep Clan, Carl Gorman comes from a noted Navajo family. HIs parents founded the first Presbyterian Mission at Chinle, Arizona. His father was a cattleman and Indian trader and his mother a fine weaver who taught her skill to other Navajo women. She also translated many hymns into Navajo. Others in the family background were leaders and excellent silversmiths.

BIRTHPLACE: Chinle, Arizona, October 5, 1907.
MARRIED: Adella Brown (div.) CHILDREN: Rudolph. Mary E. Wilson. CHILDREN: Alfred Kee, Zonnie Marie.
EDUCATION: Rehoboth Mission; Albuquerque Indian School; Otis Art Institute.
MILITARY SERVICE: U.S. Marines, World War II (code talker) Guadalcanal, Tarawa, Saipan.

HONORS: *American Indian Painters;* mentioned in numerous books; Special Honors, Fourth Division Marine Association.

EXHIBITIONS: More than 25 major exhibitions; eight one-man shows.

AWARDS: Nine major awards in various art media including oil, watercolor, ceramic painting, mosaic, silver design. Included in 23 public and private collections.

PUBLISHED WORKS: *Westways Magazine* (August 1956 and 1962, cover).

ORGANIZATIONS: Inter-tribal Indian Ceremonial Exhibit Committee; American Society for Ethno-History.

SPECIAL INTERESTS AND ACTIVITIES: Study of the rock art of the Chumash Indians; tracing pre-Columbian cultural relationships in the Americas through art forms; Overall Economic Development Program, Navajo Tribe.

FRANK DAY (MAIDU) ARTIST

Frank Day, 66 years old, is historian of his tribe. He has had no formal training as an artist and did not begin to paint until quite late in life. Developing a style and technique entirely his own, he paints entirely in the realm of Maidu history and mythology. There is no known California Indian Painter whose work has been based solely on the culture of his tribe.

Day's style is primitive but with a certain degree of sophistication. He has to his credit some 300 paintings that are mainly in private collections. There is a surrealistic feeling to his later works, all powerfully vigorous in shape, color and form.

CLARENCE H. GORMAN (NAVAJO) NATIONAL PARK RANGER

Clarence Gorman is the first Indian to be appointed a National Park Ranger.

His first assignment was duty at Mesa Verde National Park in Colorado. There, he was included in a TV documentary produced by the National Geographic Society. The film, entitled *America's Wonderland; The National Parks,* has been shown over the CBS network.

Gorman, who has been a teacher and a seasonal park ranger at Canyon de Chelly National Monument, is now superintendent of the Pipestone National Monument, Minnesota.

BIRTHPLACE: Chinle, Arizona.
MARRIED: Helen Draper. CHILDREN: Duane, Clarissa, Joceline.
EDUCATION: Northern Arizona University.
MILITARY SERVICE: U.S. Marine Corps, 1951-54 (United Nations Medal, Korea Service Medal, Presidential Unit Citation, Good Conduct Medal, National Defense Medal).

ANSON BAKER (MANDAN-HIDATSA) SUPERINTENDENT, FORT PECK AGENCY

Mr. Baker has been with the Bureau of Indian Affairs for 20 years, working on eight different reservations during that time.

The superintendency at Fort Peck is his first such position. As a career employee, he believes that the BIA is only a tool to help Indians help themselves. "The BIA shouldn't take the leading role," Mr. Baker says, predicting at the same time that "it will continue to diminish, especially from operating a reservation as a custodial institution." With the replacement of the BIA, he believes there will be increasing participation by Indians in reservation, community, and civil affairs.

As superintendent, Mr. Baker has assisted the Fort Peck Tribes in bringing an industrial plant to the reservation. An industrial park, and other long range plans are under consideration for reservation improvement.

BIRTHPLACE: Elbowoods, North Dakota, May 26, 1927.
MARRIED: Almeda Smith. CHILDREN: Thomas, Cheryl, Bonnie, Anson, Quince, James, Jefferson.
EDUCATION: North Dakota State College; Minot Business College.
HONORS: Special Recognition, Oglala Sioux Tribal Council (1960); Certificate of Superior Performance, Bureau of Indian Affairs (1964); Special Recognition, Fort Belknap Community Council (1964); Boss of the Year Award (1966; 1968); Special

Recognition, Fort Peck Tribal Industries (1969; 1970).

MILITARY SERVICE: U.S. Navy, 1945-46.

ORGANIZATIONS: American Legion.

ROSELLA HIGHTOWER (CHOCTAW) BALLERINA

Miss Hightower's parents came west by wagon train to settle in Indian Territory which was to become the State of Oklahoma. Shortly after her birth, they moved to Kansas City where her ballet training began. She studied under private teachers and, after an audition before the great Massine, she received an appointment to the Ballet Russe de Monte Carlo. She spent two years with this company; then, returning to America, became a soloist with the American Ballet Theatre.

She danced all of the great ballets in the classical repertory and then joined the original Ballet Russe for a tour of North and South America. She next became the Grand Ballerina of the newly-formed Grand Ballet of the Marquis de Cuevas. She gained international acclaim as the head of this company for many years. She also toured for two years with the Ballet Theatre of Lucie Chase at the request of the American government.

After this tour, she returned to the Theatre of the Champs Elysees and presented a number of new productions packing the house night after night. She left the company following the death of the owner and formed her own Center of Classical Dance in Cannes. This is an academy with boarding students who follow scholastic studies along with the complete formation of the classical dance.

In 1967, she was one of the four Oklahoma ballerinas who appeared in the world premier of *The Four Moons* in Tulsa.

BIRTHPLACE: Ardmore, Oklahoma.

MARRIED: Jean Robier. CHILDREN: Dominque.

447

GEORGE CLUTESI (SE-SHAHT) ARTIST/AU-THOR/LECTURER

George Clutesi spent 21 years of his life as a pile driver. Then his back was broken in an accident and for seven years he could not work. A year after the accident, he began to paint in an instinctive return to his own Indian values. It was during this time that he produced some of his finest paintings.

Although he was to become an established artist and writer, there were 13 years of hard labor ahead when he was able to work again. In the winter, he was pile driving; in the summers, he worked on the fishpackers. But, the creative process had begun and could not be denied.

Aside from painting, he has taught adult education classes on Indian culture; has appeared in TV documentaries and special programs; has travelled across Canada on lecture tours; and teaches Indian culture as a resident member of the University of British Columbia's summer staff. He has taught Indian dancing under a Canada Council Grant.

In 1967, he wrote his first book which is used as an elementary textbook in Canadian schools. His second book was published in 1969, and his third - written especially for his three sons comes out in 1971.

BIRTHPLACE: Port Alberni, British Columbia, January 1, 1905. MARRIED: Margaret Lauder. CHILDREN: George Jr., Coleen, Barbara, Carol, Edward, Guy.

448

EDUCATION: Reservation school.

EXHIBITIONS: More than 12 major exhibits; several one-man shows; three canvasses in Seattle World's Fair (1962); commissioned to paint mural at Expo '67, Montreal.

AWARDS: Citation for contributions to British Columbia, British Columbia Centennial (1959); Canada Centennial Medal, for valuable services to the nation (1967).

AUTHOR: *Son of Raven, Son of Deer* (1967); *Potlatch* (1969); *Stand Tall, My Son* (to be published 1971).

ORGANIZATIONS: British Columbia Indian Arts and Welfare Society (honorary life member); Alberni Valley Arts Society; Port Alberni Arts Council.

JAMES HENA (PUEBLO-TESUQUE-ZUNI) ASSISTANT COMMISSIONER, BUREAU OF INDIAN AFFAIRS

Mr. Hena has just been named to specialize in the Equal Employment Opportunity Program as an assistant to the Commissioner of Indian Affairs. He previously served as Director of Development, Navajo Community College, and Executive Director, Indian Community Action Programs and Program Specialist, EDA.

JOHN O. CROW (CHERO-KEE) ASSOCIATE DIREC-TOR, BUREAU OF LAND MANAGEMENT, DE-PARTMENT OF THE IN-TERIOR

Mr. Crow, a thirty-year veteran of the Bureau of Indian Affairs, was acting commissioner for one year. His experience in Indian affairs brought him to the opinion that the government's most important role as it relates to Indians is to help them help themselves. Accordingly, he developed procedures for adjusting individual tribes to the responsibilities of private citizenship once they chose to end their status as wards of the federal government.

Before entering government service, Mr. Crow played professional football. His first assignment with the BIA was as a junior clerk at the Truxtion Canyon Agency which he subsequently served as superintendent. He was next superintendent at Mescalero, Fort Apache, and Uintah-Ouray Agencies.

Transferred to Washington as deputy assistant commissioner in charge of resources he later became chief of the realty division. He was deputy commissioner of the BIA until he took his present post.

BIRTHPLACE: Springfield, Missouri, September 7, 1912.
MARRIED: Bernese M. Bonga. CHILDREN: Juanita.
EDUCATION: Haskell Institute.
HONORS: Special Service Award, Department of the Interior (1964); Career Service Award, National Civil Service League (1964); Distinguished Service Award, Department of Interior (1968).

A.E. HAGBERG (ESKIMO) VICE-PRESIDENT, MARKETING, WIEN CON-SOLIDATED AIRLINES

Mr. Hagberg was "born" for the airplane industry. As a child, he would dash to the landing strip to meet bush pilot planes when they came to the remote village where he lived. As "self-appointed cargo man" he would help unload the planes and sort and stack the mail sacks and cargo boxes.

When his family moved to Fairbanks, "Bud" Hagberg entered high school. The family had barely gotten settled with he applied for a job with Wien Airlines. He was hired to do odd jobs around the hangar after school hours.

It was apparent that his interest lay in the aviation business and he caught on quickly. He worked in various departments as mechanics's helper, cargo handler, cargo supervisor and at times flight attendant. He progressed to dispatcher, general traffic manager and eventually to vice-president of traffic and then vice-president, traffic and sales. He has been vice-president-marketing for Wien for the past two years.

In his work, Mr. Hagberg has travelled widely and generated much good will for Alaska. He is one of the originators of the World Eskimo Olympics. He comes from an interesting family, His mother is an Alaskan woman, well-known for her "Wright Parkeys," and his uncle was an Alaska Territorial Senator.

BIRTHPLACE: Haycock, Alaska.
MARRIED: Bernice Schley.
EDUCATION: Public schools; American University.
ORGANIZATIONS: Lions; Alaska Visitors Association; Alaska
Travel Promotion Association; Fairbanks Chamber of Commerce
(past president); Alaska State Chamber of Commerce (Board);
National Defense Transportation Association.

LETITIA CALDWELL (CHIPPEWA) TRIBAL LEADER

The mother of eight children, Mrs. Caldwell still finds time to
work for others. Her main interest is in Indian youth. She is a
member of the school board in the Menominee Indian Reservation School District and a member of the Advisory Committee and Curriculum Sub-Committee of the College of
Environmental Sciences, University of Wisconsin. She is also a
member of a federally-funded experimental program in education in the Menominee schools and is active in the CAP
governing board. She helped to organize the Menominee
County PTA and the annual Youth Recognition banquet. She
is secretary to the Menominee Indian Historical Foundation; a
charter member of Indian Trails, Inc., an Indian cooperative;
president of the Menominee County Woman's Club and
secretary of the Menominee County Republican Party. In
1970, she was chosen "woman of the Year" by the Business
and Professional Woman's Club.

NAPOLEON B. JOHNSON (CHEROKEE) ATTORNEY SUPREME COURT JUDGE

In his lifetime, Mr. Johnson has made an indelible imprint on society, an imprint which enures to the benefit of Indian people. His counsel and advice in promoting Indian insterests is known nation-wide.

In his state, he served six years as County Attorney; two years as City Attorney; fourteen years as District Judge of the Twelve Judicial Districts of Oklahoma; and sixteen years as Supreme Court Justice.

As the first president of the National Congress of American Indians, he served nine consecutive terms. During his tenure in office the organization gained national recognition and prestige. He was a guiding light in the formation of the Congress in 1944.

For many years, Mr. Johnson represented the Cherokee Nation on the Inter-Tribal Council of Five Civilized Tribes, and for twelve years was president of the National Hall of Fame for Famous Indians. For a number of years he was the Oklahoma Governor's representative on the Governor's Interstate Indian Council.

BIRTHPLACE: Maysville, Oklahoma.
MARRIED: Martha Lee Weber. CHILDREN: Betty Johnson Alexander.

EDUCATION: Cherokee Nation schools; Eastern University Preparatory School; Kendall College; Cumberland University (LLB).

HONORS: Honorary Doctor of Laws, Howard College; Indian Council Fire Achievement Award and honorary life membership (1955); Outstanding Indian of Year, All-America Indian Days (1955).

ORGANIZATIONS: National Hall of Fame for Famous American Indians (board); Oklahoma Historical Society (past board); Rotary International (honorary member); Scottish Rite Mason; Delta Theta Phi.

ALEXANDER MacNABB (MICMAC) DIRECTOR OF OPERATING SERVICES, BUREAU OF INDIAN AFFAIRS

Mr. MacNabb has responsibility for personnel management, plant construction, and property management. He comes to the BIA from the OEO where he served as special assistant to the director of CAP programs, as one of 15 new appointees in key executive positions announced as INDIANS OF TODAY went to press. He holds a B.A. degree from Colgate University and a J.D. from Washington and Lee.

PHIL TERRY NEW-KUMET (CADDO) PSYCHOLOGIST

Terry Newkumet is a recent graduate psychologist. After completing his college freshman year, he entered a planned program of major work in psychology, anthropology and sociology. He finished the requirements for his undergraduate degree in just 3½ years. He was already enrolled in graduate courses when he received his bachelor's degree with honors. He finished his training in the Army ROTC and was commissioned a second lieutenant in the Army Reserve.

While completing his graduate studies, Terry worked as a graduate assistant in Psychology I. Until he received his orders to report for active military duty, he worked in the public relations office of the University of Oklahoma. He is presently on active military duty.

Throughout his entire schooling, from high school on, Terry chalked up an impressive record of work and study. He was consistently an honor student, and an officer in school organizations. He was a University Scholar, one of the first group selected through tests and interviewing from 500 participants.

BIRTHPLACE: Savannah, Georgia, March 25, 1945.
MARRIED: Pamela Greenshields.
EDUCATION: University of Oklahoma (B.A., M.S.).
SCHOLARSHIPS: Bureau of Indian Affairs; Sequoyah Scholarship,

455

Association on American Indian Affairs.

HONORS: Phi Eta Sigma (honorary scholastic); Phi Beta Kappa (honorary, arts and sciences); National Merit Commendation (high school).

ROBERT J. PEREAU (DAKOTA-SISSETON) SUPERINTENDENT, GREAT LAKES INDIAN AGENCY

From previous positions as a finance specialist, wholesale salesman and retail proprietor, Mr. Pereau accepted the position of credit officer for the newly formed credit branch at the Cherokee Indian Agency.

In this branch he was responsible for the preparation and processing of a number of large loans and grants on behalf of the tribe. Among them, he developed documents and procedures to provide long term financing to the Cherokee people through the Small Business Administration and through state and national banks. This was the first long term financing received on the reservation through normal loan channels. It accelerated commercial development of the reservation and is currently a successful feature of the area.

He also developed documents and procedures to provide FHA insured financing for new home construction through banks and mortgage companies, another first for the reservation.

As superintendent of the Great Lakes Agency, he is responsible for the administration of the affairs of tribes residing in Wisconsin and Michigan.

BIRTHPLACE: Webster, South Dakota, April 12, 1926.
MARRIED: Janet Fisher. CHILDREN: Gregory, Douglas, Jory.
EDUCATION: University of South Dakota (BSC).
MILITARY SERVICE: U.S. Navy, 1944-46.
ORGANIZATIONS: Veterans of Foreign Wars; Lions.

TROMBLEY JOHN WAKEFIELD (OTTAWA) SCHOLAR

Trombley Wakefield has intently pursued a scholastic career and is now preparing to enter the legal profession. He is a student at Harvard Law School.

He has received a number of honorary scholarships and has been nominated for Rhodes, Wilson, Fulbright, and Marshall Scholarships.

BIRTHPLACE: Grand Rapids, Michigan, April 14, 1943.

EDUCATION: Dartmouth College (A.B. with distinction); London School of Economics (M.Sc. with distinction).

SCHOLARSHIPS: Alfred Sloan Scholarship; Dartmouth General Scholarship; Joseph Martin Scholarship; Harvard University Scholarship; James Martin Scholarship.

LLOYD H. NEW (CHERO-KEE) DIRECTOR, INSTITUTE OF AMERICAN INDIAN ARTS

Lloyd New is famous as a designer in leather, fabrics and fashions. His development of hand-dyed fabrics brought new excitement into casual clothing. He has been invited to participate in many important fashion shows and his textile designs have been presented in major exhibits.

Mr. New was a charter member of the crafts movement in Scottsdale, Arizona, now world famous as an arts and crafts center. In 1950, he founded Scottsdale's FIFTH AVENUE, converting it from an alfalfa field and orange grove into a street of specialty shops catering to sophisticated shoppers from around the world.

Operating under the name of Lloyd Kiva, he founded the Kiva Craft Center, comprised of 40 specialty shops, his own included. This exclusive high-fashion establishment enjoyed an international reputation for handcrafted leathers, Indian-woven tweeds and hand printed fabrics. Mr. New (Kiva) championed the regional expression and use of native form.

In 1959, Mr. New obtained a Rockefeller Foundation grant for an experimental program in art education for Indian students at the University of Arizona. In 1962, he was appointed arts director of the Institute of Indian Arts, and in 1967 to his present position as director. Under his leadership, the Institute is noted for its effective teaching techniques and high quality expressions in music, drama, creative writing, the fine arts, and crafts.

BIRTHPLACE: Fairland, Oklahoma, February 18, 1916.

MARRIED: Azalea Thorpe. CHILDREN: Jeffrey, Nancy (by previous marriage).

EDUCATION: Oklahoma State University; University of New Mexico; Art Institute of Chicago (B.F.A.).

MILITARY SERVICE: U.S. Navy (Seabees) 1941-1945) (Lieutenant, U.S. Navy Reserve).

PUBLISHED WORKS: *Forever Indian; The Gods Will Hear* (lyrics for choral works).

ORGANIZATIONS: World Crafts Council; American Crafts Council; Heard Museum (vice-president); Indian Arts and Crafts Board, Department of the Interior (commissioner); New Mexico Arts Commission; Center for Indian Arts of America (trustee).

ERNEST STEVENS (ONEIDA) DIRECTOR OF COMMUNITY SERVICES, BUREAU OF INDIAN AFFAIRS

Formerly head of the Indian CAP program in California, of the Inter-Tribal Council of California and executive director of the Los Angeles Indian Center, Mr. Stevens is newly announced in his present position. He is responsible for housing, welfare and other social aid programs.

EDWARD O. PLUMMER (NAVAJO) SUPERINTENDENT, EASTERN NAVAJO AGENCY

Mr. Plummer comes from a traditional Navajo family. He was born and raised in a hogan, cared for the family sheep, and grew up as any Navajo child coming from the same background.

Mr. Plummer was employed by the Navajo Tribe in the Lands Division for more than eleven years. He became very concerned with land ownership and use problems as they related to 25,000 off-reservation Navajo people. As chairman of the committee that dealt with these matters, he participated in the initial study and plan for resolving these problems. The committee established a number of objectives and initiated a type of land administration by which the Navajo people have their lands under their use and their own control.

As the second Navajo to serve as an agency superintendent, Mr. Plummer strongly believes that Indian people can best help themselves by becoming involved in all affairs pertaining to them. He encourages Indian parents to support their children in all educational endeavors, for it is up to "the Navajo youth to go beyond to help their people."

BIRTHPLACE: Tohatchi, New Mexico, January 7, 1928.
MARRIED: Georgia Wauneka. CHILDREN: Debra, Della (adopted).
EDUCATION: Rehoboth Mission School; Navajo Methodist Mission School; Bacone College; New Mexico Highlands University;

University of New Mexico.

SCHOLARSHIPS: Navajo Tribal.

MILITARY SERVICE: U.S. Army 1951-53, Military Intelligence, Japan.

ORGANIZATIONS: American Right-of-Way Association; New Mexico Commission of Indian Affairs; Inter-Tribal Ceremonial Association; Eastern Navajo Housing Association, Inc.; Eastern Navajo Indians, Inc.

CECILE GRAY EYES (CREE-OJIBWAY) CLOISTERED NUN

Born on the reservation and educated at an Indian school, Cecile is Sister Mary of Christ the Priest, a member of a cloistered order of *Soeurs Servantes de Jesus Marie.* She is believed to be the only cloistered Indian nun in Canada, although there are Indian members of other orders.

She was English-speaking, with a bit of Cree, before entering the all-French Order. She now speaks English with a strong French accent. She speaks and writes French fluently.

She was 21 when she first entered the order. She spent eight years preparing for her formal acceptance as a professed nun.

HOWARD C. WALKINGSTICK (CHEROKEE) SOCIAL WELFARE CONSULTANT, BUREAU OF INDIAN AFFAIRS

Howard Walkingstick is one of the outstanding social workers of the country, and is also internationally recognized for his work.

His eminent and humanitarian career, marked by an exceptional ability to work with Indian and non-Indian groups, has brought him a number of honors.

Mr. Walkingstick has been employed with the BIA in situations across the country. He has served approximately 35 tribes, pueblos, and villages in nine states. He provides a vigorous leadership for those he contacts, and has contributed greatly to the alleviation of differences between state welfare programs and the federal government. He serves on many committees and organized the first New Mexico Conference on Social Welfare which involved Indian participation. He also teaches courses in philosophies, commentaries and case studies in administration for the Army.

In his present position with the BIA, Mr. Walkingstick acts as technical Social Welfare Consultant and advisor to the Area Director. He provides consultation and technical supervision to five Indian agencies covering 35 counties in western Oklahoma, two counties in Kansas, one county in Nebraska, and liaison service to the Alabama-Coushatta tribe in Texas.

BIRTHPLACE: Tahlequah, Oklahoma, January 7, 1915.
EDUCATION: George Washington University (BA); University of

Denver School of Social Work (M.SW.); University of Chicago, School of Social Services Administration.

HONORS: *Who's Who in Oklahoma; Who's Who in the Southwest; Outstanding Personalities in the South; Dictionary of International Biography;* Distinguished Service Award, Department of Interior (1967); Distinguished Service Award, Oklahoma Health and Welfare Association (1967).

MILITARY SERVICE: U.S. Army, 1943-46.

ORGANIZATIONS: Oklahoma Health and Welfare Association; Oklahoma Rehabilitation Association; Oklahoma Mental Health Association; Caddo County Health Association; American Public Welfare Association; National Association of Social Workers; 32nd degree Mason; National Federation of Federal Employees; American Society for Public Administration.

SPECIAL ACTIVITIES: Governor's Committee of the Handicapped.

MARIA MONTOYA MARTINEZ (PUEBLO-SAN ILDEFONSO) INTERNATIONALLY FAMOUS POTTERY MAKER *

Maria Martinez stands unique as one who has developed an art into an industry, the main product of a whole community. Through her efforts, the income of San Ildefonso Pueblo was so increased from pottery sales, that it now exceeds the revenue from farm products, for many years its main source of wealth.

Maria's story is also the story of her husband, Julian, who was a janitor at the New Mexico State Museum. When Maria began to think seriously about pottery she spent hours studying ancient vessels. With the encouragement of one of the members of the museum staff, she began to apply some of the motifs to her own art. Soon her interest became more than idle curiosity - she had found her niche in life.

Hoping to build up a distinctive art form for her own people, she tried to discover the secret of some highly-polished black ware, of which only a few shreds had been found. She experimented for years, experiencing many disappointments before learning that it was the method of firing that produced the satiny-black finish so much a part of the beauty of the ancient process.

Now, though the finish was perfected, any decoration disappeared when the clay was fired, Maria again became a scientific researcher. With patient effort, she produced a fluid that fired as a dull black etched effect against the high lustre of the pottery. San Pueblo is the only Pueblo that makes this pottery today. It is easily recognized and is outstanding in quality.

Maria's perfect pieces won many prizes. The making of the pottery was hers - while Julian, who assisted so faithfully during all of the discouraging trials - was actually responsible for applying the decoration. The couple autographed their finished pieces. Pottery bearing both Maria and Julian's name is worth a fortune, today. Any individual piece of pottery produced by Maria commands a high price.

After three successive years of winning prizes, Maria refused to accept any more awards, believing that other women should have the encouragement of such recognition.

Maria's beautiful work is found in every major museum in this country and in many European museums. She still makes some pottery with her son Popovi Da, although not to the same extent she produced in her younger days. Her fascinating life story can be read in the book *Maria, the Potter of San Ildefonso,* by Alice Marriott.

BIRTHPLACE: San Ildefonso Pueblo, New Mexico, March 1887.
MARRIED: Julian Martinez. CHILDREN: Adam, John, Popovi Da, Phillip.
HONORS: Indian Council Fire Achievement Award and honorary life membership (1934); University of Colorado, honorary doctorate (1953); *Palmes d'Academiques,* French Government (1954); American Institute of Architects award (1954); Rockford College, Jane Addams Award (1955); Catholic Art Association (1960); American Ceramic Society (1968).

* *See art section*

ALBERT REIFEL (DAKOTA-BRULE) PHYSICIAN

Dr. Albert Reifel is a specialist in internal medicine, on the staff of the Sepulveda Veterans Hospital in California.

His medical training was obtained in the face of a serious handicap. At the end of his junior year in pre-med school, he contracted tuberculosis and had to drop out. Again, while on specialty residency training, lung complications developed and he had to drop out once more.

A further handicap was the lack of funds necessary for the expensive medical training. With the exception of some scholarship assistance, he had to work continuously to put himself through school.

Dr. Reifel had learned to fear tuberculosis as a child, for so many Indians were affected by it and were destroyed in the prime of life. It was this close personal contact with the dread disease, that decided him upon a medical career so that he could help his people through the use of modern medical science.

BIRTHPLACE: Parmelee, South Dakota, November 15, 1919.
MARRIED: Helen Edlund. CHILDREN: Lucy, Nancy, Kristine, Steven.
EDUCATION: University of Minnesota (B.A., M.D.).
SCHOLARSHIPS: Bureau of Indian Affairs; DAR; Massachusetts Indian Association.

467

ALEXANDER REIFEL (DAKOTA-BRULE) CIVIL ENGINEER

Alexander Reifel is a design engineer of flood controls for the U.S. Army Engineer Corps. He has been with the Engineer Corps since 1953. Prior to that, he worked for the Air Force Installation at Burbank, California, in charge of all ground facilities. He has also been with the Bureau of Reclamation working in the area of irrigation facilities, canals and dams.

Mr. Reifel believes that change in the Indian situation will come only from within the people, with mutual understanding between Indians and non-Indians, and a willingness to accept life outside the reservation.

"As boys, we lived on a small ranch near a village which had one store, a postoffice, an Episcopal Church with an Indian minister, a garage and blacksmith shop, and a country school house. We all finished our elementary schooling at the nearest public school. Sometimes we rode horseback, but mostly we walked back and forth. We knew little about the outside world, but we were not afraid to venture into it, because our Indian mother made us strong," Mr. Reifel says.

BIRTHPLACE: Parmelee, South Dakota, November 26, 1913.
MARRIED: Pakali Satterfield. CHILDREN: Michael.
EDUCATION: University of Wyoming (B.S.).
MILITARY SERVICE: U.S. Army, infantry, World War II, four years.

MOSCELYNE LARKIN (SHAWNEE-PEORIA) BALLERINA, CHORE-OGRAPHER, LECTURER, TEACHER OF BALLET

Miss Larkin's mother was a Russian dancer. She trained her daughter in her early dancing studies. She received further private training in New York City under famous teachers and at the New York City School for Professional Children.

Just before her 16th birthday, Miss Larkin was engaged by the original Ballet Russe with which she danced all over Europe, South America and the United States as a soloist and then as ballerina. She later danced with the Ballet Russe de Monte Carlo.

Miss Larkin's exceptional memory is a matter of note. She is one of the few dancers of this generation with such a vast knowledge of the classical repertoire.

In recent years, when not on tour, Miss Larkin has been featured with the Radio City Ballet and on TV programs. She has also appeared with the Danilova company in South American capitals. She is presently Artistic Director of the Tulsa Civic Ballet and teaches ballet in more than 65 schools of the Tulsa school system.

Miss Larkin conceived the idea of the Oklahoma Indian Ballerina Festival of 1957 and in 1967 she danced in the world premiere of "The Four Moons," during the year-long festival of the arts which celebrated Oklahoma's 60th year of

Statehood. The ballet was written by Louis Ballard, Quapaw-Cherokee composer and the theme has significance in Indian mythology. It featured four of the five Oklahoma ballerinas.

BIRTHPLACE: Miami, Oklahoma, January 14, 1925.
MARRIED: Roman Jasinski. CHILDREN: Roman.
HONORS: Tulsa Tribune Honor Roll; Special Citation, Governor of Oklahoma.

ANTHONY LINCOLN (NAVAJO) DEPUTY ASSOCIATE COMMISSIONER FOR EDUCATION AND PROGRAMS, BUREAU OF INDIAN AFFAIRS

The announcement of this appointment came as INDIANS OF TODAY went to press. Mr. Lincoln is the first Navajo to hold an administrative post in the BIA. He was former director of the Navajo Tribe's industrial and economic development program, and deputy to the director of the Office of Navajo Economic Opportunity.

EMERSON BLACKHORSE MITCHELL (NAVAJO) WRITER

Emerson Mitchell was still in high school when he began to write the story of his boyhood as a creative writing exercise. The story began with early childhood memories dating back to when he was four and tending his grandmother's sheep on the reservation. It ended with recollections of his early days of study at the Institute of American Indian Arts.

The writing had such charm that it was published in book form by the University of Oklahoma Press under the title of *Miracle Hill*. Few authors can boast of writing a publishable book before finishing high school; fewer do it in a second language - and Emerson used his second language in a highly individualistic way.

The book was praised by critics and Emerson, then majoring in business administration in college, was embarked on a literary career. He is currently working on a second book tentatively called *Song of the Wind*. The story is an enchanting one of a young Navajo boy who sings his way into the hearts of the animals he herds.

Emerson has lived the things about which he writes. He grew up in a hogan in the traditional ways of his people. He has a "fresh breath" approach to writing that wins the hearts of his readers, and that brings the Navajos in his stories to gentle, imaginative life.

Emerson learned his first word of English when he was seven, and in school, he says, "I almost went on the warpath trying to figure out what was meant by first, second and third person."

BIRTHPLACE: Shiprock, New Mexico, March 3, 1945.
EDUCATION: Institute of American Indian Arts; Fort Lewis College.
AUTHOR: *Miracle Hill,* University of Oklahoma Press (1968); *Grandmother's Mistake* (short story) Harcourt Brace.
AWARDS: National Poetry Day Award; Vincent Price Award for Creative Writing; Scottsdale Award for short story.

HARRY J.W. BELVIN (CHOCTAW) PRINCIPAL CHIEF, CHOCTAW NATION

Mr. Belvin's father saw to it that his son was educated, even though this meant great personal sacrifice on his part. The constant admonitions of his father to prepare for life in the white man's world was the force that enabled Harry to go on through college and to dedicate his life to the service of mankind.

Mr. Belvin says that he held steadfastly to the hand of God throughout the difficult trail that he traveled and that his moccasins were guided and his footsteps strengthened.

After his marriage, Mr. Belvin taught in the public schools of Oklahoma for fifteen years. In 1941, he was elected County Superintendent of Public Instruction. It was during this period that he was elected by referendum to the office of Principal Chief of his tribe. He has held this position continuously since 1948 - the longest tenure of any in this office in the history of the Choctaws. Mr. Belvin works hard at this job, his activities taking him coast to coast.

For ten years (1954-64), Mr. Belvin was a member of the Oklahoma Legislature, serving six years in the House of Representatives and four in the Senate. Since his retirement from the political scene, he ranches on a small scale, managing 200 head of cattle on pasture that spreads over land he rode over as a boy. He has improved his pastures to the extent that he has gained special recognition for being a good steward of the land.

Mr. Belvin says his motto is "Education and Spiritual Culture are the saving graces of my people." He advocates orderly change and discourages any semblence of violence or hostile militancy.

BIRTHPLACE: Boswell, I.T., (now Oklahoma) December 11, 1900.

MARRIED: Lucille Brightwell. CHILDREN: Louise Belvin Frazier.

EDUCATION: Southeastern State College (B.S.); University of Oklahoma (M.Ed.).

HONORS: Outstanding Indian of Oklahoma, Tulsa Indian Democratic Club (1957); Outstanding American Indian Citizen, Anadarko Indian Exposition (1959) Oklahoma Bankers Association Award, for land improvement (1964); Special Recognition Award, American Indian Institute, University of Oklahoma (1968).

ORGANIZATIONS: Inter-tribal Council of the Five Civilized Tribes; National Congress of American Indians; Association on American Indian Affairs; American Indian Institute; Choctaw-Chickasaw Confederation; Oklahoma Indian Club.

SPECIAL ACTIVITIES: Oklahoma City Area Indian Health Service Advisory Board; Surgeon General's Advisory Board on Indian Health; Jones Academy Indian School (board).

RUTH MUSKRAT BRONSON (CHEROKEE) CONSULTANT, FIELD REPRESENTATIVE, SAVE THE CHILDREN FEDERATION

Mrs. Bronson's determination to serve her people was spurred while still in college. She was sent by the YWCA as a playground instructor to the Apache reservation where she saw and experienced the way the Indians of the area lived.

In 1933, she was sent by the Student Christian Federation to represent Indians at a conference in China. She entered college on her return and was employed by the Bureau of Indian Affairs immediately after graduation. After several promotions, she became Guidance and Placement Officer concerned with government loans and scholarships to Indian students. She was also general adviser to students in college. This work demanded much personalized service and she was of great help to young Indian people in need of moral support and encouragement.

For a three year period, Mrs. Bronson was executive secretary of the National Congress of American Indians and in this capacity made an extensive survey of Indian conditions in Alaska. Then she returned to the Bureau of Indian Affairs as a health worker on the San Carlos Apache Reservation. She also was a community worker for the U.S. Public Health Service.

BIRTHPLACE: Grove, Oklahoma.
MARRIED: John F. Bronson. CHILDREN: Dolores.

EDUCATION: Mount Holyoke College (A.B.); George Washington University.
HONORS: $1,000 Henry Morganthau Award for senior considered to have accomplished the most in the first year after graduation; Indian Council Fire Achievement Award and honorary life membership (1937); Oveta Culp Hobby Award, U.S. PUblic Health Service.
AUTHOR: *Indians Are People, Too.* Friendship Press (1947).

FRED YOUNG (NAVAJO) PHYSICIST

Fred Young did not begin his schooling until he was nine years old. From Indian school education, he has advanced to the scientific laboratory in the development of scientific instruments which will increase man's knowledge of outer space.

Enlisting in the Air Force, Fred served as a ground support equipment maintenance man in England. His service completed, he enrolled for engineering studies, but decided that physics was really his field. Because he then had a family, he had to interrupt his training and work for awhile, but he returned to his studies as soon as he could.

For several years he was a research assistant in his university's physics department where he helped to design and test a space radiation measuring instrument for the National Aeronautics and Space Administration. With financial help from his tribe, he was able to complete the work for his master's degree in physics.

BIRTHPLACE: Colorado
EDUCATION: Albuquerque Indian School (Valedictorian); University of New Mexico (B.S., M.S.).

WAANO-GANO (CHEROKEE) ARTIST *

Waano-Gano, whose "other name" is Joe Noonan, is one of the foremost and most gifted of Indian artists. He is a writer and lecturer of note as well.

From his boyhood, Joe has traveled among Indians of the West, sketching the people and recording their symbology and folklore. Out of this rich background has come paintings that are likened to those of Remington and Russell. Actually, the artist has drawn or painted since he can remember, and many of his early artistic efforts were expressed in clay.

Waano-Gano paints in many mediums from stylized flat and line work, to intricate, and shaded water colors, as well as to oils. Some of his works lean to the completely surrealistic or abstract. He has experimented for ten years with painting in moonlight to produce the exact strange and unreal colors of a moonlight night. His moonlight paintings are uncanny - it is as if the ethereal light has been caught and laid on the canvas. The "moonlight nocturnes" require a specially arranged set of homemade pastels.

Much time has been devoted, by Joe, to the study of anatomy. This knowledge, coupled with an ability to produce striking and unusual paintings in which human figures are treated as geometrical forms, incorporating designs found in beadwork, basketry and pottery. His interpretations of Indian mythical personalities are gems in themselves. His services are available as a designer of textiles with Indian motifs. Additionally, he has designed more than 30 combat and transport plane insignia.

In another creative area, he directed the Hollywood Bowl presentation of *The Song of Hiawatha,* with a cast of more than 100 Indian actors, and took a personal part in every act. Friends call this versatile, creative, and sensitive man "Mr. Indian Activities."

BIRTHPLACE: Salt Lake City, March 3, 1906.
MARRIED: Nunny Reuben.
EDUCATION: Public schools; Von Schneidau School of Art; University of Southern California; private teachers.
HONORS: "Best Picture to Live With Award," Biltmore Annual (1952); First award for outstanding textile design in world-wide competition; *Who's Who in American Art; American Indian Painters; Who's Who in California.*
EXHIBITIONS: Many major exhibitions; 86 one-man shows; 27 murals.
AWARDS: More than 90 prizes and awards including design for Indian Council Fire Achievement Award Medal in national competition.
ORGANIZATIONS: American Institute of Fine Art (fellow); American Artists Professional League (fellow); Valley Artists Guild (past president); Painters and Sculptors Club (past president); California Art Club; and many others.

* *See art section*

NUNNY WAANO-GANO (KAROK) FLORAL ARTIST

Nunny is said to be the only Indian owner-designer of an F.T.D. florist shop. She is a floral artist of distinction, originating arrangements with subtle design which illustrates an extremely fine talent.

Coming from a primitive area in northern California, Nunny has won recognition through sheer courage, integrity and artistry in several fields. She has great spiritual strength handed down from the old ways of her people blended with the best of the white man's culture.

Before her marriage, she appeared in motion pictures, playing in films that starred Shirley Temple, Gary Cooper, and Tyrone Power. An accomplished violinist, she also played with country and western bands. She is a pianist of ability. For two years, with her husband, she was a member of an All-Indian radio cast which presented dramatic adaptations of Indian legends.

She is, however, best known for her exquisite flower arrangements. When asked how she creates these masterpieces, she always answers, "With love!"

BIRTHPLACE: Orleans, California.
MARRIED: Joe Waano-Gano.
EDUCATION: Sherman Institute; Bacone Junior College.

479

CHARLES C. PEAK, Jr., (CHEROKEE) MUSICIAN

As County school superintendent, Charles Peak's grandfather established the schools in Delaware County.

During Mr. Peak's college years, his intense interest in music lead to a lifetime profession. With study and personal recommendations, he earned an audition with the Navy Band in Washington. The audition for the Navy Band demanded skill in four instruments - the saxophone, bassoon, clarinet, and the string bass.

After his honorable discharge from service, Mr. Peak began work towards his Master's Degree. At the same time, he taught in a public school and conducted a 4-AAA High School music program at Ft. Worth, Texas. Several of his bands received awards as "winning organizations," and were featured at a number of state events and professional football games. Mr. Peak also performed with the Fort Worth Symphony, the Waco Symphony, and other professional musical groups.

Since 1961, however, his principal occupation has been in the investment insurance field. He says: "Opportunity is greater than ever for Indians in all fields of endeavor. In the future, it is my desire to engage in service type work and direct it, where possible, to the benefit of my people."

BIRTHPLACE: Delaware County, Oklahoma.
MARRIED: Margaret Barren. CHILDREN: (4).
EDUCATION: Seneca Indian School; Sequoyah Vocational School; Northeastern State College (B.Ed.); North Texas State University (M.Mu.).
MILITARY SERVICE: U.S. Navy, 26 months, World War II.
ORGANIZATIONS: 32nd degree Scottish Rite Mason; Karem Shrine Band (past president); Texas Shrine Band Association (secretary-treasurer).

EVELYN YELLOW ROBE (DAKOTA-BRULE) UNIVERSITY LECTURER

Evelyn Yellow Robe, the daughter of the well-known Chauncey Yellow Robe spent the first seven years of her life in South Dakota. After the death of her parents, she moved to New York to live with an older sister.

In high school she was the first girl president of the honor society. After graduation from college, she taught on the faculties of Mount Holyoke and Vassar colleges.

A special research project has been the recording of the Dakota language. In 1954, she received a Fulbright Award for the study of the physiology of the larynx at the Faculte de Medecine in Paris. During her studies abroad she lectured at medical centers in London, Hamburg, Groningen, Holland and Padua. Upon her return to the United States, she was appointed Lecturer in Otolaryngology and Assistant Director of the Voice Clinic, Northwestern University Medical School. Following her marriage she left the United States to live in Germany.

BIRTHPLACE: Rapid City, South Dakota.

MARRIED: Professor Hans Finkbeiner, M.D.

EDUCATION: Mount Holyoke College (Sarah Williston Scholar, Mary Lyon Scholar) for scholastic excellence; (B.A. Magna Cum Laude); Northwestern University (M.A., Ph.D.).

SCHOLARSHIPS: Gorse Scholarship; Illinois Federation of Women's Clubs; John Hay Whitney Fellow; Ford Fellowship.

HONORS: French Government award for excellence in French (1940); Indian Council Fire Indian Achievement Award and honorary life membership (1946).

THEODORE B. WHITE (DAKOTA-ONEIDA) SUPERINTENDENT, SAN CARLOS INDIAN AGENCY

Ted White sees employment as one of the most urgent needs of Indian people. The many land and federal programs involving hundred of millions of dollars are all worthwhile and necessary, he says, but of even greater importance is the creation of jobs for individual Indian.

"Indians who do not have work have no sense of accomplishment. This develops feelings of inferiority and a negative image that is imparted to the general public," he says.

"Work is the best way for anyone. It is the way to self-sufficiency," he emphasizes.

The new emphasis on culture has a certain value, Mr. White believes, but careful consideration should be given to avoid going "too far." It isn't possible to turn things back, he points out. Too much emphasis on culture can result in confused individuals who have no real roots in either social structure. When this is the case, culture can become a "facade." Indians can retain much cultural meaning in their professional lives, he points out, and certainly should have a sense of pride in their heritage.

BIRTHPLACE: Oneida, Wisconsin.
MARRIED: Ruby Patrick. CHILDREN: Mark, Tim.
EDUCATION: University of Wisconsin; Pepperdine College; David Lipscomb College (B.A.); Loyola University (M.S.W.).
MILITARY SERVICE: U.S. Air Force, 1942-46.
ORGANIZATIONS: Lions; Kiwanis.

WAYNE ZUNIGHA (ZUNI-DELAWARE) REGIONAL AND CITY PLANNER

Wayne Zunigha is the Executive Director of the Cherokee Tribal Planning Board for the Eastern Band of Cherokees. He assists in the coordination of the economic, social and physical development of the Cherokee Reservation, North Carolina. This means continuous work with Tribal, State and Federal agencies for reservation progress. One of his major roles is to attract tourism and industrial development to the reservation and to build toward a 12-month expanded economy.

Wayne has additional responsibilities in the field of transportation; public and private housing; the development of an industrial park; the development of recreation and winter sports; and of a shopping center; water and sewer expansion; and the over-all economic and land use development of the entire reservation.

Mr. Zunigha has been director of planning for the states of Kentucky and West Virginia.

BIRTHPLACE: Claremore, Oklahoma, September 28, 1931.
MARRIED: Patricia Miller.
EDUCATION: Oklahoma State University (B.A., MRCP).
SCHOLARSHIPS: Lavern Noyes Scholarship.
HONORS: Dean's Honor Roll; Special Award, Ohio Valley Chapter, American Institute of Planners.

483

MILITARY SERVICE: U.S. Navy, four years.

ORGANIZATIONS: American Institute of Planners; American Society of Planning Officials; Gamma Theta Upsilon.

J.C. HILL (MOHAWK) SCHOOL ADMINISTRATOR

J.C. Hill is district superintendent of schools under the federal Department of Indian Affairs on the Six Nations Reserve in Canada.

Mr. Hill has devoted most of his life to his people. He has been involved in the educational life of the reserve for more than 30 years. In that period, he has developed a school system that now totals 14 elementary schools with a total of 1,400 pupils and is staffed almost entirely by Indian teachers. He is responsible for an additional 400 reserve students who attend high schools in several counties, and for 60 who are in colleges and universities.

Through his work, Mr. Hill has introduced Indian history and values into the education of Indian children and in this, and other ways, has succeeded in preserving the important aspects of Indian culture and heritage.

He is known to his people as Skakorihonnyyennih-kowah, which translates as "Great Teacher."

In June of this year, Mr. Hill was awarded an honorary LLD from the University of Western Ontario in recognition of his work as an educator.

BIRTHPLACE: Six Nations Reserve, Canada.
EDUCATION: Reserve schools; Hamilton Teacher's College; McMaster University.
HONORS: Honorary LLD., University of Western Ontario (1970); Centennial Award, Ontario Education Association (1960).

JOHNNY YESNO (OJIBWA) RADIO PRODUCER, BROADCASTER, ACTOR

As host and co-producer of *Indian Magazine,* a weekly radio show that is aired on the CBC network and 70 independent and affiliated Canadian stations, Johnny Yesno has won a large following.

Describing his program, which goes on the air on Saturdays, Johnny says: "Our job is to gather raw material from the reserves - to get the Indian resident to describe his way of life and what he wants."

In essence, Johnny's radio program is a national forum for the opinions of Canada's peoples, linking widely separated groups and letting non-Indians hear Indian viewpoints.

Yesno studied engineering and worked as a land surveyor and engineering technician for several years, during which time he won a national championship for Indian dancing. This brought him a part as an Indian in a TV series, for which he won a special *"Wilderness Award"* because of his moving performance. He also played in the Walt Disney film, *Biography of a Grizzly.*

Johnny explains his unusual name in this way: "A government official offered an Indian chief - an ancestor of his - all the land he wanted in exchange for its mineral rights. The canny chief nodded 'yes' to the first half of the question, and 'no' to the second. No one knew his name, so it was entered in the record of the meeting as Yesno.

BIRTHPLACE: Fort Hope Reserve, Canada, November 8, 1938.
EDUCATION: University of Waterloo.
SCHOLARSHIPS: Indian Affairs Branch Scholarship.
ORGANIZATIONS: Canadian Indian Centre of Toronto (executive board).

NELLIE KIRK (NAVAJO)SOCIAL WORKER

Mrs. Kirk is the first member of her tribe to become a social worker. Her interest in this profession began when she was a teacher in a reservation school.

Studies were begun and completed, and after working for a year as a social worker on the reservation, Mrs. Kirk joined the Bernalillo County Department of Public Welfare to gain experience in an urban setting. She worked in child welfare services for almost three years and then returned to her own people. She is employed at Shiprock.

Mrs. Kirk comes from a traditional Navajo background and had to learn English as a second language.

BIRTHPLACE: Navajo reservation.
MARRIED: Virgil Kirk, judge of the Trial Court of the Navajo Tribe and president of the National American Indian Tribal Judges Association.
CHILDREN: Leon, Virgil, Jr.
EDUCATION: Arizona State University; School of Social Work, University of Oklahoma.
HONORS: Special Act Award, Bureau of Indian Affairs (1969).

486

PERCY DeWOLF (BLACK-FEET) STATE SENATOR

Mr. DeWolf is a cattle rancher who has been a member of the Montana House of Representatives for two sessions and a State Senator since 1959. He is chairman of the Banking and Insurance, and the Bills committees.

BIRTHPLACE: Browning, Montana, December 15, 1904.

MARRIED: Theo Bille-deaux. CHILDREN: Penny, Etta, Geri.

ORGANIZATIONS: Elks; Masons; Shrine; Product Credit Association (director).

CHARLES E. TRIMBLE
(DAKOTA-OGLALA)
PUBLIC RELATIONS

Charles Trimble is public information/public relations officer for the Commission on Community Relations of the City and County of Denver. In this position, he plans and implements public relations programs, including the publication of an annual report, a quarterly newsletter, and other reports. He writes and sends out news releases to the various media and creates communications programs directed at the large community in order to affect an attitudinal change toward minority peoples. He also establishes programs introducing minority people to the workings of the mass media.

BIRTHPLACE: Wanblee, South Dakota, March 12, 1935.
EDUCATION: University of South Dakota (B.A.).
MILITARY SERVICE: U.S. Army, 1957-60 - Public Information Specialist and Infantry Operations Intelligence Specialist.
ORGANIZATIONS: White Buffalo Council of American Indians (editor, *Indian Times*).

THOMAS ST. GERMAIN WHITECLOUD (CHIPPEWA) PHYSICIAN

In his boyhood, Dr. Whitecloud was a troubled youth. He began to work when he was ten, and "progressed" to farm work, truck driving, deep sea diving, mechanics, amateur boxing, and odd job man. During the depression he attended Indian schools and was "kicked out" of several.

He finally made it to college, but developed tuberculosis. Even so, he lettered in football, basketball, track and swimming. He "flunked" out of the University of New Mexico, and had a long hard struggle to get his grades up for admission to medical school, since he had finally settled on medicine as his career.

For a time, he was a physician with the Indian Service, stationed in Montana and Minnesota. Then he opened private practice in Texas where he was the only physician in the county for more than seven years. He kept a 35-bed county hospital going and delivered a total of 2,000 babies. He was also county coroner, health officer, and deputy sheriff.

When he was stricken with a malignant condition, he moved to Pascagoula, Mississippi, where he engaged in limited practice. He is now retired, but not inactive. He has founded an Indian corresponding group called Three Feather Society; is a ship's surgeon; is associated with a small hospital; and does much writing and lecturing.

While in college, Dr. Whitecloud wrote a poignant article *Blue Winds Dancing* which appeared in *Scribner's* (1938) and won first place in a Phi Beta Kappa essay contest. This is still frequently quoted.

Dr. Whitecloud says, "I lost my chagrin at being a recipient of federal help during the depression years when everybody needed help. The public put out about $10,000 on my education and they have had it back many fold."

"The Indian potential is unlimited," he says. "I wish that the public . . . and Indians . . . could know more about people of Indian blood who have gone quietly into the highly competitive society, competed, raised their children without help, and become hardworking, taxpaying citizens. On every side there are evidences of younger Indians demonstrating leadership abilities."

BIRTHPLACE: New York City, New York, October 8, 1914.
MARRIED: Barbara Ibanez. CHILDREN: Karen, Dennis, Dr. T.S. Whitecloud III.
EDUCATION: Albuquerque Indian School; Chilocco Indian School; Santa Fe Indian School; University of Redlands (A.B.); Tulane School of Medicine (M.D.).
MILITARY SERVICE: U.S. Army, paratroops, Battalion Surgeon, 2½ years, European Theatre.
ORGANIZATIONS: Lions; Civitan; Moose; American Legion; Veterans of Foreign Wars; American Medical Association; Conservation Clubs; Aircraft Owners and Pilots Association.

THOMAS ST. GERMAIN WHITECLOUD, III (CHIPPEWA)
PHYSICIAN

Dr. Whitecloud is the son of Dr. Thomas Whitecloud, also a physician. He is now completing specialty training in orthopedics at the U.S. Marine Hospital in New Orleans where he is Chief Resident.

Keenly interested in athletics - professional, amateur, and spectator sports - Dr. Whitecloud played football from grade school on through college. He was the youngest member of his team in college and he was a letterman three years.

BIRTHPLACE: New Orleans, Louisiana, December 29, 1941.
MARRIED: Mercedes Bordelon. CHILDREN: Renee, Saint.
EDUCATION: Public schools; Louisiana College (B.S.); Tulane School of Medicine (M.D.).
SCHOLARSHIPS: Louisiana Heart Association Research Grant.
HONORS: *Who's Who in American Colleges and Universities.*

CLINTON RICKARD (TUSCARORA) TRIBAL LEADER

People on both sides of the Canadian-United States border know Clinton Rickard, the Chief of the Tuscarora tribe who has worked tirelessly building understanding and communications bridges between people on both sides of the border.

Rickard, a lifetime Grand President of the Indian Defense League of America, was honored for his long career of service at the 42nd annual observance (1969) of the bridge crossing from Niagra Falls, New York, to its twin city in Canada. A special citation, authorized by the University Board of Trustees, of Niagra University, was presented in recognition of his dedicated service in behalf of the cause of human rights.

In former years, Chief Rickard has received a wide variety of honors and awards. The citation from Niagra University was of special significance because it was the first given to him by an institution of higher learning.

Even though his schooling did not extend beyond third grade, Chief Rickard has made important contributions to Indian education; to international law; and American law through his defense of INdian rights. With only limited education, he values education highly, and was one of the most active in obtaining New York legislation for improved education for Indian children.

Born at a time when Indians were not even considered to be American citizens, young Rickard volunteered for service before he was actually old enough to join the Army. He travelled around the world in the service of the United States. He saw action in the Philippine Insurrection, during the Spanish American War.

As early as 1917, Chief Rickard gave his attention to certain parts of United States legislation. He argued against the rules pertaining to the entry of illiterates to this country, stating that it was unjust to apply such rules against American Indians. His arguments won his cause for him. Later, an even more determined, and much more prolonged fight centered around the Immigration Act of 1924 which violated the rights guaranteed to Indians by the Jay Treaty of 1794.

Chief Rickard spoke and wrote to many groups about this injustice. As a result of his campaign, a bill was introduced which exempted Indians born in Canada from the 1924 Immigration Act and permitted them to continue to cross the border without hindrance. The bill, signed by President Coolidge in 1928, confirmed the rights for Indians for which Chief Rickard had fought so hard to retain.

In 1930, in a celebrated murder case involving two Seneca women, Rickard forced the U.S. Attorney to defend the women, calling attention to the section in the U.S. Code which required that Indians be defended by federal attorneys. He was further helpful in proving the women's innocence.

From this celebrated case came much interest in Indian education. Chief Rickard was sought after as a speaker by civic groups. Today, New York State has a creditable record with special funds available for Indians interested in going beyond high school. Such great gains were made in Indian education that it is now impossible to find illiterate Indians on any New York reservation.

Chief Rickard worked for honor and justice without regard

for any material benefits to himself. Frequently, he neglected his own farm and personal interests to help free those falsely accused to make certain that civil rights were restored to those who had been deprived of them. There are always those who are willing to act as critics of talented and dedicated individuals. Rickard is generally recognized for his breadth of vision, as well as for his honor and integrity.

When the Tuscaroras were locked in a legal struggle with the New York State Power Authority over reservation land in the 1950's, it was no surprise to find Chief Rickards in the fight. The Tuscaroras did not win this battle, but they had made their stand, and held firmly to their principles.

Chief Rickard is now devoting much time taping and recording the Tuscarora language so that it will not be lost. Hopefully, this effort during his twilight years will help his people to retain this important part of their heritage.

BIRTHPLACE: Tuscarora Reservation, May 19, 1882
MARRIED: Beulah Mt. Pleasant. CHILDREN: Edith Rickard Hill, Eli, Beverly, Onalee Rickard Eustis, Karen Rickard Jacobson, Eunid, Norton, Lois Rickard Henry.
HONORS: Citation, Order of Purple Heart (1962); Cited for Distinguished Service, Peter Doctor Memorial Scholarship Fund (1930); honorary member, several Boy Scout troops.
ORGANIZATIONS: B.M. Butler Post, Spanish American War Veterans (commander); Masons; Veterans of Foreign Wars.

INDEX